£19.95

DI034115

UNIVERSITY OF WINNIPEG
LIBRARY
DISCARDED
Winnipeg, Manitoba R3B 2E9

POPULAR OPPOSITION TO THE 1834 POOR LAW

KD
3310
.K51
1986

Popular Opposition to the 1834 Poor Law

John Knott

CROOM HELM
London and Sydney

© 1986 John Knott
Croom Helm Ltd, Provident House, Burrell Row,
Beckenham, Kent BR3 1AT
Croom Helm Australia Pty Ltd, Suite 4, 6th Floor,
64-76 Kippax Street, Surry Hills, NSW 2010, Australia

British Library Cataloguing in Publication Data

Knott, John William
  Popular opposition to the 1834 Poor Law.
  1. Great Britain. *Poor Law Amendment Act 1834*
  2. Poor—Great Britain—History—19th century
  I. Title
  344.104'36258
  ISBN 0-7099-1532-2

Printed and bound in Great Britain
by Billing & Sons Limited, Worcester.

CONTENTS

LIST OF TABLES

For my Mother and Father

The 1834 Poor Law was one of the most important and controversial pieces of legislation passed in early nineteenth-century Britain. At a single blow the New Poor Law (as it quickly became known) overthrew more than two hundred years of tradition in the shape of the Elizabethan Poor Law, and introduced an entirely new and restrictive national poor relief policy. The existing system of parish relief based on individual need was abandoned, and local government in England and Wales transformed with the creation of a centralised bureaucracy to administer uniform regulations. It is not surprising therefore that the 1834 Poor Law has come to assume a dominant role in British historiography: it has been seen variously as a symbol of the ascendancy of the middle class and of middle-class values in British public life, and as a key element in what some people have called the nineteenth-century revolution in government.[1] Despite the attention paid to the legislations' ideological and political implications, however, it is only recently that historians have begun to scrutinise the storm of popular protest which greeted attempts to implement the New Poor Law. It is that campaign of popular opposition which is the subject of this book.

Historical orthodoxy has it that the campaign of popular opposition to the 1834 Poor Law was the product of 'ignorance'. Redlich and Hirst, for instance, claim that 'every arsenal of superstition and ignorance were ransacked to provide reasons against [Poor Law] reform'. And they contrast this with the actions of that 'small section ... of the better organised workmen, instructed and led by Francis Place, [who] saw that the measure was framed in the true interests of labour'. Derek Fraser agrees, telling us that the campaign was 'spurred by fear and anger'. Fear and anger about what, we are not told, simply that the results were 'riots'. Even the few historians who have specifically written about popular opposition to the 1834 Poor Law have tended to perpetuate these views. Thus we are told by Michael Rose that 'emotional propaganda ... played on the fears of the working classes'. He does admit that political arguments against the New Poor Law were put forward, but claims that these were only important in arousing the middle class. Nicholas Edsall, in the only book devoted solely to the anti-poor law movement, is equally reluctant to admit that popular opponents of the 1834 Poor Law might have been acting rationally. We are told, for instance, that popular protests in the rural south of England were either an example of 'spontaneous rioting', or the result of 'pathetic misconceptions'. One can search his book for an illustration of the popular beliefs and assumptions which gave rise to these 'misconceptions', but in vain. Even in the industrial north of England, we are told, the campaign of popular opposition was merely one of 'spontaneous resistance'.[2]

I mention this not to ridicule the work of those who first described the campaign of popular agitation against the New Poor Law, but to illustrate how my approach differs from theirs. It is my contention that the campaign of popular opposition to the 1834 Poor Law was a self-conscious process guided in almost every instance by a coherent and rational system of beliefs and assumptions. And I will therefore be arguing that it was not 'pathetic misconceptions' which guided popular opponents of the New Poor Law, but the ideas they shared. While charting the rhythms of the anti-poor law movement, I hope to show precisely what those ideas were, where they derived from and how they affected later political thought.

This book is a revised and shortened version of a doctoral dissertation submitted in the Department of History, Research School of Social Sciences, the Australian National University. I owe much to all those who helped me while researching and writing that thesis. My first and greatest debt is to my supervisor, Dr F.B. Smith, who shared with me his extensive knowledge of nineteenth-century British history, and was a constant source of enthusiasm and encouragement. I would also like to thank Professor Norman McCord of the Department of History, the University of Newcastle-upon-Tyne, for the generous help and hospitality he extended towards me while I was researching this book in Britain during 1978-9. Others who assisted include Mr Tony Barta, Dr Alan Haigh, Professor K.S. Inglis, Professor Oliver MacDonagh, Dr A.W. Martin and Dr Pauric Travers. The process of revision has been a long and arduous one (I estimated three years, it has taken nearly four). My thesis examiners, Dr Stuart Macintyre, the late Mr J.M. Main and Dr Dorothy Thompson, all had constructive comments to make which made the process of rewriting easier. Dr Alan Atkinson, Dr Heather Gregory, Mr David Kent, Professor R.S. Neal, Mrs Jacqui Parkinson and Dr F.B. Smith kindly read draft chapters and Mrs Marian Robson typed the final manuscript. To all of them I offer thanks, although the end result remains my responsibility.

In a move to rationalise the administration of local government in Britain, the national government recently redrew the boundaries for some of the counties of England, Scotland and Wales. In order to remain compatible with the primary sources I have referred to the pre-April 1974 county boundaries throughout the text.

Notes

1. E. Halevy, *A History of the English People in the Nineteenth Century*, vol.III (Ernest Benn, London, 1950), p.210. For the full debate over the question of whether there was really a revolution in nineteenth-century government, including a reprint of Oliver MacDonagh's seminal article, see P. Stansky (ed.), *The Victorian Revolution* (New Viewpoints, New York, 1973).

2. J. Redlich and F.W. Hirst, *History of Local Government in England* (Macmillan, London, 1971), p.115; D. Fraser, *Evolution of the British Welfare State* (Macmillan, London, 1973), p.47; M.E. Rose, 'The anti-Poor Law Movement in the North of England', *Northern History*, vol.I (1966), pp.79 and 81; N.C. Edsall, *anti-Poor Law Movement, 1834-44* (Manchester University Press, Manchester, 1971), pp.31, 38 and 258.

ABBREVIATIONS

BL	British Library
BMBA	Bolton Metropolitan Borough Archives
BML	Barnsley Municipal Library
CMBA	Calderdale Metropolitan Borough Archives, Halifax
Hansard	*Hansard's, Parliamentary Debates*
HO	Home Ofice
JRULM	John Rylands University Library, Manchester
KMBA	Kirklees Metropolitan Borough Archives, Huddersfield
LCA	Leeds City Archives
LRO	Lancashire Record Office, Preston
LWMA	London Working Men's Association
MCLA	Manchester City Library, Archives Department
MCLH	Manchester City Library, Local History Department
PLC	Poor Law Commission
PP	*Parliamentary Papers*
PRO	Public Record Office
Report	'Report from His Majesty's Commissioners for Inquiring into the Administration and Practical Operation of the Poor Laws', *PP*, 1834, vols XXVII-XXX and XXXIV-XXXIX
SCA	Salford City Archives, Irlam
SCL	Sheffield City Library
TH	Transport House, London
UCL	University College, London
VCH	*Victoria County History*
WRO	Wigan Record Office, Leigh
WYRO	West Yorkshire Record Office, Wakefield

PROLOGUE:
POMP AND PROTEST

A million people were said to have watched Queen Victoria's coronation procession on Thursday, 28 June 1838. The diarist Charles Greville described the scene: 'From Buckingham Palace to Westminster Abbey ... there was a mass of people; the seats and benches were all full, every window was occupied, the roofs of the houses were covered with spectators'.[1] The whole nation, it appeared, wanted to catch a glimpse of the Young Queen dressed in her coronation robes, wearing a crown and carrying the orb and sceptre, pass through the streets of her capital in the state coach. Victoria was overwhelmed:

> multitudes ... millions, of my loyal subjects ... were assembled in *every spot* to witness the Procession... I really cannot say *how* proud I feel to be the Queen of *such a Nation*.[2]

The coronation of a young and popular girl of nineteen had provided the Whig government under Lord Melbourne with an opportunity to revive the pomp and splendour of the full state occasion. Parliament voted £200,000 for the coronation, four times the amount spent on the coronation of Victoria's uncle and predecessor, William IV. The formal state procession, discontinued since the coronation of George III, was revived; and to ensure that the maximum number of people would be able to share in the spectacle, special stands were erected along the route. Bands played festive music in the parks, a two-day fair was held in Hyde Park, there were balloon ascents, illuminations and firework displays. 'The great merit of this coronation', wrote Greville, 'is that so much has been done for the people: to amuse and interest *them* seems to have been the principal object.'[3]

While London was the focus of the nation's coronation day celebrations, it was by no means unique in its display of public loyalty. Throughout Britain in rural hamlets, towns and the new industrial cities there were processions, dinners and balls to help mark the occasion. In most centres employers treated their workers to a paid holiday so they could participate in the festivities. School children, both day and Sunday school scholars, were a particular focus of

1

attention. Everywhere children were given an opportunity of displaying their loyalty to the Crown; they paraded, sang and were treated to celebratory teas. More often than not their participation earned them a small gift, most usually a loyal medal.

Like all public rituals, the coronation celebrations had the potential of going astray and seriously embarrassing their organisers. The determining factors were whether loyalty to the Crown and the values it symbolised were strong enough to overcome any alternative shared values, and whether, even if people were loyal to the Crown and accepted the values it symbolised, they would necessarily perceive the authorities as also adhering to those same values. By licensing a display of public loyalty, the authorities also (unwittingly) afforded an opportunity for public protest.

Called upon by the authorities to join in the local coronation day procession, the Committee of the Manchester and Salford Trades' Union advised their members to refuse to participate. They emphasised that they were 'not wanting in love and loyalty to the Queen', but experience had taught them 'the folly of such idle pomp and useless parade'. They continued:

> We regret that our government should have agreed to spend so much money upon a Coronation whilst so many of our fellow-labourers are out of employment, and very many of them pining in hunger, and literally starving to death...
>
> We ... find the wealthy in and out of Parliament conspiring against the labouring poor to deprive them of the rights of industry, and withholding from them the political rights and liberties of freeborn British subjects; at the same time they call upon us to testify our allegiance to that very system of government which offers us no protection – which manifests no sympathy for the destitute poor of our country, but upon all occasions takes advantage of the power they possess to treat us as slaves, stigmatize us as combinators, and persecute us as criminals.

The present government was accused of having 'hardened the heart' of the Queen and of having 'sworn enmity' against the labouring classes. Such conduct was 'undermining the throne, alienating the affections of the people, and bringing the throne and laws into contempt'.[4]

Members of the Trade Unions were reminded that their organisations had been 'brought into existence by the baseness of ... [the] political system and the consequent tyranny of capitalists, whom the laws allow to ride rough-shod over prostrate labour'. They were therefore urged

> On no account [to] allow themselves to be duped by their employers with gifts of money, drink, and feasts, in order to induce them to join in the procession... Let the authorities send their delegates in vain; join neither [the] procession nor the idle throng that gapes on it; but betake yourselves to some more rational mode of testifying your loyalty to the Queen, and your hatred of those base minded wretches who fatten upon your labour, and poison her royal ear against the prayers of her suffering subjects.[5]

Boycotted by the Trade Unions, the coronation day procession at Manchester was not the success that the authorities had hoped for. The only working people to join heartily in the procession were the Temperance Societies and the Irish. 'There was a profuse expense without taste, and a long procession without people', commented the radical *Champion and Weekly Herald*. As if to compound the authorities' discomfort, even their request that 'no *political flags* should be shown on the occasion' was ignored. A large green and white flag with the slogan 'Repeal of the New Poor Law, Universal Suffrage, Annual Parliaments and Equitable Adjustments' was flown from the popular-radicals' meeting rooms.[6]

Manchester was not the only northern town to see members of the labouring classes refuse to participate in the coronation day celebrations, or use those celebrations as a means of protest. At Leeds the boycott staged by the Trades Unions resulted in the procession resembling a funeral rather than a celebration. And, according to the *Leeds Times*, it would have been 'nearly as sorrowful', had not the laughter and jeers of the crowd 'served a little to enliven the scene'. The festivities at Keighley were interrupted by 'some facetious opposition from a section of the "Northern Democrats" '. At Elland a black flag with the inscription 'mourn for the follies of the people' was flown over the route of the procession. And at Huddersfield the local authorities actually found themselves the unwilling hosts of a large contingent of popular radicals, 'one of them bearing a tri-coloured flag inscribed "Liberty and Love" '. When the loyalists attempted to sing the national anthem, they were interrupted by the popular radicals. After a delay the anthem was again proceeded with, 'till the commencement of the third stanza, when the Rad[ical]s again interfered with shouts and groans, and a large proportion singing a nonsensical verse about the poor laws'. The Huddersfield authorities' attempt to silence the protesters caused stones to be thrown and a *mêlée* to break out.[7]

The general holiday called to celebrate the coronation at Newcastle-upon-Tyne presented the popular radicals with an opportunity to hold their own counter-demonstration. A procession of the Trades, with flags and banners flying and music playing, marched from St Nicholas' Square to the town moor, where they held a meeting. One of the first speakers, James Ayr, a Newcastle working-man, contrasted 'the unmeaning mummery of the coronation ... going on in the Metropolis' with the meeting they were holding 'to assert the rights of human nature'. He warned the government that the working people were uniting in defence of their common interests and that they would no longer allow themselves to be led away by 'gaudy trappings'. 'If they saw the gewgaws of royalty on the one side they [would be sure to] see the damnable [Poor Law] bastile on the other.' Another speaker, George Smith, an operative coachbuilder, said they had waited patiently for six years for the benefits of Reform, but 'instead of benefit murder was its result'. 'They immured the needy, the old and the helpless in [Poor Law] bastiles, and poisoned them in their dungeons with water gruel; and what other name could he give it but ... murder.'[8]

The popular radicals of Ashton-under-Lyne held a meeting in the market place before the local coronation day procession got under way. Nearly 5,000 people assembled to hear, amongst others, the demagogic leader of a local sect, the Reverend Joseph Rayner Stephens, assert the rights of human nature and forcefully attack the New Poor Law. While acknowledging that it was their 'constitutional duty' to swear allegiance to the Queen, the Ashton protesters drew attention to what they saw as the reciprocal nature of the relationship between sovereign and subject. '[A]llegiance ... is loyally given by a free people, in return for that protection, which the sovereign is bound to afford the subject.' In particular they asked to be protected from Her Majesty's Government, which, they claimed, was

> continuing to employ the bludgeon of an unconstitutional police, and the bayonets of the soldiery, to compel Englishmen to surrender their ancient liberties, and to abandon their hearths and homes to the brutal invasion of the three traitor kings [the Poor Law Commissioners], who exercise a power greater than that of the crown, are alienating the affections of the people, and driving them, in self-defence, to the last and most solemn step, which the

constitution requires them to take.

The Queen was entreated 'to dismiss from her council the men who have deceived the royal ear, abused the trust reposed in them, and by so doing endangered the public peace and the very existence of the throne itself'. Her Majesty was also 'implored to restore forth the old constitutional rights of the poor [the Old Poor Law], and all the acknowledged rights of the people at large, as nothing short of this will suffice to save the country from anarchy, and make her majesty what the constitution requires her to be – worthy [of] the love and reverence of a loyal, peaceable, prosperous and happy people'.[9]

At Oldham the popular radicals held their own meeting to celebrate the coronation day in what they termed a 'rational and becoming manner'. A large procession led by the Middleton Working Men's Association and including other groups from the neighbourhood, all bearing flags and banners, marched into Oldham. One of the banners had 'a figure of Justice trampling upon Corruption'; below were the words 'Equitable Adjustments'. Another had a painting of the Peterloo massacre. And the handloom weavers from Failsworth brought a large cart, in which was placed a loom with a 'Jacquard' on top and a 'poor weaver' in the act of weaving a piece of 'fancy goods'. This 'emblem of usefulness and misery' excited great compassion amongst the crowd and quite a few pence were collected to reward the handloom weavers for the pains they had taken to show their actual condition and distress.[10]

The chairman of the Oldham meeting, the radical shopkeeper Alexander Taylor, told those present that he had expected great things from the Reform Bill, but that he had been 'deceived'. The reformed Parliament had 'never passed a single measure for the good of the people', but instead had passed that 'infamous bill, the new poor law – the most accursed law that ever passed any legislature in the world to rob the people of their *rights*'. Taylor called upon all those present to 'fearlessly tell the Parliament that we are not satisfied with their proceedings, which have been altogether cruel and unjust towards the poor'. He ended with a plea that they do all they could 'to get the New Poor-Law Act repealed'.[11]

John Knight, an old-time supporter of the radical cause, proposed to the meeting that the following memorial be sent to the Queen:

That in the opinion of this meeting, the Poor Law Amendment Act is at direct variance with the constitution of England, and of the chartered rights of Englishmen, as set forth by the Magna Charta, and the Bill of Rights; and inasmuch as it deprives them [the labouring population] of the free use of their lives and limbs, by shutting them up in a prison called a poor law workhouse, and as it endangers and jeopardises their lives, when labouring under misfortunes over which they have no control, by compelling them to subsist upon food, so small in quantity, so impure, and so obnoxious in quality, as to produce disease and premature death, it is, therefore, our duty legally and constitutionally to resist this most tyrannical, infamous, and cruel law, by all the means that may be within our reach; and as this is the day of her majesty's coronation, we deem it to be a proper and fitting opportunity, to assemble a public meeting, in order to memorialise her majesty to remove this most obnoxious law from the Statute Book; and as a first step ... to dismiss immediately from their present traitorous employment the three Poor Law Commissioners.[12]

The memorial was accepted unanimously and the meeting closed with three cheers for Richard Oastler, the Reverend Stephens and Feargus O'Connor – the leaders of the anti-poor law movement – and three groans for those who were attempting to abridge the rights of human nature, the Poor Law Commissioners.

II

It would be easy to dismiss the coronation day protests in the north of England (there were none below the Trent) as a mere aberration and of little significance. Apart from the Newcastle-upon-Tyne meeting, none of the protests attracted much attention outside their immediate locality; and, compared with those who attended the London festivities or took part in local celebrations, the number of protesters appears quite small.[13] But the boycotting of the loyal processions at Manchester and Leeds by large sections of the working population and the staging of protests in many of the smaller textile towns are not to be dismissed lightly. Numerical support alone is not always the best means of judging popular sentiment: to protest on the same day as the monarch's coronation required a degree of commitment and determination which far outweighed the relatively small numbers involved. Not of course that the protesters were being disloyal – all of the protesters took great pains to stress their loyalty to the Crown – but by opposing the authorities they did leave themselves open to a charge of disloyalty. Furthermore, as the Manchester and Salford Trades' Union Committee were aware, a whole range of inducements could be offered to encourage people to join in the loyal celebrations. Even for people who might normally be distrustful of the authorities' motives and behaviour, such enticements would be hard to refuse. At the time of another coronation nearly eighty years later, Robert Roberts recalled that the gift of a 'medal, a bun, an orange, a banana and a small box of chocolates' was enough to produce a schoolful of loyal subjects for King George V.[14] Participation in the coronation day celebrations was not based solely on loyalty to the Crown: bribery, curiosity and pressure to conform were just as important. That there was even one protest meeting on the same day as Victoria's coronation, however, must be taken as an indication of widespread popular ill-feeling towards the government and its policies.

Although a variety of issues were raised by the protesters – the failure of the Reform Bill, a demand for universal suffrage, the tyranny of 'capitalists' – there was one overriding issue which concerned all of them, the New Poor Law. The Manchester and Salford Trades' Union Committee gave as one of their main reasons for boycotting the coronation day procession, that the 'system of Government . . . manifests no sympathy for the destitute poor'. At Huddersfield it was a 'verse about the poor laws' which the popular radicals sang in place of the third stanza of the national anthem. The protesters at Ashton-under-Lyne saved their most severe criticism for the 'three traitor kings', the Poor Law Commissioners. And at Oldham it was for a repeal of the 'accursed' New Poor Law that the meeting memorialised the Queen.

Passed in 1834, the Poor Law Amendment Act (or New Poor Law, as it was more popularly called) was viewed with hatred and horror by most of the labouring population of Britain. Why? Superficially one might answer that the New Poor Law was seen as treating poverty as crime and robbing Englishmen of the rights and liberties that they had enjoyed for over two hundred years under the Old Poor Law. But while such an answer is perfectly correct, it is also inadequate. To talk of the loss of rights and liberties is meaningless, unless that transaction is placed within the context of that complex web of beliefs, customs, values and assumptions which guided popular responses to the Old and New Poor Laws. Furthermore, such a web of beliefs was neither uniform nor immutable: they varied between urban and rural communities, and were liable to modification over time. Thus, as we shall see, although the campaign of popular opposition to the New Poor Law started as a clash between two world views, moral economy versus political economy, it ended up in Chartism as a class struggle for political representation. Finally, a distinction has to be made between the New Poor Law as a system of poor relief and as the product of a new ideology. For the labouring population of England and Wales there was something sinister and frighteningly different about the New Poor Law: it was viewed as turning social relationships, human values and Christian worship on their head. The purpose of the New Poor Law, claimed the Chartist newspaper the *Northern Star*, was to 'enable the High Priests of this modern Moloch, to offer up a human sacrifice to the household Gods of "Capital" '.[15]

By reviving the full ritual of the coronation, the government had hoped to reaffirm the harmony and unity of the nation as a whole. In a large measure they were successful. The London celebrations were a resounding triumph for the authorities. But the further one moved away from the capital and the closer one got to the northern manufacturing towns, with their traditions of popular radicalism, the louder were the cries of dissent. For all the pomp and pageantry in London, it was the 'poor weaver' and his loom, being dragged into Oldham on the back of a cart, which provided the most powerful and moving image of Victoria's coronation day. One detects in this poignant symbol of 'usefulness and misery' the bewilderment of ordinary men and women aggrieved at the disjunction between life as they experienced it and the state of society as the authorities, the constructors of social knowledge, wished it to be seen. Popular opposition to the 1834 Poor Law stood near the centre of this growing unrest.

Notes

1. C. Greville, *Memoirs, Part 2,* vol.I (Longman Green, London, 1885), p.108.
2. Queen Victoria's Journal, 27 June-2 July 1838, quoted in C. Woodham-Smith, *Queen Victoria* (Alfred A. Knopf, New York, 1973), p.157.
3. Greville, *Memoirs*, p.109.
4. 'Coronation. The Officers and Members of the Trades Unions in Manchester and Salford' (handbill), PRO, HO 40/38, f.59.
5. Ibid.
6. *Champion and Weekly Herald*, 8 July 1838. Victoria's coronation day was not the only occasion on which the Manchester authorities were embarrassed by the lack of popular support for a 'loyal' demonstration. The large crowds at Chartist demonstrations reflected badly on the smaller Queen's birthday parade. The authorities had their successes: W. Napier, *The Life and Opinions of General Sir Charles James Napier*, vol.II (John Murray, London, 1857), p.39, tells how the Queen's birthday parade of

May 1839 was used to stage a massive military display and thereby remind the Chartists (who were to hold a demonstration of their own two days later) that any attempted armed rising was bound to fail. The Manchester authorities ultimately abandoned the arena of public demonstration completely. 1840 saw the last of the annual Queen's birthday parades in Manchester; thereafter the Chartists, Corn Law Repealers and other popular groups had the field to themselves.

7. *Leeds Times*, 30 June 1838; *Leeds Mercury*, 7 July 1838; *Halifax Guardian*, 30 June 1838.

8. *Northern Liberator,* 30 June 1838. Contemporaries spelt 'bastile' with one *l.* The French spelling, 'bastille', was not adopted in England until late in the nineteenth century. I have used 'bastile' throughout the text.

9. *Manchester and Salford Advertiser*, 30 June 1838.

10. *Champion and Weekly Herald*, 8 July 1838.

11. Ibid.

12. *Northern Star*, 7 July 1838.

13. The respectable London press (including *The Times*, which opposed the New Poor Law) carried no reports of the protest meetings. Presumably it would have been disloyal to have mentioned them. Based on provincial newspaper reports an estimated 30,000-50,000 people took part in the coronation day protests.

14. R. Roberts, *Classic Slum* (Penguin, Harmondsworth, 1977), p.142.

15. *Northern Star*, 7 April 1838.

PART ONE

CONTEXT

1 THE OLD POOR LAW

Popular opposition to the New Poor Law was founded on expectations created by the Old. Unfortunately, our view of the Old Poor Law continues to be dominated by the *Report* of the 1832 Royal Commission. Despite criticism of the *Report's* prejudiced views, selective use of evidence and unstatistical methods, many historians persist in presenting us with what is little more than a rehash of its findings. The Old Poor Law, we are invariably told, 'demoralized the agricultural labourer', 'had the effect of keeping down wages', and 'imposed a heavy burden on the ratepayers'.[1] As Mark Blaug has pointed out, such uncritical acceptance of the views contained in the *Report* of the 1832 Royal Commission 'has seriously distorted the history of the Industrial Revolution in Britain'.[2] More particularly it has distorted our understanding of popular opposition to the 1834 Poor Law. To correct this distortion and help us view the campaign of popular opposition to the New Poor Law in context, it is necessary to re-examine the Old Poor Law, the way it operated, and (most important of all) the expectations to which it gave rise.

I

During the sixteenth century, as the state absorbed many of the powers and functions of the Church in England, it became responsible for the system of public relief which had previously been regulated by canon law. The poor laws enacted by successive Tudor governments were a development both of this canonistic tradition and of the customary charitable practices which operated within families and local communities. Many of the features of the Tudor poor laws which are usually claimed as important innovations – the recognition that society had a duty to provide for the impotent poor through an established public authority, the rule that each parish should support its own poor, the principle of compulsory poor relief contributions – were present in the informal system of poor relief which had operated in England since medieval times. Where the Tudor poor laws did break new ground, apart from the changes made to the administrative machinery, was in attempting to deal in a constructive manner with the 'new' problem of able-bodied unemployment.[3]

The economy of sixteenth-century England was in transition. Agriculture was increasingly becoming commercialised and there was a growth in commodity production. The accompanying social and economic upheavals – enclosures, unemployment, population movement (and growth?), rising prices – had combined to produce widespread destitution amongst the newly created class of day-labourers. This in turn placed an intolerable burden on existing poor relief schemes and charitable institutions. Successive Tudor governments, sensitive to the dangers of social unrest, sought to overcome these problems. Working through the local Justices of the Peace, the central authorities began to experiment with different methods of allaying distress, preventing vagrancy and maintaining social stability. The series of Tudor poor law provisions passed between 1531 and 1601 were the result.[4] The last of these enactments, the 1601 *Act for the Relief of the Poor*, the 'beloved 43rd of Elizabeth', was to form the basis of poor relief in England and Wales for the next 232 years.

The 1601 Act instituted a three-tier system of administration. At the top were the central authorities, the Crown, Privy Council and Parliament, with responsibility for determining overall policy. Next came the local magistrates, the Justices of the Peace, whose duties were supervisory, and included such activities as appointing officers, auditing accounts and settling disputes. And finally, at the bottom, came the parish authorities who were responsible for the detailed day-to-day work of administering poor relief.[5]

Under the terms of the 1601 Act, parishes were made responsible for the relief of all destitute persons living within their bounds. Funding was to be provided by the levying of a compulsory rate on 'every inhabitant ... and every occupier of land'. Unpaid parish officials, 'Overseers of the Poor', were to collect this poor-rate and control its expenditure. The overseer's first task was to help those who could achieve some degree of independence: young children, whose parents were unable to keep and maintain them, were to be set to work; older children of poor parents were to be provided with apprenticeships; and adults who were able-bodied, but had no work, were either to be 'set on work', or given 'necessary relief' until they were able to regain their independence. Of course, anyone refusing to work was liable to be gaoled. To those unlikely ever again to achieve independence — 'the lame, impotent, old, blind' and the like – the overseers were simply to give relief.[6]

With the passage of the 1598 and the 1601 Acts the Privy Council began to show a greater interest in the administration of poor relief. Initially its orders and proclamations did not differ greatly from those of an earlier period: it continued to enforce indirect measures for relieving the poor by ensuring adequate supplies of corn for the markets and controlling its price. But gradually, as it became more directly involved in the administration of poor relief, the Privy Council's orders related more and more to ordinary relief, pensions for the old and work for the unemployed.[7] Contemporary legal handbooks indicate the way in which magistrates and parish authorities interpreted these orders. One of the most popular of these handbooks makes the distinction, common at the time, between three classes of poor persons. There were the 'poore by impotency and defect', the aged, crippled, blind, lunatic and diseased, who were to be provided with enough to sustain them properly. Then there were the 'poore by casualty', the sick, those 'overcharged with children', the able-bodied unemployed and those who were the victims of accidental loss, who were to be provided with work and further relieved according to their needs. And finally there were the 'thriftless poore', rogues and vagabonds who were deserving of no sympathy or relief, and who were to be dealt with under the harsh provisions of the Vagrancy Act.[8]

The active involvement of the central authorities in poor relief reached its peak in 1630 with the issuing of the 'Book of Orders', and the formal embodiment of the Privy Council as 'Commissioners of the Poor'. Between then and the outbreak of the Civil War (and including the period of Charles I's personal rule) the central authorities' involvement in poor relief matters was almost continuous. In fact, so effectively did the central authorities intervene during this period that at least one historian argues that it was not until the twentieth century that Britain was again to see 'so much provision of work for the able-bodied or so complete a system of looking after the more needy classes'.[9]

The outbreak of civil war ended the central authorities' active involvement in poor relief. Henceforth, the magistrates and parish authorities were to enjoy virtual autonomy in the administration of poor relief, albeit an autonomy tempered by the legacy of the central authorities' period of active involvement. In all but the remotest parts of England and Wales a system of poor relief had been established, which with periodic tinkering was to remain in force for the next two hundred years.

II

The Old Poor Law slowly extended its influence well beyond the simple provision of poor relief. More than any other piece of legislation, it directly affected the lives and well-being of ordinary men and women. This is partly explained by the Old Poor Law having originally been both an instrument for the maintenance of law and order, and an arm of paternal government; and partly by its having been written in such general terms that 'the Poor' could be interpreted as meaning the labouring population as a whole. Furthermore, there was a natural tendency for the parish bureaucracy, once established, to become the *de facto* administrator of a variety of related laws and regulations. Thus we find laws relating to employment, vagrancy, bastardy, charity, the welfare of maimed soldiers, the treatment of plague victims, the maintenance of roads, the playing of games, drinking, the hunting of game and the building of Houses of Correction intimately connected with the administration of poor relief and the responsibility of the local magistrates and parish officials.[10]

The wide powers available to the parish authorities not only meant that they had a great deal of power over the poor, but that 'they were [also] expected to do more for them'. Freed from central control, the administrators of poor relief began to implement the Old Poor Law in ways which were not necessarily in accordance with the principles of the legislation itself. Relief in aid of wages, assistance for large families, the provision of housing, apprenticeships for poor children, and help so people could earn their own livelihood and again become independent, were just some of the benefits which became available to a wide section of the labouring population under the Old Poor Law. As Dorothy Marshall has observed: 'the parish was not only a relieving, but, in some cases, a preventative agent'.[11]

The prevention of destitution took many forms. The one which has attracted most attention was relief in aid of wages, or as it was better known, the allowance system. Unfortunately, the dominant position assumed in British historiography by 'Speenhamland' has tended to distort our view of the operation of the allowance system. Accepted wisdom has it that the Berkshire magistrates who met at Speenhamland in 1795 introduced the concept of relief in aid of wages into Britain; that their sliding scale of allowances, varying with the price of bread and the size of families, corrupted and debased the operation of the Old Poor Law; and that it eventually forced the introduction of much-needed reform in the shape of the New Poor Law.[12] In fact, the allowance system was in operation at least a century and a half before 'Speenhamland'.[13]

Under the terms of the 1601 Act, the practice of subsidising the wages of someone in full-time employment could be justified on two grounds: setting the able-bodied to work, and the care and welfare of the children of poor parents. In both cases parish officials soon realised that it was much cheaper and simpler to give an allowance. As early as 1629 the Privy Council had acknowledged this practice by issuing orders which allowed the magistrates to 'otherwise relieve' the able-bodied unemployed should the provision of work prove impossible. From granting outdoor relief to the unemployed, it was logical that parish officials should next help people to retain their jobs when wages began to fall during periods of economic depression. In Colchester, for instance, the 'baize makers' whose wages had been reduced to fourpence per day, had them 'made up' to tenpence per day out of the parish poor relief fund. Parish officials also realised it was cheaper and simpler to give an allowance to those labourers 'overcharged with children' than attempt to find better paid work for them. Certainly the practice had become widespread by 1697 when John Locke condemned the system whereby 'a great number of children [gave] ... a poor man title to an allowance from the parish'.[14]

Surviving parish records for the seventeenth, eighteenth and early nineteenth centuries indicate that a small, but ever present, proportion of poor relief was given under the allowance system.[15] During periods of exceptional hardship, the allowance system could be used to relieve a large proportion of the labouring population. At the end of the eighteenth century it was the agricultural labourers who benefited most from the operation of the allowance system; by the beginning of the nineteenth century it was the outworkers in the decaying handicraft trades. Foremost amongst these were the handloom weavers.

During the late 1820s, as the once-prosperous trade of cotton handloom weaving was challenged by the introduction of the powerloom, the wages of the skilled handloom weavers began to fall dramatically. Forced to work exceedingly long hours for a pitiful wage, the handloom weavers turned to the parish for help. There was no uniform scale of allowances, but in most northern parishes 'it was the practice to make up the earnings of the family to 2s. or in some cases 1/6 a head'.[16] Gilbert Henderson, Assistant Commissioner to the 1832 Royal Commission, reported how the system operated in Manchester:

those employed on work of a common description usually make out a case for relief when they have three or more children under ten years of age; printed forms are used for the purpose of ascertaining from their employers the amount of their earnings and their character for industry; and after enquiring into their means of subsistence, the deficiency is usually made up to 2 shillings a head for each member of the family.[17]

Not all parishes had systematised their operations to this extent, but most tried to alleviate the weavers' suffering. At Oldham the Select Vestry introduced a retraining scheme. Situations were 'procured for many of them in the power-loom factories' and their families maintained by the parish whilst they were 'learning to work at the power-looms'.[18] In the smaller villages and towns, however, where the majority of handloom weavers lived and worked, retraining was not practicable. The new powerloom sheds tended to be built in the existing large factory towns; and furthermore they required the labour of women and children to operate them, not adult men. For most handloom weavers the choice was therefore either to move to the overcrowded towns, in the hope of finding some sort of work, or to stay in the small handloom weaving villages and eke out an existence as best they could.[19] The Old Poor Law, through the allowance system, was able to offer some measure of support to these victims of technological change; it saved jobs, protected the young and enabled people to avoid becoming totally dependent on parish poor relief.

Opponents of the Old Poor Law consistently argued that relief in aid of wages was open to abuse. The criticisms are so well known that they hardly need repeating: workers tended to become lazy and unruly once they knew that wages would automatically be 'made up' to a fixed amount out of parish funds; and the guarantee of a minimum income destroyed all incentive to work.[20] There is little evidence of this ever happening. The allowance system did not encourage 'sloth' among the handloom weavers according to Henderson. He reported to the 1832 Royal Commission that this was because the amount decided upon was to supplement a full week's work and if the recipient worked harder he kept the extra income.[21] Those Assistant Poor Law Commissioners charged with introducing the New Poor Law into the north of England in the late 1830s also reluctantly admitted that there was little abuse of the allowance system. Alfred Power thought this was due to

a very close spirit of economy in relieving the poor...; a great degree of hardihood & independence in the mass of the people; the existence of numerous clubs and societies, providing against the contingency of sickness & embracing large numbers of the operative classes; and ... a disposition on the part of the medical men, to make moderate charges upon the township for attendance upon pauper patients.[22]

Charles Mott believed the explanation was to be found in the custom of selecting for parochial officers 'only men of great respectability without reference to political or religious feeling'. On one point all commentators agreed: the handloom weavers and other depressed persons were 'reluctant to apply for relief'.[23] Samuel Roberts, a Sheffield cutler who served his town for more than twenty years as an overseer of the poor, explained why. 'It is a mistaken idea', he wrote,

that the greater part of the Poor Rates are bestowed on improper objects – for instance, on able bodied men; men capable of working and able to produce work. Likewise that such men and their families look forward, with a kind of longing desire, to get, and remain, on the list of paupers. The very reverse of this is certainly the fact... [Even] when want of employment absolutely compels them to seek temporary relief from the parish, [far] from regarding it with satisfaction ... nine times out of ten they shrunk from it with horror, and it is only resorted to at last from absolute necessity... [F]ar from idleness being considered as an enjoyment, the great complaint of all workmen was, *the irksomeness of being unemployed.*[24]

Rent relief was another important means of preventing destitution. One of the largest areas of expenditure under the Old Poor Law, it has received little attention from historians.[25] Under the terms of the 1601 Act the parish was given power to erect 'convenient houses of dwelling for the ... impotent poor' on waste ground. It did not take long before the able-bodied were also being helped with housing at parish expense. In the north of England the practice appears to have commenced during the Civil War. The widespread dearth and want of employment at that time combined to render many labouring families destitute. Rents fell due with people unable to pay, and numerous evictions took place. Many of those evicted, like James Cowpe of Westhoughton, near Wigan, took their cases to court. Cowpe petitioned the Lancashire Quarter Sessions that he, his wife and four children were faced with starvation, 'because of the Exterodinary darth and want of work'. As a consequence, he told the Bench, he had been unable to pay his rent and been put out of his house. The Bench, sympathetic to the plight of such families, ordered that the churchwardens and overseers provide him and his family with a house.[26] Gradually, as the parish officials came to understand and accept the court's views on the housing of the poor, they began to ensure that people were not thrown out of their homes because of their failure to pay rent.

Surviving parish records indicate that by the eighteenth century the practice of paying at least part of a pauper's rent was well established. Of the twenty-two 'permanent poor' in the parish of Barrowford Booth, near Colne, Lancashire, in 1717, twelve had at least part of their rent paid out of parish funds. In extreme cases parish authorities were even prepared to pay all the rent. Nor were rent subsidies restricted to the 'permanent poor', they could also be used to assist the able-bodied poor on low incomes. At Barnsley, Sam Thornly, a linen weaver who had suffered 'misfortune', was only one of many full-time workers to have a proportion of his rent paid out of parish funds. The 1832 Royal Commission concluded that, apart from direct cash payments, the most common form of relief to be given to the able-bodied was 'that of relieving the applicants, either wholly or partly from the expense of obtaining house-room'.[27]

III

The Old Poor Law's benefits were tempered by coercion and stigmatization. The settlement laws, the compulsory wearing of badges, the Vagrancy Act and the workhouse were the price the labouring population paid for the Old Poor Law's protection. Nevertheless, it was not unusual to find their application moderated by a mixture of incompetence, expedience and humanitarianism.

Following the passage of the 1662 *Act for the Better Relief of the Poor*, parish officials had the power to remove and ship back to the parish in which they were 'legally settled' any person who did not inhabit a dwelling worth at least £10 a year, and who was liable (no matter how vaguely) to become chargeable on the parish poor rate.[28] This and later settlement laws have traditionally been seen as restricting the free movement of labour and generally contributing to the hardship experienced by the poor.[29] In practice, the settlement law's effects were nowhere near as clear cut as that. Certainly in the north of England, the settlement law appears to have done nothing to restrict the free movement of labour into the towns. In fact the settlement law might even have assisted it. Town authorities had nothing to fear from an influx of labour from the rural parishes, because the cost of removal (or as was more likely, the cost of providing outdoor relief) had to be borne by the recipient's home parish. At least one historian has seen the settlement law as yet another way in which the agricultural sector subsidised the growing industrial sector. Put simply: 'The factory got the labour; then in sickness and [old] age the rural parish got the relief bill.'[30]

The settlement law's effects were mixed. Certainly there were many occasions on which pregnant women, the sick and the aged were treated with callous disregard by penny-pinching officials. But equally there were many paupers who were able to use the threat of being removed back to their home parish as a means of obtaining outdoor relief from their overseer. Joseph Pennington was using the settlement law to advantage when he wrote to the Atherton overseers from Huddersfield in December 1831 to claim that he and his family of ten had 'not a web in the looms' and were in dire need of relief. He asked whether they were to be sent relief 'or are we all to be brought to you'. And to ensure the overseers did not delay in ordering relief to be paid, Pennington warned that if he did not hear from them quickly he would assume 'it is your will that we should come, and must apply to the overseers here to bring us'.[31] With few employment opportunities available for the poor in their home parishes, overseers were very susceptible to such pressure. Thomas Ainsworth of Clayton in Dale, Lancashire, explained to the Poor Law Commissioners that most of the paupers in the parish were 'resident at a distance in the manufacturing Towns', and as a result the parish was 'continually receiving threats from some of them that unless we send them relief they would come to us with a removal order, or a letter & Bill from the overseer of the town stating that he had relieved them and taken out an order'. The high cost of removal and/or litigation meant the parish authorities were helpless in these circumstances. '[W]hatever the charge', admitted Ainsworth, 'we always found it best to pay'.[32]

Attached to the 1697 Settlement Act was a clause requiring paupers to wear a badge on their right shoulder, bearing the letter P and the initial of their parish. The requirement has often been construed as an attempt to attach a stigma to the recipients of poor relief, but this was clearly not the intention of those who passed the legislation. It was to ensure 'that the money raised only for the relief of such as are well impotent as poor, may not be misapplied and consumed by the idle, sturdy and disorderly beggars'.[33] The wearing of badges was designed to block fraud, not punish the poor. As it happened, pauper badges soon fell into disuse. There were several reasons for this. In the smaller parishes, common knowledge was already doing the job for which the badges were intended, and it was hard to justify the expense and effort involved in their use. And in the larger parishes and towns, those at whom the badges were aimed – persons falsely claiming relief – could evade its provisions without much difficulty. Periodically the practice of making paupers wear badges was revived by enthusiastic individuals seeking to tighten up the administration of local poor relief, but by and large their use had ceased by the time the relevant legislation was repealed in 1810.[34]

The Old Poor Law's protection did not extend to the undeserving poor. Any person who refused to work could be gaoled under a clause of the 1601 Act, or, as was much more likely, dealt with under the harsh provisions of the Vagrancy Act. Passed contemporaneously with the Old Poor Law, the Vagrancy Act was the penal arm of the poor relief system. Any person 'going about begging', who obtained a livelihood by undesirable means, who refused to work for regular wages, or who was simply unable to give 'a good account of themselves', risked being 'whipped until his or her body be bloody', imprisoned in one of the newly constructed Houses of Correction, or after repeated offences, transported for up to seven years.[35] (Vagrants were also liable to be shipped back to their home parish or last place of residence after the passage of the settlement laws in 1662.)

The undoubted ferocity of the Vagrancy Act gives a false impression of its effectiveness. At different times and in different places the legislation was put into action with ruthless vigour, but enforcement was never more than spasmodic. Searches for vagrants were rare and the system of rewards for the capture of vagrants was widely abused. The law actually penalised the conscientious parish, which more often than not had to incur the cost of dealing with vagrants. It was cheaper for parish officials to warn off vagrants by threatening them with arrest and whipping, rather than proceed against them with the full rigour of the law. Furthermore, the very savagery of the Vagrancy Act militated against its effectiveness. A public whipping was provided for any woman who gave birth to a bastard child in a parish to which she did not belong or for any cripple found begging outside his home parish.[36] By the end of the eighteenth century humanitarians were questioning whether one 'could devote an unhappy human being to the whipping post or House of Correction merely for asking for charity?' And constables who attempted to arrest vagrants were more likely than not to find themselves surrounded by a hostile crowd demanding the prisoner's release.[37]

The Vagrancy Act was amended in 1824. The system of rewards for the capture of vagrants was abolished, as was the penalty of whipping. Henceforth vagrants were to be classified as common criminals and punished by imprisonment with hard labour. Vagrants were to be dealt with under the provisions of the Old Poor Law if destitute, and the removal of all persons was to be regulated by the existing settlement laws rather than by special vagrancy provisions.[38] Although the 1824 legislation went some way towards ameliorating the harshness of the old Vagrancy Act, it still did not manage to draw a clear distinction between the different categories of people who were brought within its scope. Reputed thieves, friendless beggars and paupers who proved troublesome to the authorities were all liable to suffer the same punishment, imprisonment with hard labour.

One pauper who made a nuisance of himself and was caught up in the Vagrancy Act was Joseph Wood of Barnsley. A handloom weaver by trade, Wood was one of hundreds thrown out of employment by the depression in the Barnsley linen industry in the late 1820s. The parish provided him with occasional work on the roads for eightpence a day, but it proved inadequate to support himself, his wife and two young children. As a result Wood and his wife began to harass the parish officials. On one occasion Martha Wood even followed an overseer down the street begging for relief, much to the official's annoyance. In desperation she went before the magistrates to plead her case. The bench ordered that she immediately be given two shillings and sixpence to buy food for the family. No sooner had the family sat down to eat, however, than Joseph Wood found himself under arrest. He was charged with having neglected his family, refused work and having annoyed the overseers. He was sentenced to one month in the Wakefield House of Correction. The magistrates admitted that the sentence was intended as a 'warning', but they showed some compassion for the family by ordering that Martha and the children receive five shillings a week from the parish poor relief fund while Wood was imprisoned.[39]

It is not clear how many paupers fell victim to the Vagrancy Act. Clearly the legislation could be used to entrap not only those who sought to take advantage of the community's generosity, but also some of those who were simply sick, friendless, destitute or troublesome.

Nevertheless we should be wary of concluding that large numbers of paupers were subjected to the Act's harsh provisions. Although some 15,000 people were gaoled under the provisions of the Vagrancy Act in 1832, this was still tiny when compared with an estimated pauper population of one million.[40] The Vagrancy Act might have encouraged caution on the part of paupers, but it did not discourage them from applying for relief.

Of all the impositions placed on the recipients of poor relief under the Old Poor Law, the workhouse was undoubtedly the most important. In 1696 the City of Bristol obtained a Local Act of Parliament allowing it to take over the administration of poor relief in its nineteen city parishes. Traditionally this has been viewed as the beginning of the workhouse system. The Bristol 'Mint', the huge workhouse which the merchants of the city established for the confinement of the vagabond poor, quickly became a model for similar institutions throughout England. As it happens, the Bristol 'Mint' was not the breakthrough it might first appear. A workhouse could clearly be justified under the 1601 Act's provisions for setting the poor to work and for gaoling those who refused to work. A number of the new Houses of Correction functioned as workhouses at the beginning of the seventeenth century, although they later degenerated into common gaols. And during the 1630s, several parishes, chiefly in textile towns, reported to the Privy Council that they had established places where the unemployed could be given supervised work.[41] Accurate information on how many of these early workhouses were established, or how long they stayed in operation, is not available. Chance references, however, indicate that they were much more common than is usually supposed.[42]

For most parishes, the absence of any positive legal provision might have deterred them from establishing one of these early workhouses. It was only the more prosperous towns which could apply for a Local Act of Parliament which would give them positive permission to build a workhouse. The 1722 Act removed all these difficulties. Under the terms of this Act, parishes could obtain premises for use as workhouses and enter into contracts with people to manage the house. One of the Act's most important provisions, however, was to allow parish authorities the power to deny relief to those who refused to enter the workhouse. By applying this 'workhouse test', overseers could seek to eliminate the idle and undeserving poor from their books. At least that was the theory. Apart from an amendment made in 1795, allowing magistrates the power to grant outdoor relief in cases of temporary need, the Act remained in force until the arrival of the New Poor Law in 1834.[43]

The experience of the town of Leeds, which established its first workhouse following the passage of the 1722 Act, was typical. In March 1725 the Leeds Vestry decided that a workhouse should be hired or erected 'for keeping lodging and maintaining the Poor'. A committee was appointed and in due course a house near Northbar, which had formerly been used as a Charity School, was converted for use as a workhouse. By June 1726 the house was ready for occupation and the Vestry issued orders that 'all the Charity-Children who have now Town pay be brought into this house'. It was also decided that the town's Aldermen would be requested to 'inspect their respective liberties, and give an account of what poor persons they find proper to be rec[eive]d into this house who are capable of working'. Over the next week a list of those who were to be offered the workhouse was drawn up. There were 7 men, 11 women and 33 children on the list. Three of the men, 5 of the women and 19 of the children refused to go into the house, and the committee ordered that their relief payments be stopped.[44]

The Leeds establishment was initially intended to function as a proper *work*house. Shubaal Speight, his wife and two sons were hired by the workhouse committee for £50 a year, to attend the house and 'teach the Children and others ... to spin with the dutchwheel and to card to it'. The thread that they produced was to be made into material to clothe the inmates. The workhouse was also to tender for work from outside commercial sources. Apart from making the inmates work, the workhouse committee also turned their thoughts to the education of the children under their care. In October 1726 the committee decided that any child in the workhouse who was 'untaught' should receive lessons from 'the Woman who Teacheth Reading'. It was also resolved that when vacancies occurred at the town's Charity School, workhouse children were to be given preference.[45]

Within twelve months the Leeds workhouse was encountering difficulties. A number of the adult inmates were refusing to work. The committee, who would brook no disobedience, warned one of the troublemakers, Jane Skelton, that if she continued to disobey instructions to work, the workhouse master had orders to 'turn her, and her sister and mother out of this house'. Perhaps more importantly, the workhouse was also finding it increasingly difficult to obtain work from outside commercial sources. By November 1727, outside work had dried up completely. The workhouse master, Robert Milnor, was ordered to obtain as much wool as he could to keep the inmates busy until further work came in. Apparently the outside work did not materialise, because in January 1728 the Leeds Vestry ordered the workhouse closed. The inmates were sent back to their respective divisions and the workhouse fittings sold up to help pay off its debts.[46]

The closure of the Leeds workhouse after a little over two years' operation was not unusual. In theory the workhouse appeared an admirable idea. By making the paupers work, the parish saved money and the work-shy were kept off the rates. In practice it often proved more expensive to operate a workhouse than it did to relieve the poor by the simple expedient of granting them all outdoor relief.[47] The difficulty was that the advocates of workhouses were misinformed (often wilfully) about who were the main recipients of poor relief. It was often claimed that there were large numbers of able-bodied paupers (both male and female) receiving outdoor relief, who could be forced to work to cover the cost of their relief. This was not the case. An examination of almost any list of paupers for the eighteenth and early nineteenth centuries (see Table 1.1) reveals that the vast majority of poor relief recipients were aged persons. It was true that during periods of economic depression the number of able-bodied paupers increased dramatically, but it was unlikely in those circumstances that a workhouse could have obtained any paid work for its inmates

Table 1.1: Recipients of Outdoor Poor Relief, Halifax, 1802

Category	Percentage of outdoor paupers
Widows and aged women	47
Old men	13
Infirm and idiots	7
Women with bastards	13
Men with large families	20

Source: Halifax List of Out-Poor, 22 April 1802, CMBA, MISC:283. Other records show a similar pattern: Mirfield Survey of the Poor, Farside Moore Hamlet, 1816, KMBA; Higham Parish, Details of the Poor, 1829, MCLA., L1/41/18; Atherton Overseer's List of Paupers, 25 March 1838, WRO, TR Ath/C9/8/1; Hindley Overseer's List of Paupers, 1828-9, WRO, TR Hi/Misc; F.M. Eden, *The State of the Poor* (Frank Cass, London, 1966), vol.II, pp.371-3.

anyway. The workhouse had to obtain its work from the same outside commercial sources which had failed to provide work for the able-bodied paupers in the first place. As it happened, most workhouses were almost exclusively inhabited by 'old women and children'.[48] Even at times of prosperity, it is unlikely that such inmates could earn enough to cover the cost of operating a workhouse. Unprofitability was the reason why the Leeds workhouse closed in 1728 and it was the reason why workhouses in general tended to degenerate into mere poorhouses – refuges for the aged, the sick, the infirm, the lunatic and the homeless young. Periodically the idea of establishing a workhouse in which the paupers would be made to earn their keep was revived by enthusiastic parish officials, but invariably the result was the same.[49]

In September 1738, a decade after it had closed, the Leeds workhouse at Northbar was reopened. This time there was no mention of setting the inmates to work, although this does not mean the workhouse's punitive function had been entirely abandoned. Israel Grimes was ordered to 'be kept within the gates [of the workhouse] for the space of three months', and William Cockshat, who had been found 'beating the children', was ordered to be 'confined in the dark hole for twenty four hours'. But generally the workhouse now assumed a more benevolent role. It provided shelter for those in need. Mary Scholfield was allowed into the workhouse, 'till she be well'. George Coare, 'aged over seventy', was taken into the care of the workhouse, 'he having the misfortune in Breaking his Ribs and Never likely to recover'. And John Lamb was still allowed to obtain his 'victualls' from the workhouse after he had obtained work with Robert Ripley for three shillings a week – thus effectively having his income supplemented by the free board and lodgings he received at the workhouse.[50]

What proportion of paupers received relief inside a workhouse under the Old Poor Law? Although Parliament obtained returns from every parish in England and Wales in 1776, 1804 and 1813-15, the imprecision of the questionnaires and replies leaves them only useful for gaining an impression. The 1804 returns, for instance, list 1,970 'workhouses', but it is unclear how many were places where the inmates actually worked and how many were simply almshouses. Some of these so-called workhouses had accommodation for only two people. Nevertheless, on the basis of the returns (see Table 1.2) it appears that fewer than 10 per cent of paupers were even relieved in a workhouse. Furthermore, few parishes or townships had access to a workhouse. Of the 14,600 parishes and townships which sent in their returns in 1804, only 3,765 maintained paupers in any form of workhouse. The situation had improved slightly by 1815 (see Table 1.3), but even so, three out of four parishes had no access to a workhouse. In the industrial northern counties the ratio of parishes to workhouses went as high as eight to one.[51] When Alfred Power, the Assistant Poor Law Commissioner responsible for introducing the New Poor Law into the West Riding of Yorkshire, arrived there in 1836 he was shocked to learn that there was no workhouse in the whole of the Holmfirth district of the Huddersfield Union, one of the largest and most populous Poor Law Unions in England.[52]

Table 1.2: Percentage of Paupers Receiving Relief inside a Workhouse, 1804 and 1813-15

Year	England & Wales	Cheshire	Lancashire	W.R. Yorkshire
1804	6.70	1.04	4.77	4.10
1813-15	9.90	3.07	9.53	7.10

Sources: 'Abstracts ... Maintenance of the Poor', *PP*, 1803-4, vol.XIII; 'Abstract ... Poor in England 1813-1815', *PP*, 1818, vol.XIX.

Table 1.3: Workhouse Distribution and Access, 1804 and 1813-15

		Ratio of parishes to workhouses in		
Year	England & Wales	Cheshire	Lancashire	W.R. Yorkshire
1804 (Distribution)	7.42:1	15.84:1	8.37:1	6.51:1
1813-5 (Access)	3.88:1	8.05:1	2.83:1	4.27:1

Sources: 'Abstracts ... Maintenance of the Poor', *PP*, 1803-4, vol.XIII; 'Abstract ... Poor in England 1813-1815', *PP*, 1818, vol.XIX.

IV

It has become something of a cliché among historians to say that prior to 1834 and the introduction of the New Poor Law, there was no 'system' of poor relief in Britain; that what we term the Old Poor Law was little more than a 'multitude of practices within (and sometimes without) the framework of a complicated aggregation of law'.[53] In a sense this is perfectly true: except for the early seventeenth century there was no systematic enforcement of a uniform national policy. But such a view is also misleading. The Old Poor Law might not have been controlled by uniform rules and regulations, but its implementation was informed by a commonly held system of beliefs and values concerning the rights of the poor and the obligations of the community to help those in need. To claim that there was no 'system' of poor relief before 1834 is to be blind to the existence of such 'moral economy' notions and to misinterpret the Old Poor Law's most important attribute, its flexibility.[54]

Poor relief under the Old Poor Law was a personal service in which the recipients were generally relieved in familiar surroundings by people who were personally known to them. This close contact meant that parish poor law officials were usually well placed to judge the circumstances and needs of the poor and destitute. It was first-hand knowledge and individual assessment, rather than the rigid enforcement of a uniform national policy, which decided whether an applicant would be helped and what form that relief would take. This meant that assistance given could be (and often was) as varied as the circumstances of the person in need. Thus after Mr Thomason had ridden a horse over Widow Cunliff, she was not only given relief, but the Halliwell parish officers decided that Thomason should be prosecuted at the 'expence of the Township'. William Thackray's home parish of Sandal Magna paid his contributions to the Friendly Society where he suffered a prolonged bout of unemployment. The Pennington overseers paid a wet nurse to care for Richard Collier's child following the death of his wife. And 'Old Nanny' was allowed pasture and a saddle for her donkey after she had explained her difficulties to the parish officials.[55] Such relief might not have been sanctioned by a uniform national policy (and strictly speaking it might not even have been in accordance with the law), but it did assist those in need and ultimately the parish itself.

Flexibility in poor relief even extended to assisting those who had previously taken advantage of the Old Poor Law. Thus Sam Mather, despite his reputation for being 'a great rascal' who had 'given ... trouble at various times', found sympathy and help from the parish officials when he succumbed to a crippling back ailment. Certainly the innocent were never made to suffer for the behaviour of others. Even when applicants were reputed to be of 'bad character', parish officials were loath to refuse relief if they had families to support. William Pearson, the vestry clerk for Crosthwaite and Lythe, spoke for most poor-law officials when he expressed the view that even 'if the labourer spends his summer earnings improvidently, we do not suffer his wife and children to starve and go naked on that account, we are obliged to relieve them'.[56]

This concern for the welfare of the family underpinned much of the Old Poor Law. Whether it was rent relief, the allowance system or help to the disabled, the maintenance fo the family structure and familial values informed the parishes' response. The Chartist Robert Lowery recalled how when sudden death robbed a family of its breadwinner

> the practice [was] to relieve the widows with families liberally at first, so as to enable them, with some of the club money and the aid of friends, to get into some mode of employment, such as keeping a mangle, a child's school, or a little shop... This policy kept the house together, as it was called, gave security to the family tie, and encouraged them to hope for better days, while to withhold relief, except they went into the [work]house, would have broken their spirits, destroyed their family bond, and rendered them incapable of struggling to maintain themselves.[57]

Such practices had the advantage of lessening the burden on the ratepayers, of course: people in need tended to seek the help of family first, and overseers were always quick to ascertain whether an applicant for relief had relatives who were in a position to render assistance. But this should not detract from the widespread community support for those familial values which helped guide the Old Poor Law's operation.

V

The flexibility, accessibility and familial values of the Old Poor Law nourished popular beliefs about natural justice and the 'rights' of the poor. This is not surprising: the Old Poor Law, after all, was a product of Elizabethan paternalism – with its notion of 'Commonweal' – and had been shaped by the autocratic but benevolent rule of Charles I. Furthermore, the wide range of benefits available under the Old Poor Law – relief in aid of wages, assistance for large families, the provision of housing, apprenticeships for poor children, help so people could earn their own livelihood and again become independent – encouraged the poor to expect sympathetic treatment from their local officials. In most cases these expectations were fulfilled. The ratepayers at Hatfield in Yorkshire, for instance, justified their liberal treatment of 'widows and poor women' by saying 'it is hard that those who have given the Parish the advantage of the Labours of their youth should not be supported in their Age'. One tenant farmer even ventured the opinion that 'Poor Folk have as much right to bread as the rich, and that they niver can have, till every man has land enif to keep a coo'.[58]

The moral economy notions of the rights of the poor operated within a framework of paternalism and deference. Provided the local authorities recognised their obligation to assist those in need, and so long as they acted in accordance with customary practices, there was no need for the poor to assert their right to relief. However, any rending of that web of paternalism could see such rights forcibly invoked. In East Anglia between 1769 and 1785 there was a series of violent protests against the huge Houses of Industry which were built in the area to replace the existing system of outdoor relief. The agricultural labourers and artisans fought against this blatant denial of their right to outdoor relief. The new Houses of Industry were repeatedly attacked by armed bands and in 1768 one of them (known locally as 'Bulcamp Hell') was burnt to the ground.[59]

As the new ideas of political economy gained ascendancy amongst the ruling elite of Britain in the late eighteenth and early nineteenth centuries, there was increased friction with the traditional moral economy notions embodied in the customary practices of the Old Poor Law. From the 1790s onwards the champions of political economy sniped at the existing system of poor relief. The Old Poor Law was condemned for promoting idleness, improvidence and degradation; it was said to be a spur to population growth; and with its constantly rising costs was even rumoured to be eating into the estates of the gentry. In this litany of extravagance there was one aspect of the Old Poor Law with which the apostles of political economy were especially incensed: the notion that the poor had a 'right' to relief. 'I am not at all disposed to consider legal relief as a *right* of the Poor', insisted S.W. Nicolls.

The great body of the Poor, Have no more distinct claim on the property of the country at large, than any single pauper has on a private fortune . . . The Poor ought to be informed of this; they ought to know that they are in the enjoyment of a *bounty*, not in the perception of a *right*.[60]

It was in response to attacks on the customary rights of the poor that the paternalistic notions of a moral economy began to merge with the more assertive traditions of 'free-born Englishmen'. Forced to justify their right to poor relief under the Old Poor Law, the labouring population of England and Wales came to see it not as a handout, not as a dole, not as something to be gratefully received, but as a thing they had earned or inherited – something which belonged to them. William Cobbett, that supreme spokesman for the popular conscience, warned those who wished to abolish the Old Poor Law

> that the labouring people of England, inherit, from their fathers, not any principle, not any doctrine, not any rule or maxim relative to this matter, but the habit of regarding parish relief as *their right*... These projectors [of poor law reform] ought to have known something of the habit of the people's mind in this respect. Every one of them looks upon it that he has a species of property in his parish; they talk of *losing* their parish as a man talks of losing his estate... Now, men may talk, and do whatever else they please, as long as they please, they will never persuade the labourers of England, *that a living out of the land is not their right in exchange for the labour which they yield or tender.*[61]

A recurrent theme of popular protest throughout the late eighteenth and early nineteenth centuries was the belief that 'free-born Englishmen had a right to be relieved'.[62]

Cobbett even sought to give historical backing to the notion that the poor had a right to relief. In his *History of the Protestant 'Reformation'* he claimed the Medieval Church had held its lands in trust for the poor. Although these lands had been plundered over the intervening centuries, Cobbett insisted that the poor still had claim to them, a claim which was recognised by the rights the Old Poor Law gave them:

> the right to live in the country of our birth; the right to have a living out of the land in exchange for our labour...; the right, in case we fell into distress, to have our wants sufficiently relieved out of the produce of the land, whether that distress arose from sickness, from decrepitude, from old age, or from [an] inability to find employment...

Such rights were part of an ancient social compact between the landowners and the Church on the one hand, and the labourers on the other.

For a thousand years, necessity was relieved out of the product of the Tithes. When the Tithes was taken away by the aristocracy, and by them kept to themselves, or given wholly to the parsons, provision was made out of the land, as compensation for what had been taken away. That compensation was given in the rates as settled by the poor-law. The taking away those rates was to violate the agreement, which gave as much right to receive, in case of need, relief out of the land, as it left the landowner a right to his rent.[63]

The implication of such a belief was clear: any denial of the rights of the poor ultimately threatened the rights of property.

VI

I hope a somewhat different picture of the Old Poor Law has emerged from this account than the customary one of a corrupt and depraved system which encouraged pauperism. I have tried to describe a system of poor relief, not from the point of view of its critics (measuring it against a nineteenth- or twentieth-century ideal), but from the point of view of those it benefited and most deeply affected, the labouring poor. Far from being the great evil its detractors were later to claim, the Old Poor Law tried to cope in a humane manner within a relatively poor economy with the problems of indigence, unemployment, illness, old age and death. It was not perfect and sometimes it was harshly administered, but guided by widespread community concern for the poor and weak it did offer some measure of protection against utter destitution.

The Old Poor Law played an essential role in the domestic economy of the labouring family. It maintained 'the real income of workers by tying wages to the cost of living; it provided unemployment compensation together with a scheme to promote private employment; and it coupled both of these to a family endowment plan'.[64] There were few working men and women who were not grateful at some stage for the help and assistance the Old Poor Law gave. If, for whatever reason, they became destitute and were unable to maintain themselves or their family, they could expect relief. They could expect help in sickness, infirmity, old age and death. They could expect assistance if they were unemployed or when earning inadequate wages. They could expect to be buried, have their children apprenticed, be assisted in childbirth, and helped in recovering payment from the father of their illegitimate child. They might be fortunate and never require to be helped in any of these ways, but that still did not lessen their dependence on the Old Poor Law. In an age when famine was still a real threat, illness and death could have the most catastrophic consequences for a family, land enclosures were forcing the rural peasantry to become increasingly dependent upon wage labour, and people were moving into the new industrial towns, the Old Poor Law offered ultimate protection against possible destitution. Was it any wonder that the labouring population of England and Wales came to regard relief under the Old Poor Law as their *right*? It was this old moral economy notion, that the poor had a *right* to relief, which was to clash head-on with the political economy beliefs embodied in the New Poor Law.

Notes

1. S.G. Checkland, *The Rise of Industrial Society in England* (Longman, London, 1964), p.274, N. Gash, *Aristocracy and People* (Edward Arnold, London, 1979), pp.33-4, and D. Roberts, *Victorian Origins of the British Welfare State* (Yale University Press, New Haven, 1960), pp.38-9, all repeat the litany. Such views have become so much a part of conventional wisdom that supporting evidence is rarely listed; but when it is, it is invariably the *Report, PP*, 1834, vols XXVII-XXX and XXXIV-XXXIX, or the writings of its supporters.

2. M. Blaug, 'The Myth of the Old Poor Law and the Making of the New', *Journal of Economic History*, vol.XXIII, 2 (June 1963), p.152.

3. J.R. Tanner, *Tudor Constitutional Documents* (Cambridge University Press, Cambridge, 1948), pp.470-1; B. Tierney, *Medieval Poor Law* (University of California Press, Berkeley, 1959), pp.130-2.

4. K. Polanyi, *The Great Transformation* (Octagon, New York, 1975), pp.34-5, 70; S. and B. Webb, *English Poor Law History, Part I* (Longmans Green, London, 1927), pp.60-5. Although the 1601 Act, 43 Eliz.I, c.2, was only passed as a temporary measure, it was continued by the parliaments of James I and Charles I.

5. G.W. Oxley, *Poor Relief in England and Wales, 1601-1834* (David & Charles, Newton Abbot, 1974), p.14.

6. 43 Eliz.I, c.2.

7. Oxley, *Poor Relief*, pp.16-7; E.M. Leonard, *The Early History of English Poor Relief* (Cambridge University Press, Cambridge, 1900), p.142-52.

8. M. Dalton, *The Countrey Justice*, 1635 edn, p.100, quoted in Leonard, *English Poor Relief*, pp.139-40.

9. The 1630 'Book of Orders' is reprinted in F.M. Eden, *The State of the Poor*, vol.I (Frank Cass, London, 1966), pp.156-60; Leonard, *English Poor Relief*, p.132.

10. Ibid., pp.137-8, lists some of the major statutes passed between 1597-1644 that were connected with the Old Poor Law.

11. D. Marshall, *The English Poor in the Eighteenth Century* (George Routledge & Sons, London, 1926), p.2.

12. Eden, *State of the Poor*, vol.I, p.575, helped establish the tradition by calling wage subsidies 'a deplorable evil' and singling out 'Speenhamland' for particular abuse. G. Nicholls, *A History of the English Poor Law*, vol.II (Putman's Sons, New York, 1898), pp.116, 132, took up the cry: 'Speenhamland' was 'a source of great and universal abuse', and 'was extensively adopted in other counties'. Later historians have

repeated the claim. Webb, *English Poor Law History, Part I*, pp.180-1, tells us that between '1795 and 1833 the principle of making up wages by Outdoor Relief, according to a definite scale depending on the price of bread and the number of children in the family, spread to nearly every county in England and Wales'. More recently M.E. Rose, 'The Administration of Poor Relief in the West Riding of Yorkshire, c.1820-1853', unpublished D.Phil. thesis, Oxford, 1965, p.13, has claimed that the allowance system in the north of England grew up as a result of 'Speenhamland'.

13. Instances of the allowance system operating in the seventeenth century are to be found in: A.W. Ashby, 'One Hundred Years of Poor Law Administration in a Warwickshire Village' in P. Vinogradoff (ed.), *Oxford Studies in Social and Legal History*, vol.III (Clarendon Press, Oxford, 1912), p.155; E.M. Hampson, *The Treatment of Poverty in Cambridgeshire, 1597-1834* (Cambridge University Press, Cambridge, 1934), p.37; G.W. Oxley, 'Permanent Poor in South-West Lancashire under the Old Poor Law' in J.R. Harris (ed.), *Liverpool and Merseyside* (Augustus M. Kelley, New York, 1969), p.27-8; Webb, *English Poor Law History, Part I*, p.172. It appears that J.R. Poynter, *Society and Pauperism* (Routledge & Kegan Paul, London, 1969), p.79, was correct to question whether 'Speenhamland' was really deserving of its fame.

14. Leonard, *English Poor Relief*, p.153; Webb, *English Poor Law History, Part I*, p.172; Hampson, *Treatment of Poverty*, p.48; H.R.F. Bourne, *The Life of John Locke*, vol.II (Scientia Verlag, Salem, 1969), p.384.

15. Whiston Petition 1654, LRO, QSP/259/12; Tyldesley and Shackerley Overseers Accounts 1703, LRO, QSP/916/26; Atherton Overseer's Correspondence 1718-1841, WRO, TR Ath/C8; Sutton Overseer's Accounts 1769, Chethams Library, Mun A7/14; Halliwell Township Book 1787-1813, BMBA, PHA/1/2.

16. *Extracts from the Information Received by His Majesty's Commissioners, as to the Administration and Operations of the Poor-Laws* (B. Fellowes, London, 1833), p.340.

17. *Report, PP*, 1834, vol.XXVIII, p.920.

18. Ibid., p.917.

19. D. Bythell, *Handloom Weavers* (Cambridge University Press, Cambridge, 1969), pp.254-7.

20. H.B. Gascoigne, *Pauperism; Its Evils and Burden Reduced* (Baldwin Cradock & Joy, London, 1818), p.12, claimed that 'the ease with which many obtained money [from the parish], induced others to apply'. And Lord Althorp, *Hansard*, 3rd series, vol.XXII (1834), col.878, told the House of Commons when introducing the New Poor Law that relief paid to the poor in their own dwellings was 'a great mistake', as all 'feelings of independence on the part of the labourers had been almost entirely extinguished'.

21. *Extracts*, p.340.

22. Power to PLC, 9 March 1839, PRO, MH 32/64.

23. Mott to PLC, 9 March 1839, PRO, MH 12/6039; *Extracts*, p.356; Power to PLC, 21 October 1837, PRO, HO 73/53.

24. S. Roberts, *Defence of the Poor Laws* (n.p., Sheffield, 1819), p.33, my italics.

25. An exception is N.D. Hopkin, 'The Old and New Poor Law in East Yorkshire, c.1760-1850', unpublished M.Phil. thesis, Leeds, 1969, p.12.

26. Petition of James Cowpe for a Habitation, 1650, LRO, QSP/32/12. Other examples are to be found in LRO, QSP/8, 32, 64.

27. Barrowford Booth Overseer's Accounts 1717, MCLA, L1/41/8/1; Barnsley Parish, Overseer's Account Book, 10 January 1774, BML; *Report, PP*, 1834, vol.XXVII, p.8.

28. 13 & 14 Car.III, c.12. The Act was slightly amended and legal settlement more clearly defined in 1691, 3 & 4 M.&W. c.11, and again in 1697, 8 & 9 Will.III, c.30. In

36   *The Old Poor Law*

1795, 35 Geo.III, c.101, the legislation was modified again to allow removal only after a person had actually applied for relief.

29. Critics of the Settlement Laws include: Webb, *English Poor Law History, Part I*, p.330; Ashby, 'One Hundred Years', p.80; J.D. Chambers, *Nottinghamshire in the Eighteenth Century* (King & Son, London, 1932), p.266; and Marshall, *The English Poor*, p.248. Not all historians agree with the criticisms: E.J. Hobsbawm, 'The Tramping Artisan', *Economic History Review*, 2nd series, vol.III, no.3 (1951), p.303, says the settlement law 'hardly incommoded the artisan'. He expressed similar views about the rural labourer in E.J. Hobsbawm and G. Rude, *Captain Swing* (Norton, New York, 1975), p.46.

30. J.S. Taylor, 'The Impact of Pauper Settlement, 1691-1834', *Past and Present*, 73 (November 1976), p.66.

31. Pennington to Atherton Overseas, 3 December 1831, Atherton Overseer's Correspondence, WRO, TR Ath/C8. For other examples of such thinly veiled threats see: Hindley Overseer's Correspondence, WRO, TR Hr/Cl; Sandal Magna Poor Law Correspondence, 1820-1829, LCA, SM 22/1; and (according to Taylor, 'Impact of Pauper Settlement', p.68) the correspondence of Stephen Garnett, overseer of Kirkby Lonsdale, Westmoreland Record Office, Kendal, WPR/19.

32. Ainsworth to PLC, 31 January 1835, PRO, MH 12/5529. *Extracts*, p.359, reports Assistant Commissioner Henderson as observing that the practice of relieving out-paupers in the large towns, rather than removing them, operated to the benefit of everyone concerned.

33. 8 & 9 Will.III, c.30; see also Oxley, *Poor Relief*, p.54.

34. A.E. Davies, 'Some Aspects of the Operation of the Old Poor Law in Cardiganshire, 1750-1834', *Ceredigion*, vol.6, no.1 (1968), pp.19-20, says Cardiganshire was one of the few areas in Britain still to be enforcing the wearing of badges when the legislation was repealed by 50 Geo.III, c.52.

35. 39 Eliz.I, c.4; Webb, *English Poor Law History, Part I*, p.352.

36. 17 Geo.II, c.5; L. Radzinowicz, *A History of English Criminal Law*, vol.IV (Stevens & Son, London, 1956), pp.18-20; G.M. Ayers, *England's First State Hospitals and Metropolitain Asylums Board 1867-1930* (University of California Press, Berkeley, 1971), p.224, fn.4. The whipping of women was abolished in 1792.

37. Radzinowicz, *English Criminal Law*, pp.21-3, [John Scott], *Observations on the Present State of the Parochial and Vagrant Poor* (n.p., London, 1773), p.4; Webb, *English Poor Law History, Part I*, pp.371-6.

38. 5 Geo.V, c.83; G. Taylor, *The Problem of Poverty 1660-1834* (Longman, London, 1969), p.55.

39. 'Incidents in a Pauper's Life, An Account of Joseph Wood' in J. Wilkinson, 'Barnsley Diaries', unpublished MS, BML.

40. Radzinowicz, *English Criminal Law*, p.25, estimates that one-fifth of all vagrants were involved in other sorts of crime. The estimate of the pauper population in 1832 is based on 'Abstract ... Poor in England 1813-1815'. *PP*, 1818, vol.XIX, which gives a total pauper population of 940,627 in 1815, and 'Fourteenth Annual Report PLC' *PP*,1848, vol.XXXIII, Appendix B. no.2, which puts the number at 1,199,529 in 1840.

41. M. Ignatieff, *A Just Measure of Pain* (Macmillan, London, 1978), p.13; Leonard, *English Poor Relief*, pp.255-7; S. and B. Webb, *English Poor Law History, Part II*, (Frank Cass, London, 1963), pp.83-6, 116-20.

42. See A. Redford, *The History of Local Government in Manchester*, vol.I (Longmans Green, London, 1950), pp.173-4; *VCH, Shropshire*, vol.VIII, p.167; and S.H. Waters, *Wakefield in the Seventeenth Century* (Sanderson & Clayton, Wakefield, 1933), p.59.

43. 9. Geo.I, c.7 (1722); 22 Geo.III, c.83 (1782) allowed the establishment of

'Union' workhouses; 36 Geo.III, c.23 (1795) contained the amendments allowing outdoor relief.

44. Leeds Vestry Workhouse Committee Minute and Order Book, 6 March 1725, 18 and 25 June 1726, LCA, LO/M/1.

45. Ibid., 9 July, 22 October 1726.

46. Ibid., 24 June, 18 November 1727, 12 January 1828.

47. Eden, *State of the Poor*, vols.II & III, *passim*, has many examples of this. At Market-Weighton (ibid., vol.III, p.864) the parish authorities explained that they only had a few paupers in their workhouse because 'the Poor could be maintained at a cheaper rate out of the house'.

48. Ibid., vol.II, pp.35, 296, 343, 370 and vol.III, p.811.

49. Webb, *English Poor Law History, Part I*, p.411.

50. Leeds Vestry Workhouse Committee Minute and Order Book, 22 September 1738, 27 October 1744, 4 May 1748, 19 April 1749, 6 April 1948, LCA, LO/M/1-3.

51. 'Report ... Overseers of the Poor', *PP*, 1777, First Series, vol.IX; 'Abstracts ... Maintenance of the Poor', *PP*, 1803 4, vol.XIII; 'Abstract ... Poor in England 1813-1815', *PP*, 1818, vol.XIX. For a discussion of their failure as statistics see: J.S. Taylor, 'The Unreformed Workhouse, 1776-1834' in E.W. Martin (ed.), *Comparative Development in Social Welfare* (Allen & Unwin, London, 1972), p.58, and P. Grey, 'Parish Workhouses and Poorhouses', *Local Historian*, vol.10, 2 (1972), p.73.

52. Power to PLC, 28 January 1840, PRO, MH 12/15065.

53. Poynter, *Society and Pauperism*, p.1. Similar views are expressed by Webb, *English Poor Law History, Part I*, p.424, K. de Schweinitz, *England's Road to Social Security* (University of Pennsylvania Press, Philadelphia, 1947), p.79, Marshall, *English Poor*, p.251, and Rose, 'The Administration of Poor Relief', p.11.

54. This analysis is informed by E.P. Thompson, 'The Moral Economy of the English Crowd in the Eighteenth Century', *Past and Present*, 50 (February 1971), pp.76-136.

55. Halliwell Township Book, 22 October 1789, 6 May 1797, BMBA, PHA/1/2; Thackray to Firth, 21 December 1818, and Firth to Thackray, 14 January 1819, Sandal Magna Poor Law Correspondence, LCA, SM22/1; Pennington Overseer's Accounts, 3 July 1823, WRO, TR Pen/C1/84

56. Davidson to Atherton Overseers, 21 December 1831, Atherton Overseers Correspondence, WRO, TR Ath/c8; *Extracts*, p.173; R.N. Thompson, 'The New Poor Law in Cumberland and Westmoreland (1834-1871)', unpublished PhD thesis, Newcastle-upon-Tyne, 1976, p.24.

57. R. Lowery, 'Passages in the Life of a Temperance Lecturer' in B. Harrison and P. Hollis (eds.), *Robert Lowery: Radical and Chartist* (Europa, London, 1979), p.96.

58. Pilkington to Chadwick, 20 October 1834, Chadwick Papers, UCL, CP 1585.

59. Webb, *Poor Law History, Part 1*, pp.141-2; A.J. Peacock, *Bread and Blood* (Gollancz, London, 1965), p.32; Ignatieff, *A Just Measure of Pain*, pp.13-14.

60. S.W. Nicolls, *A Summary View of the Report and Evidence Relative to the Poor Laws* (n.p., York, 1818), p.31.

61. *Cobbett's Two-Penny Trash*, vol.I, no.6 (December 1830), p.137.

62. A. Digby, *Pauper Palaces* (Routledge & Kegan Paul, London, 1978), p.216. See also I.J. Prothero, *Artisans and Politics in Early Nineteenth-Century London* (Dawson, Folkestone, 1979), p.70, who gives an example of the Spitalfield weavers asserting 'their *right* to relief from the rich'; and J. Obelkevich, *Religion and Rural Society* (Oxford University Press, London 1976), p.75, who points out that until the 1870s the agricultural labourers of South Lindsey still regarded outdoor relief as their right.

63. W. Cobbett, *History of the Protestant 'Reformation' in England and Ireland*

(Myres, Baltimore, 1826); W. Cobbett, *Tour of Scotland*, pp.101, 108, quoted in W. Reitzel (ed.), *The Autobiography of William Cobbett* (Faber, London, n.d.), pp.224-5.

64. Blaug, 'Myth of the Old Poor Law', p.152.

UNIVERSITY OF WINNIPEG
LIBRARY
DISCARDED
Winnipeg, Manitoba R3B 2E9

On Thursday, 14 August 1834, the *Act for the Amendment and better Administration of the Laws relating to the Poor in England and Wales* received royal assent.[1] Notwithstanding its conservative title and wording, the Act constituted a radical reform of the existing system of poor relief. In part a product of Philosophical Radicalism, the New Poor Law (as it quickly became known) overthrew more than two hundred years of tradition by introducing an entirely new and restrictive national poor relief policy, and it transformed the system of local government in England and Wales with its creation of a centralised bureaucracy to administer the new policy. While some recent scholars have argued that the New Poor Law was not as radical as it has often been portrayed,[2] there is no denying that many contemporaries viewed it as a near-revolutionary measure. Edwin Chadwick, who more than anyone else could claim authorship of the New Poor Law, saw it as 'the first piece of legislation based on scientific or economical *[sic]* principles'. John Walter, Tory MP for Berkshire and owner of *The Times*, agreed that it was based on entirely new principles but found no virtue in this. He told the House of Commons that

> it was impossible to conceal the fearful importance of the ... measure. It was an attempt, not to alter or improve, but to abolish at one stroke the whole body of our Poor Laws, and to substitute another body of laws, totally different in principle and practice, in their place.

Samuel Roberts, a retired Sheffield cutler and prominent philanthropist, was shocked by what he saw as the inhumanity of 'this comet of Lucifer'. And Richard Oastler, the Tory Radical who had earned the support of urban workers for his staunch advocacy of factory reform, noted with irony that the ' "first-fruits" of "Reform" and "Liberal Principles" ... should have turned out to have been a robbery of the RIGHTS of the poor'.[3]

Proposals to reform the Old Poor Law were not new. In 1692 John Locke had suggested that the system of poor relief be altered and throughout the eighteenth century there was a steady stream of proposals for reform.[4] But it was not until the 1790s that the rising cost of poor relief, famine and the fear of revolution combined to give any real urgency to the debate over reforming the Old Poor Law. While traditionalists and humanitarians sought to lessen the burden to the poor, others, informed by the new ideas of political economy, proposed more drastic solutions.

The Reverend Thomas Robert Malthus was undoubtedly the most influential of the early political economy critics of the Old Poor Law. Although he was only to have an indirect effect on the eventual shape of the New Poor Law, Malthus's natural law critique of the Old Poor Law transformed debate on the subject and paved the way for the reforms of 1834. In *An Essay on the Principle of Population*, the first edition of which was published in 1798, Malthus set out what he saw as the natural law governing population growth. Put simply, he claimed that population had a tendency to grow at a much greater rate than the rate of increase in subsistence. And because of this population growth was only restrained within the limits of subsistence by the operation of natural checks, 'misery and vice'. The consequence, according to Malthus, was that misery and vice 'must necessarily be severely felt by a large portion of mankind'.[5]

Malthus's natural law of population had important implications for the operation of the Old Poor Law. To start with, it suggested that no distribution of money, no matter how great, could possibly raise the general standard of living for the poor and destitute. 'Suppose', argued Malthus,

that by a subscription of the rich the eighteen pence a day which [labouring] men earn now was made up to five shillings, it might be imagined, perhaps, that [labourers] ... would then be able to live comfortably and have a piece of meat every day for their dinners. But this would be a very false conclusion. The transfer of three shillings and sixpence a day to every labourer would not increase the quantity of meat in the country. There is not at present enough for all to have a decent share. What would then be the consequence? The competition among the buyers in the market of meat would rapidly raise the price from sixpence or sevenpence to two or three shillings in the pound, and the commodity would not be divided among many more than it is at present... [W]hen subsistence is scarce in proportion to the number of people, it is of little consequence whether the lowest members of the society possess eighteen pence or five shillings. They must at all events be reduced to live upon the hardest fare and in the smallest quantity.[6]

Furthermore, any relief given to the unproductive pauper could only be at the expense of the deserving independent labourer. This was true even of relief given in the workhouse:

The quantity of provisions consumed in workhouses upon a part of the society that cannot in general be considered as the most valuable part diminishes the shares that would otherwise belong to the more industrious and more worthy members, and thus in the same manner forces more to become dependent. If the poor in the workhouses were to live better than they now do, this new distribution of the money of the society would tend more conspicuously to depress the condition of those out of the workhouses by occasioning a rise in the price of provisions.[7]

Malthus claimed that he was describing the effects of an immutable law of nature and, in his *First Essay* at least, that he could offer no solution to the inevitable 'recurrence of misery' – such things were 'beyond the power of man'. But he could suggest palliatives. In 1798 he suggested three: 'the total abolition of all the present parish laws'; the encouragement of 'agriculture above manufacturers, and ... tillage above grazing'; and finally (and rather surprisingly in view of his opinions) the establishment of county workhouses, 'for cases of extreme distress'. Malthus stressed that these workhouses were not to be 'comfortable asylums', but places where 'the fare should be hard, and those that were able obliged to work'.[8]

With the publication of the *Second Essay* in 1803, Malthus's view hardened. He no longer shied away from recommending the firm action which logically followed from his views. The workhouse proposal was abandoned and he now urged the abolition of the entire poor law system. As a first step, and as a matter of urgency, Malthus suggested that the government 'disclaim the *right* of the poor to support'. His proposal for abolition was simple: 'I should propose a regulation to be made, declaring, that no child born from any marriage, taking place after the expiration of a year from the date of the law, and no illegitimate children born two years from the same date, should ever be entitled to parish assistance'.[9] Thus, within a generation, the entire poor law system would be abolished. Malthus also recommended that private charities be more strictly controlled. Large charities, with their lack of discrimination, were as pernicious as the Old Poor Law and should be abandoned. Small voluntary charities, on the other hand, were acceptable, because the recipients could not help but feel grateful and those who were refused charity could not complain of injustice or a denial of their 'rights'. But he stressed that discrimination had to be exercised at all times. The deserving poor were the only genuine 'objects of charity'; and if the idle were also to be given charity it had to be with the greatest care.[10] Malthus even hinted at something like the principle of less-eligibility as a guide for giving charity to the poor. 'We may', he wrote,

> take upon ourselves, with great caution, to mitigate the punishments which they are suffering from the laws of nature, but on no account to remove them entirely. They are deservedly at the bottom in the scale of society; and if we raise them from this situation, we not only palpably defeat the end of benevolence, but commit a most glaring injustice to those who are above them. They should on no account be enabled to command so much of the necessaries of life as can be obtained by the wages of common labour.[11]

Few works have provoked such heated controversy as Malthus's *Essay on the Principle of Population*. This persuasively written book, with its claim to having discovered one of the iron laws of economics, transformed debate over the Old Poor Law and captivated the minds of a generation. Even defenders of the Old Poor Law were forced to accommodate their arguments to Malthus's principles. William Godwin, whose optimistic view of future development had provoked Malthus to write his *First Essay*, initially admitted the truth of Malthus's principles 'in the fullest extent', although later he was to direct his fury against all things Malthusian.[12] While Malthus himself was probably sincere in his claims that he deplored misery and welcomed such improvements as were possible, not all his followers were so benevolent or so well intentioned. Hard-hearted and selfish people found in Malthus's writings a doctrine which relieved them of any obligation to help the poor and needy. It was this doctrinaire Malthusianism which John Weyland, magistrate and member of the Board of Agriculture, branded as 'utterly subversive of this country and the moral and political welfare of its inhabitants'. Other outraged conservatives and popular radicals added their voices to the growing controversy. Robert Southey accused Malthus of defending plagues, of pitting his 'science' against God's Laws, and of 'detestable hard-heartedness'. And William Cobbett embarked on a lifetime of campaigning against the 'hard-hearted doctrine' of the 'check-population philospher'.[13]

The end of the Napoleonic War brought economic depression, unemployment, and renewed public criticism of the Old Poor Law. Malthusian views predominated. The Reverend John Davison, fellow of Oriel College Oxford, produced a thoughtful and comprehensive work on poor relief which quickly gained a considerable reputation. For the most part it supported the Malthusian cause. Davison suggested that relief to the able-bodied should be abolished within ten years and that relief to the impotent should be more strictly supervised.[14] S.W. Nicolls wrote a pamphlet denying that the poor had a 'right' to relief, read Malthus's *Second Essay* and within a year produced an even more doctrinaire work calling for immediate abolition.[15] James Ebenezer Bicheno, lawyer and botanist, was if anything even more outspoken and doctrinaire. The Old Poor Law, he claimed, stood in the way of progress: it encouraged marriage, removed hunger as the chief stimulus to labour and discouraged the worthy poor. Its results were low wages and near universal vice and misery. '[W]e must return', wrote Bicheno, 'to the operation of the natural law from which we have departed; and not regret it because some unhappiness and misery may be the consequence'.[16] Hunger, apparently, would provide the destitute with a splendid opportunity to regain the path of moral righteousness.

The most influential pamphleteer of the post-war years was undoubtedly the Right Reverend John Bird Sumner, Bishop of Chester (and future Archbishop of Canterbury). A cautious, moderate man, his *Treatise on the Records of Creation* did much to reconcile God and Malthus in the minds of conscientious Christians. Sumner claimed God had created the world and the laws of nature not to provide indolent satiety, but as a sphere where virtue might be exercised under the pressure of adversity. Thus poverty and social inequality provided the best conditions for the development of man's moral character. Equality would not end immorality and vice, but would only see the 'great occasions of virtue cut off for ever'.[17] To this creed of social complacency, Sumner added Malthus's principle of population. The pressure of population ensured that unequal state of society in which every person was placed in the condition best calculated to improve their faculties and virtue. The scarcity of subsistence produced not only the division of property, but the division of rank; and the pressure of population put a premium on economy and individual exertion. Without poverty and inequality life would be a 'dreary blank'. How inconceivable, argued Sumner, that God had not provided scarcity for precisely this reason. The Old Poor Law, by acting as a barrier to the operation of the principle of population, obstructed the creation of the virtues proper to the labouring classes. 'This evil', claimed Sumner, 'can only be remedied by a return to the natural course'.[18] But Sumner hesitated about advocating total abolition. The Old Poor Law was faulty and should be severely limited, but rather than immediate abolition he sought its gradual replacement with enlightened charity, education, friendly societies, savings banks and similar self-help schemes. Sumner's *Treatise*, with its Malthusian critique of poor relief and pious justification of existing social inequalities, did much to convince devout Christians that the Old Poor Law should be replaced.[19] A decade and a half later Sumner's views were again to be heard, when he sat as a member of the 1832 Royal Commission of Inquiry into the Poor Laws.

Malthusian criticism of the Old Poor Law reached its climax with the Report of the 1817 House of Commons Select Committee into poor relief. The criticism was perhaps all the more dramatic because it came not from the pen of any political economist or doctrinaire Malthusian, but from a large committee whose forty members included men of a variety of parties and opinions. The Report (which was reputedly written by Sir Thomas Frankland Lewis, future chairman of the Poor Law Commission)[20] accepted in full the Malthusian critique of the Old Poor Law. Public relief, it was alleged, demoralised the labourer, served 'to separate ... the interests of the higher and lower orders', encouraged 'an unlimited demand on funds', and ultimately pulled down the level of wages paid to the independent labourer. The Report approved of the Scottish system of private charity and the deterrent effect of the workhouse system, and recommended a limit on poor law expenditure, together with the encouragement of parish schools and benefit clubs, and an improved system of poor relief administration.[21]

That the 1817 House of Commons Select Committee baulked at endorsing an immediate abolition of the Old Poor Law was a cause of some anger amongst the more doctrinaire Malthusians.[22] It also illustrated an inherent weakness in the Malthusian solution to the problem of poor relief. Malthus and the other economic law opponents of the Old Poor Law were uncompromising in their proposals and refused to consider anything less than total abolition; yet total abolition was too drastic a solution to be seriously entertained by the majority of parliamentarians. As it was, the House of Lords responded to the Commons Select Committee Report by establishing their own rival Select Committee to find a more acceptable solution. The Lords Inquiry criticised again the abuses in the Old Poor Law, but was much more cautious in its recommendations.

[T]he Committee are ... decidedly of the opinion, that the general system of these laws, interwoven as it is with the habits of the people, ought, in the consideration of any measure to be adopted for their melioration and improvement, to be essentially maintained... [T]he subject is in its nature so extensive and difficult, that little more can be expected ... from any exertions that can be made by individuals, or perhaps from the collective wisdom of Parliament, [and] that such alleviation of the burthens as may be derived from an improved system of management, ... [will only come] from rendering the laws more simple in execution.[23].

The Lords Select Committee Report was a recipe for inaction, and successive Tory Governments under Liverpool, Canning, and Wellington happily complied.[24] Reform of the Old Poor Law had to await the formation of the first Whig ministry in twenty-three years and the acceptance of an entirely different solution to the problem of poor law reform, a solution suggested by the work of the Philosophical Radical, Jeremy Bentham.

II

The moral philosopher and reformer Jeremy Bentham first turned his attention to the system of poor relief in 1787. Examining William Pitt's proposed Poor Law Amendment Bill, Bentham concluded that the proposed humanitarian reforms could lead only to waste and corruption. Bentham was particularly critical of Pitt's system of outdoor relief and a clause which allowed an individual possessing £30 worth of property to remain eligible for relief. According to Bentham, the continuation of relief to idle and profligate persons would reduce the independent labourer's incentive to work. If Bentham's criticisms were a preview of those made in the *Report* of the 1832 Royal Commission, so too was his remedy. He proposed the establishment of large and strictly controlled workhouses where paupers would be maintained at a standard only slightly above starvation.[25]

Criticism of Pitt's Poor Law Bill was only the beginning of Bentham's effort to alter the Old Poor Law and over the next couple of years he devoted himself to exploring the subject in detail. Bentham started from the assumption that all civil laws, like the Old Poor Law, had to meet four specific aims: subsistence, security, abundance and equality. He recognised that the aims of security and equality could come into conflict, but resolved that security was the superior aim and should take precedence.[26] Security, especially the security of property, was what distinguished civilised society from the savage: without it there could be no effective industry, no reliable subsistence and no abundance. 'When security and equality are in conflict', Bentham wrote,

> it will not do to hesitate a moment. Equality must yield . . . The establishment of perfect equality is a chimera; all we can do is to diminish inequality.[27]

Unlike many other writers on poor relief, Bentham was careful to distinguish between poverty and indigence.

> Poverty is the state of everyone who, in order to obtain *subsistence*, is forced to have recourse to *labour*. Indigence is the state of him who, being destitute of property ... is at the same time, either *unable to labour*, or unable even *for* labour, to procure the supply of which he happens thus to be in want.

Poverty was thus 'the natural, the primitive, the general and the *unchangeable* lot of man'. It was not only impossible to remove poverty, but the attempt should not even be made. Poverty, through the labour for necessities, acted as the spur for the creation of all wealth. Only indigence was to be pitied and relieved.[28]

Although Bentham rejected the notion that the indigent had a 'natural right' to relief, he agreed that it was necessary to pass legislation to guarantee relief: it was contrary to the basic principle of utility and the general aim of security that a person should starve to death while food existed, and only a legal provision could ensure that this did not happen.

If the condition of persons *maintained* without property *by the labour of others* were rendered more eligible, than that of persons maintained by their *own* labour then, in proportion as the existence of this state of things were ascertained, individuals destitute of property would be continually withdrawing themselves from the class of persons maintained by their own labour, to the class of persons maintained by the labour of others: and the sort of idleness, which at present is more or less *confined* to persons of *independent* fortune, would thus extend itself sooner or later to every individual ... till at last there would be *nobody* left to labour at all for anybody.[30]

Although he did not give it the name, this was clearly the basis of the less-eligibility principle' of 1834.

Bentham was a system builder, and the result of his thoughts on poor relief was 'Pauper Management Improved', an elaborate plan for a centrally governed poor relief system. Five hundred large workhouses, each capable of holding 2,000 inmates, were to be erected throughout the country. They were to be spaced at intervals of ten and two-thirds miles, so as to be accessible to people on foot. These were no ordinary workhouses, but Panopticons, Bentham's famous twelve-sided industry-houses, designed on the principle of 'central inspectability'. Health, morals, and the prevention of annoyance required the classification and separation of the inmates, and Bentham planned it in great detail. The diseased and lunatic were to be separated from the healthy, the morally corrupt from the innocent, male from female, and those with extra comforts from the rest, to prevent 'unsatisfiable desires'. All the inmates were to be set to work. The bed-ridden were to inspect the goods manufactured by the healthy, and the blind were to be taught to knit. Piece-work was to be the rule, and all the paupers were to be made to work off the value of the relief they received before being allowed to leave the house.[31] Managing the whole scheme would be a National Charity Company, who would run the enterprise on strict business lines, making a profit from the paupers' labour. Bentham was confident that within twenty years the Company would have repaid the capital outlay of £4—6 million and reduced the poor rate to nothing.[32]

Like most of Bentham's schemes, the Pauper Plan was never put into effect. There was an attempt in 1798 to set up a National Charity Company to collect information which would enable detailed planning to take place, but it attracted little support. His proposal was considered by a Parliamentary Committee in 1811, but rejected.

Bentham eventually received £23,000 compensation from the government for the work he had undertaken.[33] Although rejection marked the end of Bentham's personal involvement in poor law reform, his ideas and principles were not forgotten. Both at a national and a local level, Benthamite thinking on reforming the Old Poor Law continued to win converts.

In 1808, the Reverend John T. Becher, a magistrate active in local poor law affairs, persuaded the parish of Southwell in Nottinghamshire to erect a new workhouse on the Benthamite principles of 'inspection, classification and seclusion'. At a time when prices were rising and most parishes were extending their outdoor relief schemes, it was a bold step. Built to house eighty-four inmates, the workhouse was to incorporate Bentham's ideas on central inspectability, with a lodge at the centre and wings extending on each side. If success is to be judged in terms of a scheme's ability to reduce expenditure, the Southwell experiment was a triumph. By 1824, the annual cost of poor relief in the parish had been reduced from £2,254 to £760.[34]

Becher's success at Southwell inspired a number of imitators. They included his cousin, the Reverend Robert Lowe of Bingham, Nottinghamshire, the Reverend Thomas Whately of Cookham, Berkshire, and J.H.L. Baker of Utley, Gloucestershire. In 1823 Becher succeeded in extending his system to the forty-nine parishes within the Thurgarton Hundred. A new workhouse was built at Upton, again incorporating Benthamite principles. The able-bodied were only to be relieved in the workhouse, where they were to be set to work breaking stones, shovelling gravel, and doing other tasks designed to drive them off the parish rates. The strict regime had the desired effect. Although the workhouse had been built to house 71 persons, in 1827 it held only 54 inmates, 23 men, 17 women and 14 children.[35]

Apart from reducing the cost of poor relief, Becher's system had other unforeseen benefits: a well-administered workhouse made an effective instrument of social discipline. 'In all our views and reasonings on the subject', wrote the one-time acting overseer at Southwell (and future member of the 1834 Poor Law Commission), George Nicholls,

we contemplated the workhouse as little more than an instrument of economy... It was not until these results began to be developed, at Bingham and Southwell, that the full consequence of the *mitigated kind of necessity* imposed on the working classes, by a well-regulated workhouse, were understood and appreciated. We saw that it compelled them, *bred* them, to be industrious, sober, provident, careful of themselves, [and] of their parents and children...[36]

Here then, or so dogma insisted, was the answer to the Malthusian dilemma: a poor relief system which, instead of encouraging pauperism, taught the labouring population to be industrious and independent. The apparent success of Becher and the other local reformers, in applying Bentham's principles to poor relief, was to have a profound impact on the shape of the New Poor Law.

III

Humanitarians and political radicals had traditionally been amongst the severest critics of the Old Poor Law. Throughout the second half of the eighteenth century a succession of humanitarians (including Jonas Hanway, Thomas Gilbert and George Rose) condemned the existing system of poor relief for its cruelty towards the poor and sought humane reform. And in 1792 Tom Paine, the patron saint of popular radicalism in Britain, had no hesitation in describing aspects of the Old Poor Law as 'instruments of civil torture', oppressive to ratepayers and paupers alike. He proposed that parish relief be replaced by a nationally funded system of family allowances, education subsidies, old-age pensions, funeral expenses and a scheme of public employment for the casual poor.[37] Needless to say Paine's prophetic suggestion was ignored by the legislature of the day. As the clamour against the Old Poor Law from Malthusians and Benthamites grew in intensity, however, humanitarians and political radicals alike were increasingly forced to defend the existing system of poor relief.

Samuel Roberts, a successful cutlery manufacturer with a philanthropic bent, first sought appointment as an Overseer of the Poor for Sheffield in 1804 because he was opposed to the system's treatment of the poor. For his efforts in reforming the town's poor relief system he earned the accolade, the 'Pauper's advocate'. Fifteen years later Roberts could be found vigorously defending the Old Poor Law against attack. He admitted it was often imperfectly administered, but believed that in the final analysis the Old Poor Law was based on humane principles.[38]

It was the same with William Cobbett. At the beginning of the nineteenth century Cobbett was severe in his criticism of the Old Poor

Law. What particularly incensed him was the way in which the allowance system encouraged farm labourers to accept pauperism, and sink 'quickly and contentedly into that state, from which their grandfathers, and even their fathers, shrunk with horror'.[39] Later, in response to persisted attacks on the Old Poor Law (and in the light of his experiences of political oppression in Regency Britain) Cobbett's views changed. He remained concerned about the increasing acceptance of pauperism by farm labourers, but now blamed 'the Thing' – public debts, heavy taxation, enclosures and the Funds – for perverting the operation of the Old Poor Law. '[T]he opulent have no right to withhold aid from the distressed', thundered Cobbett,

> even where the distress has arisen from actual misconduct. What, then, must be the magnitude of the guilt of those, who first cause the distress, and then deny relief to the distressed person? Poverty, in some degree, is the lot of mankind; but if we take a survey of the state of nations, we shall find, that a very small portion of it really arises from any fault in the poor themselves; and that its principal cause is some vicious institution, some course of misrule, which enables the rich to rob, degrade and oppress the labouring classes.

In Cobbet's opinion, outdoor poor relief had first been manipulated to hold down rural wages and create a permanent reserve of cheap labour, and when the poor rates rose dramatically the political economists put forward the fallacious argument that the Old Poor Law alone was to blame.[40]

All political radicals agreed that the Old Poor Law should not be singled out for criticism, but not all would have agreed with Cobbett's uncompromising defence of the Old Poor Law. Certainly many urban radicals were as critical about the administration of parish poor relief as any political economist. London radicals, for instance, spent a good deal of time and energy campaigning against the mis-use of the poor rate, which often went on lavish dinners for officials rather than on relief for the poor. Similarly, when political radicals campaigned against the 'close' or select vestry system in the late 1820s, their criticisms usually centred on the corruption and maladministration present in the parochial poor relief system.[41] It would probably be fair to say that many political radicals hoped for some reform of the Old Poor Law before 1834, although certainly not the sort of drastic reforms proposed by either Malthusians or Benthamites.

IV

Three successive bad harvests for the years 1828 to 1830, a continued rise in the cost of poor relief and the Swing Riots of 1830 made reform of the Old Poor Law inevitable. The landed interest might have been prepared to pay the increased rates if it had guaranteed social stability, but when south-east England was shaken by rural unrest in 1830, the fate of the Old Poor Law was sealed. It was no longer a question of whether the Old Poor Law would be reformed, but only when and how.

The Whigs, under Earl Grey, came to power on 17 November 1830 committed to political reform, but with no clear policy on the question of reforming the Old Poor Law. If anything they were even more deeply divided on the subject than the Tories. Although Grey's government included among its supporters an influential group of Philosophical Radicals and political economists, who favoured a radical reform of the Old Poor Law, it was also dependent on the support of the more traditional-minded Whigs who did not, as yet, support drastic reform. The new government's first instinct was therefore to delay. Unfortunately for them, Parliament was in no mood to procrastinate. A succession of private members' bills and an inconclusive House of Lords Select Committee investigation helped keep the issue of poor law reform very much alive. The various debates reveal a wide diversity of opinion on the best means of dealing with the problem of poor relief: traditional Tories wanted to set the poor to work on allotments; liberal Tories, imbued with the ideas of Malthus and other political economists, preferred subsidised emigration; and the Whigs could only propose a political solution, reform of the system of representation. The Philosophical Radicals were the only faction to stand out as zealous advocates of immediate and radical reform. Henry Brougham, their parliamentary spokesman, and by now Lord Chancellor, promised early and dramatic reform of the Old Poor Law.[42] The government was caught in a dilemma: deeply involved in the struggle over the Parliamentary Reform Bill, and lacking a firm proposal for poor law reform of their own, they faced a Parliament eager to institute any suggestion which might help. A solution of sorts was provided by Thomas Hyde Villiers's proposal that the government appoint a Royal Commission to investigate the Old Poor Law and make recommendations for its reform.[43] Cabinet eagerly accepted the idea.

A Royal Commission of Inquiry was a well established procedure by 1832. Between 1800 and 1832 no fewer than sixty Commissions had been appointed.[44] It was the first time, however, that a Royal Commission had been set up to investigate the poor law. A seven-member Commission was initially appointed. Three of the members had strong Tory connections: the chairman, Charles James Blomfield was Bishop of London, John Bird Sumner was Bishop of Chester, and William Sturges Bourne was a former Tory MP and author of the 1817 Vestries Act. These lent the Commission dignity and prestige. The other four members were Whigs, with strong links to Benthamite and political economy circles: Nassau William Senior, the former Drummond Professor of Poltical Economy at Oxford, was a member of the influential Political Economy Club and chief economic adviser to the government; Walter Coulson, barrister and former journalist, was also a member of the Political Economy Club and at one time had been secretary to Jeremy Bentham; Henry Gawling was an uncle of the Benthamite law reformer C.H. Bellenden Ker; and the Reverend Henry Bishop, an Oxford don, was an acquaintance of Senior's. (Edwin Chadwick, another former secretary of Bentham's, and James Traill were to be added to the Commission in 1833).

Underlying the whole approach of the 1832 Royal Commission were new, so-called scientific, methods of investigation. Adam Smith had suggested some fifty years earlier that the correct method for investigating social and economic conditions was to collect the maxims of prudence and morality, and join them together 'by one or more general principles from which they were all deductible, like effects from their natural causes'. This 'scientific' approach had been further developed in the intervening decades by the influential Professor of Moral Philosophy at Edinburgh, Dugald Stewart, his counterpart at Oxford, Richard Whately, and the utilitarian James Mill. They claimed that the proper method of investiating social and economic conditions was one guided by the principles of political economy and moral philosophy. Such principles would provide the connecting links which joined together the vast body of factual material, highlighting some events and ignoring others. They would tend to ignore, for instance, the testimony of 'practical men' – politicians, magistrates, overseers, churchwardens – who acted as receptacles for bad theory. And they would inevitably highlight the testimony of those who were accustomed to broad generalizing. The testimony of such men would in turn become the basis for developing even better theory. Accordingly the learned opinions of the political economists and moral philosophers were to be given precedence over the views of 'practical men'. And any investigation of pauperism was to be undertaken only by persons acquainted with the principles of political economy and moral philosophy.[45]

To assist the Royal Commission, twenty-six Assistant Commissioners were appointed. It was an important innovation. Paid a daily allowance, they were sent out to various parts of the country to collect information and report back to the Royal Commissioners in London. Senior was responsible for drawing up their instructions. He defined not only the scope and character of their investigations, but also the procedures they were expected to follow and even the conclusions they were expected to reach. The Assistant Commisioners were allocated a specific district and told to collect 'those facts from which some general inference may be drawn and which form the rule rather than the exception'. And to make sure the general inference they should draw had not escaped their attention, they were informed that relief to the able-bodied had caused 'the idleness, profligacy, and improvidence, which now debase the character and increase the numbers of the population ... of the southeastern districts'.[46]

The Royal Commission's views were clearly influenced by the criticism of the Old Poor Law which had been growing since the 1790s. It was assumed that before 1795, before Speenhamland, the Old Poor Law had been well administered; and that it was only after the introduction of large-scale outdoor relief for the able-bodied that the system of poor relief in southern England had become debased. The corollary of this was that conditions in southern England were worse than in the industrial north; that the maladministration of poor relief in the south caused rural distress; and that superior administration in the north accounted for the presumed higher standard of living enjoyed by the industrial labouring class. It was assumed, of course, that the northern counties were free of such evils as relief in aid of wages.[47] Guided by these assumptions the Royal Commission decided to investigate in detail only a few urban and rural counties to show the inevitable results of good and bad administration. The vast majority of counties in England and Wales were scarcely touched.

Before the investigation had even started, the Royal Commission had declared its intention to recommend a return to the system of poor relief that it believed to have existed prior to Speenhamland. They indicated that they had no intention of eliminating relief to the impotent; but they were going to make it more difficult to obtain. The Assistant Commissioners were instructed to discover 'the degree in which the public provision of sickness and old age interferes with the exercise of prudence'. The Royal Commissioners were also determined to modify the bastardy laws. They asserted that the Old Poor Law acted as 'a punishment to the father, a pecuniary reward to the mother, and a means by which the woman obtains a husband, and a parish rids itself of parishioners'. However, it was on relief to the able-bodied that the Royal Commissioners concentrated their attack. They regarded the allowance system in all its forms – roundsmen, labour-rate, or bread scale – as the main cause of the Old Poor Law's failure. Seeking to discredit outdoor relief, the Assistant Commissioners were instructed to determine what effects the allowance system had on 'the industry, habits, and character of labourers, the increase in population, the rate of wages, the profits of farming, the increase or diminution of farming capital, and the rent and improvement of land'.[48] The Royal Commissioners were aware that able-bodied unemployment existed, but accounted for it in terms of the corrupting influence of outdoor relief. They were to give the abolition of outdoor relief to the able-bodied their highest priority.

Mindful of the need to begin educating public opinion, the Royal Commissioners decided to take up Brougham's suggestion that they make available to the public the results of their preliminary investigations. *Extracts from the Information Received by His Majesty's Commissioners* was published in book form early in 1833. Every effort was made to give it as wide a circulation as possible. The catalogue of poor law abuses contained in the *Extracts* would help prepare the public to accept a drastic reform of the Old Poor Law.[49]

Only one of the seventeen preliminary reports published in the *Extracts* contained a clear proposal to reform the Old Poor Law. The work of Edwin Chadwick, it was based on Bentham's principle of pauper management. Chadwick proposed that all outdoor relief to the able-bodied be abolished and replaced by relief in a strictly administered workhouse. He also proposed that salaried officials, or contract management, replace unpaid magistrates and overseers as the administrators of poor relief. Chadwick believed his investigations had established the efficiency of Bentham's principle of less-eligibility. His report and recommendations appeared so outstanding to the Royal Commissioners that it was published in its entirety.[50] As the only report to make clear recommendations (and recommendations in line with the Royal Commission's preconceived views), Chadwick's report was virtually adopted by the Royal Commission as its own.

Chadwick had shown himself to be a master of the new, 'scientific' methods of inquiry and Senior was one of the first to recognise the significance of his achievement. Senior quickly recommended to the government that Chadwick be promoted to the position of Royal Commissioner. His suggestion was accepted, and henceforth the work of the Royal Commission would be shared between Senior the political economist and Chadwick the Benthamite legislator. Using the principles of political economy, Senior would condemn the inherent abuses in the Old Poor Law and Chadwick, guided by Bentham's science of legislation, would have the task of constructing a new system of poor relief.[51] The *Report* which the Royal Commission presented to the House of Commons on 21 February 1834 reflected the division of labour between the two men. The first part of the *Report*, the work of Senior, exposed and condemned the corrupting influence of the Old Poor Law. The second part, the work of Chadwick, set out the recommendations and remedial measures that were thought necessary to produce a poor relief system free from abuse.[52] These recommendations were to form the basis of the New Poor Law.

Despite its claim to be 'scientific', the *Report* presented a biased and distorted view of the Old Poor Law and of the conditions experienced by the poor generally. The shoddy research findings, the defective methods of investigation and Senior's and Chadwick's readiness to claim scientific knowledge for their views induced them to write a doctrinaire *Report*. They disregarded contrary evidence, ignored the beneficial aspects of the Old Poor Law and wherever possible stressed its debilitating effects. The distortions contained in the *Report* of the Royal Commission had their desired effect: a shocked and concerned Parliament accepted drastic reform of the Old Poor Law. But this was not the *Report's* only outcome. An unforeseen legacy of Senior and Chadwick's doctrinaire *Report* was the delay it caused to the improvement of social welfare legislation in Britain. The spectre of outdoor relief to the able-bodied and an extravagant poor relief system eating up the wealth of the nation would terrify middle-class voters in the nineteenth century in much the same way as the Red Menace was to do in the twentieth century.

V

The Bill which resulted from the recommendations of the Royal Commission was cleverly conceived and written. Conservative in title and wording, opponents found it a difficult Bill to attack. The ploy was so successful that Francis Place, a staunch advocate of poor law reform, accused the government of having 'castrated the Poor Law Bill'. The government also decided to treat the Bill as a non-party measure, and with the tacit support of Sir Robert Peel (and a willingness occasionally to misrepresent the intentions of the Bill), they were able to adopt the disarming tacts of conciliation and compromise.[53] Furthermore, Whig, Tory and Philosophical Radical alike, were, by 1834, willing to accept that the rising cost of poor relief made reform absolutely necessary. Thus under the general heading of economy, and ignorant about the true nature of the Bill, most members of Parliament could agree to support a radical reform of the Old Poor Law.

Passage of the Bill was further assisted by the political crisis which accompanied its introduction. Before the legislation had even been debated in the House of Lords, Grey had resigned as Prime Minister and had been replaced by Viscount Melbourne. One historian has claimed recently that this crisis 'scarcely interrupted the course of the New Poor Law'.[54] He is correct, but I would want to put it even more strongly: the political crisis actually served to draw attention away from the New Poor Law and ease its passage through Parliament.

There was opposition, of course, both in Parliament and in the country at large. In Lancashire a number of the more populous parishes held meetings to protest against the Bill. A meeting of the ratepayers of Bolton summed up the attitude of these early public protests: the proposed amendments to the Old Poor Law would be too expensive, the creation of a centralised Poor Law Commission would threaten ancient liberties, and local officials knew best how to deal with their own paupers.[55] In Parliament a small group of ultra Tories and popular radicals mounted a sustained attack on the Bill. John Walter ridiculed the *Report* of the Royal Commission by pointing out that the 'questions have been put with a view to draw out answers corresponding with the preconceived opinions of the Commissioners'. John Fielden was more concerned about the justice of the Bill, reminding the House of Commons

> that the labouring man has no control whatever over the price of his labour, and that this House has constantly refused, under an affectation of principle, to regulate ... that he may receive a due reward for the labour that he performs. As I have found that this House is unwilling to do that which is to keep the people from

poverty, I will resist this act which punishes them for being poor.

Fielden's fellow MP, for Oldham, the grand old man of popular radicalism, William Cobbett, came to the point more quickly: he branded the Bill 'the Poor Man Robbery Bill'.[56] Despite Cobbett's powerful rhetoric, the opposition in the Commons failed dismally. Only in the House of Lords did opponents of the Bill succeed in making amendments. Some of the harsher provisions of the bastardy clause were watered down and the new measure was initially limited to a five-year life. Nevertheless, the Act which was passed into law on 14 August 1834 was essentially the same as that which had been outlined in the *Report* of the 1832 Royal Commission.[57]

The New Poor Law established a centralised bureaucracy, the Poor Law Commission, with power to regulate poor relief and lay down the conditions under which it was to be granted. The Commission also had power to disallow relief to any pauper who infringed its regulations. Although the Act made no specific mention of the new policy which was to apply, the *Report* made it perfectly clear that it was to be the Benthamite principle of 'less eligibility'. The Poor Law Commission would insist that all relief to the able-bodied and their families (except for medical attendance) was to be restricted to a 'well-regulated workhouse'.[58]

To ensure the proper administration of its policies the Poor Law Commission was empowered to unite existing parishes and townships into Poor Law Unions. These Unions were to be administered by Boards of Guardians elected by ratepayers and property owners on a multiple voting system.[59] The Poor Law Commission also had the power to prescribe the number and property qualifications of the Guardians, as well as their duties. To avoid offending the powerful landowners, Justices of the Peace within each Union were made Guardians *ex officio*. Once the administrative structure within a Union had been established the Poor Law Commissioners could order the building of a workhouse, with the consent of either the Guardians or a majority of the voters. Without the agreement of the Guardians or voters, the Commissioners could order the expenditure of up to £50 to alter or enlarge an existing workhouse. The Commissioners were to control the qualifications, duties and salaries of Union officials – clerks, relieving officers, workhouse masters and the like – although the power to make appointments to these positions was left in the hands of the Guardians, an important source of patronage. Needless to say, the

Poor Law Commissioners retained the power to dismiss any paid
Union official. Finally, to ensure that their regulations and orders were
carried into effect, the Poor Law Commission could appoint Assistant
Commissioners to oversee the administration of relief.

The Settlement and Bastardy Laws were also altered by the New
Poor Law. Settlement by hiring and service, or by residence in any
tenement which did not pay rates, was abolished. This was a major
change: since 1697 most claims to settlement had been earned through
apprenticeship or hiring.⁶⁰ Henceforth, birth and marriage were to be
the main sources of settlement. It also had the unforeseen consequence
of making the occupiers of poor cottages, who had previously had their
rates paid by the landlord, responsible for paying their own rates.
Alterations to the Bastardy Laws threw the full economic consequences
of illegitimacy on the mother. Although the authors of the New Poor
Law had intended to free the fathers of bastard children from all legal
responsibility, this was amended by the House of Lords. The fathers of
illegitimate children could still be sued for maintenance, but before the
Quarter Sessions, not, as previously, the Petty Sessions. This
effectively meant a curtailment of the mother's right (although not the
parishes') to sue the putative father for maintenance. No money
received by the parish officials at the Quarter Sessions could be paid
over to the mother. The only concession given to the mothers of
illegitimate children was that the laws relating to the punishment of
'lewd' women were repealed.

VI

In 1834 Parliament attempted to solve the problem of poor relief in
England and Wales by bringing the Old Poor Law into line with the
precepts of political economy. It was a solution which many of those
who voted for the Bill felt uneasy about. The Duke of Richmond was
concerned that rural rebellion might result from the denial of outdoor
relief to the able-bodied. And the Marquis of Lansdowne needed
reassuring that the New Poor Law did not punish poverty as a crime.⁶¹
Both eventually voted in favour of the Bill. In the wake of a half-
century of persistent criticism of the Old Poor Law, the rural violence
of 1830-2, and the Royal Commission *Report*'s bleak picture of a
rapacious poor relief system eating up the wealth of the country, the
ruling elite of Britain appeared to have little choice but to accept a
radical reform of the Old Poor Law. The Poor Law Amendment Bill

passed both Houses of Parliament with surprisingly large majorities. What did those members of Parliament who voted for the New Poor Law hope would be achieved by the legislation? John Pratt, one of the barristers engaged to assist in drafting the Bill, claimed it had two aims: 'To raise the labouring classes, that is to say, the bulk of the community, from the idleness, improvidence, and degradation, into which the ill administration of the laws for their relief has thrust them'; and to 'arrest the progress, and ultimately to diminish the amount of the pressure on the owners of land and houses'.[62] Tory, Whig and Philosophical Radical could find common ground here: the New Poor Law was to save the labouring population from pauperism, and save the property-owning class money. The landed interest, in particular, hoped that a lessening of pauperism would in turn lead to a decrease in rural unrest. Subsequent events were to show them to be sadly mistaken.

Notes

1. 4 & 5 Will.IV, c.76.
2. E. Halevy, *A History of the English People in the Nineteenth Century*, vol.III (Ernest Benn, London, 1950), p.210, undoubtedly oversimplified matters when he called the New Poor Law 'the first victory of the Benthamites'. But to deny the Benthamite connection completely, as A. Brundage, *The Making of the New Poor Law* (Hutchinson, London, 1978), and D. Fraser (ed.), *The New Poor Law in the Nineteenth Century* (Macmillan, London, 1976), do, is equally misleading. U.R.Q. Henriques, *Before the Welfare State* (Longman, London, 1979), p.39, is probably correct when she describes the New Poor Law as 'a very careful dovetailing of new institutions with survivals of the old order'.
3. [E. Chadwick], 'Preface' to J. Bentham, 'Observations on the Poor Bill, introduced by the Right Honourable William Pitt' in *The Works of Jeremy Bentham*, vol.VIII (William Tait, Edinburgh, 1843), p.440; *Hansard*, 3rd Series, vol.XXIII, col.830; S. Roberts, *Lord Brougham and the New Poor Law* (Oldfield, London, 1838), p.20; R. Oastler, *The Rights of the Poor to Liberty and Life* (Roake & Varty, London, 1838), p.vi.
4. H.R.F. Bourne, *The Life of John Locke*, vol.II (Scientia Verlag, Salem, 1969), pp.377-91; J.R. Poynter, *Society and Pauperism* (Routledge & Kegan Paul, London, 1969), ch.2, *passim*; R.G. Cowherd, *Political Economists and the English Poor Laws* (Ohio University Press, Athens, 1977), ch.1, *passim*.
5. T.R. Malthus, *An Essay on the Principle of Population, as it Affects the Future Improvement of Society* (first published 1798; Penguin, Harmondsworth, 1976) (hereafter *First Essay*), pp.71-2. In the so-called second edition, which was in fact an entirely new work, T.R. Malthus, *An Essay on the Principle of Population; or a View of its Past and Present Effects on Human Happiness*, 2 vols, (first published 1803; Murray, London, 1826) (hereafter *Second Essay*), moral restraint was added as a third possible check to population growth.
6. Malthus, *First Essay*, pp.94-5.
7. Ibid., p.97.

8. Ibid., pp.101-2.

9. Malthus, *Second Essay*, vol.II, pp.337-8. Malthus was not the first writer to advocate abolition of the poor laws: T. Alcock, *Observations on the Defects of the Poor Laws* (R. Baldwin, London, 1752), and J. Townsend, *A Dissertation on the Poor Law* (n.p., London, 1786), had earlier advocated abolition.

10. Malthus, *Second Essay*, vol.II, pp.365-70.

11. Ibid., vol.II, pp.371-2.

12. W. Godwin, *Thoughts occasioned by the Perusal of Dr Parr's Spital Sermon*, p.56, quoted in Poynter, *Society and Pauperism*, p.166.

13. J. Weyland, *Observations on Mr Whitbread's Poor Bill and on the Population of England* (n.p., London, 1807), p.64; *Quarterly Review*, vol.VIII (1812), pp.319-27, quoted in Poynter, *Society and Pauperism*, p.174; *Cobbett's Political Register*, 14 March 1807.

14. J. Davison, *Considerations on the Poor Law* (University Press, Oxford, 1817), pp.116-19.

15. S.W. Nicolls, *A Summary View of the Report and Evidence Relative to the Poor Laws* (n.p., York, 1818), and S.W. Nicolls, *A View of the Principles on which the Wellbeing of the Labouring Classes Depends* (Darton Harvey & Longman, London, 1819).

16. J.E. Bicheno, *An Inquiry into the Nature of Benevolence* (n.p., London, 1819), p.133.

17. *J.B. Sumner, A Treatise on the Records of Creation* (n.p., London, 1818), p.92.

18. *Quarterly Review*, vol.XVII (1817), pp.398-40, quoted in Poynter, *Society and Pauperism*, p.231.

19. Ibid., p.229, argues that Sumner's *Treatise* provided his contemporaries with what Poley's *Principles* had provided an earlier generation, justification of the existing social state.

20. Poynter, *Society and Pauperism*, p.246.

21. 'Report of the Select Committee of the House of Commons appointed to consider of the Poor laws', *PP*, 1817, vol.VI, pp.4-10.

22. J. Durthy, *Letters on the Agricultural Petition and on the Poor Laws* (n.p., London, 1819), p.10.

23. 'Report of the House of Lords Select Committee on the Poor Laws', *PP*, 1818, vol.V, pp.7 & 10.

24. There were minor amendments: 59 Geo.III c.12 provided for the election of Select Vestries and the appointment of paid assistant overseers. But more substantial changes such as William Sturges Bourne's attempt to outlaw the allowance system in 1818, James Scarlett's Bill to abolish relief to the able-bodied in 1821, and Michael Nolan's 1822 reforms were all defeated. See Poynter, *Society and Pauperism*, ch.9, *passim*, and Cowherd, *Political Economists*, chs.6 & 7, *passim.*

25. J. Bentham, 'Observations on the Poor Law Bill introduced by the Right Hon. William Pitt', *Works*, vol.VIII, pp.440-61.

26. J. Bentham, *The Theory of Legislation* (Trubner, London, 1864), pp.102-9.

27. Ibid., p.120.

28. Bentham Papers, UCL, Box CLIII a.21, quoted in Poynter, *Society and Pauperism*, p.119. The same definition and argument was used by the 1832 Royal Commission.

29. Bentham, *Works*, vol.II, pp.533-4.

30. Bentham Papers, UCL, Box CLIII a.25-6, quoted in Poynter, *Society and Pauperism*, pp.125-6.

31. J. Bentham, 'Outline of work entitled Pauper Management Improved', *Works*, vol.VIII, pp.369-439.

32. S.E. Finer, *The Life and Times of Sir Edwin Chadwick* (Methuen, London,

1952), p.44.
33. Poynter, *Society and Pauperism*, pp.141-2.
34. J.T. Becher, *The Anti-Pauper System* (Simpkin & Marshall, London, 1834), pp.2, 37.
35. 'Report of the Select Committee of the House of Lords appointed to Consider of the Poor Laws', *PP*, 1831, vol.VIII, p.222.
36. Quoted by H.G. Willink, 'Life of Sir George Nicholls' in G. Nicholls, *A History of the English Poor Law* (Putnam's Sons, New York, 1898), vol.I, pp.xiii-xiv.
37. Cowherd, *Political Economists*, pp.2-11; T. Paine, *The Rights of Man* (first published 1791; Dent, London 1969), p.245-57.
38. C. Holmes, 'Samuel Roberts and the Gypsies' in S. Pollard and C. Holmes, *Essays in the Economic and Social History of South Yorkshire* (South Yorkshire County Council, Barnsley, 1976), p.235; S. Roberts, *Defence of the Poor Laws* (n.p., Sheffield, 1819).
39. *Cobbett's Political Register*, 16 July 1808.
40. W. Cobbett, *The Rights of the Poor* (first published 1833; Samuel Mills, London, 1890), p.4; Cobbett's most scathing attack on the political economists was his 'Letter to Parson Malthus', *Cobbett's Political Register*, 8 May 1819.
41. J.W. Brooke, *Democrats of Marylebone* (Cleaver, London, 1839), pp.20-5; F. Sheppard, *London 1808-1870: The Infernal Wen* (Secker & Warburg, London, 1971), pp.23-7.
42. Cowherd, *Political Economists*, pp.182-93; *Hansard*, 3rd series, vol.IV, cols.261-7, 284-5.
43. T. Mackay, *History of the English Poor Law*, vol.III (Putnam's Sons, New York, 1900), pp.25-7.
44. H.M. Clokie and J.W. Robinson, *Royal Commission of Inquiry* (Oxford University Press, Oxford, 1938), pp.58-9.
45. A. Smith, *The Wealth of Nations*, E. Cannon (ed.) (McGraw-Hill, New York 1937), p.724; D. Stewart, *Collected Works*, vol.II, W. Hamilton (ed.) (Constable, Edinburgh, 1854-8), pp.222-31, and vol.III, pp.332-5; R. Whatly, *Introductory Lectures on Political Economy* (n.p., London, 1832), pp.43-5; J. Mill, *Selected Economic Writings* (University of Chicago Press, Chicago, 1966), pp.365-8.
46. Finer, *Sir Edwin Chadwick*, p.49, says Chadwick was the only Assistant Commissioner to be paid a retainer's fee in addition to the daily allowance; [N.W. Senior], 'Instructions to the Assistant Commissioners', *Report, PP*, 1834, vol.XXVIII, pp.248-55. S. and B. Webb, *English Poor Law History, Part II* (Frank Cass, London, 1963), vol.I, p.90, claim that the instructions were printed but not published; that they were without bias; and that Chadwick was the author. The Webbs were wrong on all points: see S.L. Levy, *Nassau W. Senior* (Augustus M. Kelley, New York, 1970), p.307, n 176.
47. [Senior], 'Instructions', *Report, PP*, 1834, vol.XXVII, p.255.
48. Ibid., pp.250-1.
49. *Extracts* (Fellowes, London, 1833), was published in octavo rather than the official folio format so it could be circulated as an ordinary book. Brougham also sought the help of the novelist Harriet Martineau in educating the public over the poor law question. The result was H. Martineau, *Poor Laws and Paupers, Illustrated* (2 vols, Charles Fox, London, 1833).
50. *Extracts*, pp.200-338. Chadwick's report occupies almost a third of the volume.
51. N.W. Senior, *An Outline of the Science of Political Economy* (Allen & Unwin, London, 1951), pp.2-3.
52. *Report, PP*, 1834, vol.XXVII, pp.146-202, lists twenty-two specific recommendations.
53. Place to Parkes, 21 April 1834, Place Papers, BL, Add MSS, 35154, f.193; Webb, *English Poor Law History, Part II*, vol.I, pp.100-1; Poynter, *Society and*

Pauperism, p.322, writes that Brougham horrified Senior when he introduced the Bill into the House of Lords with an abolitionist diatribe. The story of the drafting and passage of the New Poor Law has recently been told by Brundage, *Making of the New Poor Law*, ch.3, and O. MacDonagh, *Early Victorian Government, 1830-1870* (Weidenfeld & Nicolson, London, 1977), ch.6.

54. Brundage, *Making of the New Poor Law*, p.68.

55. *Manchester Chronicle*, 31 May 1834; *Bolton Chronicle*, 24 May 1834; Darbishire to Heywood, 27 May 1834, Heywood Papers, BMBA, 2HE/30/6.

56. J. Walter, *A Letter to the Electors of Berkshire* (James Ridgway, London, 1834), p.20; *Hansard*, 3rd series, vol.XXXVI, col.1014; ibid., vol.XXIV, col.388.

57. 4 & 5 Will.IV, c.76.

58. *Report, PP*, 1834, vol.XXVII, pp.127, 146.

59. Ratepayers rated at less than £200 a year were to have one vote, and one further vote for every extra £200 up to a maximum of three votes. Property owners were to have votes in accordance with the 1818 Vestries Act, 58 Geo.III, c.69.

60. J.S. Taylor, 'Impact of Pauper Settlement', *Past and Present*, no.73 (November 1976), p.52, suggests that the majority of poor during the eighteenth century obtained settlement in this manner.

61. Nassau Senior's Journal, Stirling Library, University of London, MS.173.

62. J.T. Pratt, *Act for the Amendment and Better Administration of the Laws Relating to the Poor* (B. Fellowes, London, n.d.), p.i.

PART TWO

PROTEST

3   'OUR RIGHTS WE WILL HAVE'

Implementation of the New Poor Law moved ahead rapidly. Within ten days of the Act receiving royal assent the Poor Law Commission had been appointed. Its three members were Thomas Frankland Lewis, chairman, George Nicholls and John George Shaw-Lefevre. The architect of the legislation and a man who had hoped to be appointed as a Commissioner, Edwin Chadwick, was named secretary to the Commission. Nine Assistant Commissioners were quickly recruited (eventually the number would rise to twenty-one) and by the beginning of November 1834 were at work in the Home Counties. Against Chadwick's advice, the Poor Law Commissioners decided to establish the New Poor Law in the south of England first; the Assistant Commissioners, who were to create its administrative framework, would move north later, when the system was successfully operating in the south.[1]

The Assistant Commissioners' procedure was to meet with the 'respectable inhabitants' of their allotted districts, inspect the parish books, draw up tables of average poor rates, find out which towns acted as commercial and judicial centres, examine existing workhouses, and, on the basis of this information, divide the district into viable Poor Law Unions. All this took time, of course, and it was not until the Spring of 1835 that the first Poor Law Unions had been declared, Boards of Guardians elected and Union officials appointed. At first the Assistant Commissioners encountered little opposition. There were, for example, few cases of existing overseers refusing to co-operate. Most of the 'respectable inhabitants' appeared to welcome the New Poor Law. Even the Boards of Guardians' elections caused little dissension, with the majority of candidates being elected unopposed. Opposition to the New Poor Law in the south of England arose after the New Poor Law Unions had been declared; it arose among the labouring population as the old system of relief was being phased out and the new regulations introduced.

I

The Milton Union, near Sittingbourne in Kent, was among the first to experience a display of popular opposition to the New Poor Law. By the end of April 1835 the New Poor Law Union of Milton had been declared, Guardians elected and poor relief handed over to the new relieving officers. The new Board of Guardians decided, in consultation with Sir Francis Bond Head, the Assistant Commissioner, that the change in administration should be accompanied by a change in policy. Henceforth allowances for children were to be reduced and relief to be given in tickets redeemable for goods rather than in cash. On Thursday, 30 April 1835, the day the new policy was introduced, there was a disturbance at the village of Bapchild. The relieving officer and a Guardian were mobbed and their books and papers destroyed. Over the next few days there were other disturbances, and at Milton itself the Guardians were stoned as they rode away from their weekly meeting.[2]

The Milton authorities responded hesitantly at first and, after consulting with Assistant Commissioner Head, agreed to make some concessions. The able-bodied would continue to receive relief on the new reduced scale, but all other classes of paupers would go back to receiving relief on the old scale, half in cash. The chairman of the local Bench, the Reverend Dr Poore, was not very confident about the concessions working, however, and began swearing in special constables. A few days later a crowd of several hundred agricultural labourers, many armed with 'bludgeons', assembled outside the Doddington workhouse where the relieving officer was dispensing poor relief. As the paupers came out of the workhouse they were met by the protesters who demanded to know what they had received. On being told 'money and a ticket', the crowd insisted the paupers go back inside, return the ticket to the relieving officer, and demand money instead. The protesters, many of whom had come from the neighbouring villages of Newham and Lenham to confront the relieving officer, claimed the giving of relief by means of a ticket was 'illegal'. They said that they had 'come to assist the Doddington people and see that they have their Rights'. The Doddington protesters responded with shouts of 'and our Rights we will have'. The labourers finally agreed to withdraw after the relieving officer promised to lay their complaint before the next Board of Guardians' meeting.[3]

A more serious disturbance took place on the following Thursday, 7 May 1835, at Rodmersham, a small village near the centre of the

Milton Union. A large crowd gathered outside the local church where the relieving officer and Guardians were interviewing applicants and issuing relief tickets. As fast as the tickets were handed out to paupers, the protesters confiscated them. When one of the overseers foolishly intervened he was assaulted and forced back into the church which was quickly surrounded by the angry crowd. After some four hours of being bottled-up in the church, those inside decided to make a break for it. They were chased for over a mile by the protesters and pelted with stones and mud. Near exhaustion, they were only saved from further discomfort by the opportune arrival of a detachment of troops.[4]

This marked the end of concessions by the authorities. Police were brought down from London and within a few days the ringleaders had been arrested. Agitation did not immediately cease: some arrests were only made with the greatest difficulty and when the prisoners were taken off to Canterbury Gaol their escort was stoned. But by and large the campaign of popular opposition in the Milton Union was quelled.

The pattern of disturbance in the Milton Union was repeated, with minor variations, throughout south-east England. In the Ampthill Union in Bedfordshire, the protesters anticipated the alterations to the poor relief system. The new relieving officer, James Osborn, was mobbed in the village of Lidlington when he arrived to collect information from the parish overseer. A large crowd of women followed him into the house of the overseer, pinned him up in a corner, and 'vowed they would not have bread instead of money'. Osborn was only allowed to leave after he had borrowed £3 16s 0d from the local overseer and paid off the women. The next day, at the village of Millbrook, Osborn was again stopped by an angry crowd who demanded money from him before they would let him go. When the authorities attempted to arrest those who had assaulted the relieving officer, a large crowd marched on Ampthill to confront the Guardians. The Guardians tried to reason with the protesters, but when it was admitted that the new poor relief regulations were to be introduced – clothing and food handouts replacing cash payments – there were loud cries of 'no bread' and 'blood and bread'. The upshot was that the crowd began stoning the workhouse with the Guardians huddled inside. After the Riot Act had been read the protesters slowly drifted off, allegedly to spend the rest of the afternoon drinking beer at the public houses.

The next day twenty-one London policemen arrived in Ampthill and together with a force of special constables and twenty to thirty gentlemen on horseback, began rounding up the trouble-makers. Five men and four women were taken into custody that first day. (A total of nineteen people were eventually arrested.) The speed of the arrests apparently 'astonished' many of the labourers, and the Clerk of the Board of Guardians informed the Poor Law Commissioners that the local officials 'anticipated no further difficulties'.[5]

In the wake of the disturbances at Ampthill a sensationalist broadsheet appeared, claiming to give a 'Full, True and Particular Account of that Dreadful Riot'. Readers were told that Ampthill had been in a state of riot for a week, that magistrates and Guardians had been assaulted, that the gentry had been 'much alarmed' and forced to flee the town, that the workhouse had been 'pulled down' and that the troops 'couldn't disperse the mob without using violent means'. Thirty rioters were supposed to have been killed and sixteen placed in Bedford Gaol to await trial.[6] Such an account bore little relation to actual events at Ampthill, but it does indicate the sorts of wild rumours and tense atmosphere present in the areas where the New Poor Law was being introduced.

Protests against changes in poor relief could occasionally become mixed up with protests over rates of pay. In June 1835 the farmers in the Docking Union, Norfolk, announced that they had lowered the pay rates for mowing hay. Although the agricultural labourers were obviously dissatisfied with the move they took no action to oppose it until the same farmers, this time in their capacity as poor law guardians and overseers, decided to alter the existing poor relief system. The labourers delayed their protest because they expected their already low wages to be made up under the allowance system. As long as the regulations governing poor relief remained the same, so did their overall income. The first indication that the labourers had of the changed regulations was when a number of farm labourers at the village of Bircham applied to the overseer for relief. Instead of being given cash relief, they were offered tickets redeemable for shop goods and flour. The men swore they would not accept such relief and 'declared that the system would be resisted by the whole parish'. On the following Monday, 22 June 1835, all the labourers in Bircham and the adjoining parishes 'turned out'. One of the leaders, George Bennett, told the crowd that they were 'bound in a bond of blood, and blood would be spilt before this is finished'. The strikers had chosen their time well: most of the grass had just been cut and was on the ground ready for collecting. The labourers told one of the farmers that 'they would go back to work if they could have money of the parish as usual'.[7]

The Guardians, who were all farmers or landowners, decided to resist the labourers' demands. They were supported by the Assistant Commissioner and former Arctic explorer, Captain Sir Edward Parry RN. The strike had been in progress for a week when a Mr Hunter of Barwick sent two of his men to the farm of Mr Kitton, one of the Bircham overseers, to assist him with gathering the hay and sowing his turnips. As soon as the men attempted to leave Kitton's farmyard to work in the field they were assaulted by a large crowd and Hunter, who had accompanied them, was 'dragged from his horse and severely ill-treated'. The authorities responded by dispatching the governor of the Walsingham Bridewell and a party of constables to Bircham to arrest the ringleaders. They succeeded in securing one of the men they sought, but on attempting to arrest a second were met by an angry crowd of farm labourers, armed with 'heavy bludgeons'. One of the constables was knocked down by the crowd and Mr Hunter, who was present to help identify those who had earlier assaulted him, was again dragged from his horse. This time he had had the foresight to have armed himself with a pistol, however, and threatened to shoot anyone who came near him. The party, with their single prisoner, fled back to Walsingham.[8]

Angered by the day's events, the labourers resorted to more traditional means of protest. Eight to nine hundred labourers 'marched under orders' that night to the home of Mr Kitton, whose attempt to break the strike had provoked the morning's violence. They smashed every door, window and piece of furniture in the house, piled the debris on the floor and set it alight. The labourers next moved on to the home of another overseer, Mr Hebgin, and destroyed it in a similar manner. Hebgin, his wife and child were forced to scramble over a wall to safety. The crowd were by now fast running out of suitable targets. The home of another unpopular farmer, Mr Nurse, was stoned and the night's activities concluded with the sacking of the home of Kitton's son-in-law, Mr Howlett. With a short time that dwelling had also been gutted.[9]

The military did not arrive until noon the next day, by which time the area was again calm. Nevertheless arrests were made and a total of eight people were later convicted for their part in the disturbances. They received prison sentences ranging from three months to two years. As for the strike, it continued for a week more and then petered out.[10] Despite this, the situation in the area remained tense, with 400 special constables on stand-by in case of a renewed outbreak. Just how effective this force would have been was the cause of some concern to the local authorities, however, because the Docking magistrates informed the Home Secretary that although the farmers were unanimously in favour of the New Poor Law, they were also 'intimidated by the labourers, and from a fear of damage to their property by incendiarism and otherwise, are deterred from taking an active part in the preservation of the peace'. As for the petty tradesmen, they were 'all opposed to the measure, and desirous of throwing every obstacle in the way'. The Home Office's rather unhelpful advice was to prosecute those ratepayers who refused to do their duty.[11]

Throughout the course of the anti-poor law protests in the Docking Union, the labourers were supported by artisans and small shopkeepers. Officials in other Poor Law Unions noted similar patterns of support. Some even claimed that the shopkeepers and tradespeople were behind the protests – a view which appears to have owed more to officialdom's willingness to believe the agricultural labourer incapable of independent thought and action than it did to any hard evidence. Artisans and shopkeepers opposed the New Poor Law partly because they feared being economically disadvantaged by the new regulations. As the Reverend Dr Poore explained to the Home Office, the labourers in the Milton Union had been 'urged on by the little shopkeepers whose Trade will be entirely injured if Bread, Meat etc is to be procured by contract'.[12] But we should be wary of assuming that self-interest was the only motivation behind the petty tradespeople's opposition. The tradesmen and small shopkeeper shared with the agricultural labourer a belief in the values of an earlier moral economy. Certainly a concern for (and a recognition of the community's obligation to) the poor, the weak, the aged and the infirm was as important as self-interest. Nowhere was this solicitousness for those in need more clearly demonstrated than in the widespread opposition shown by labourers and tradespeople alike to alterations in workhouse relief.

II

The first organised protest against changes in the management of workhouse relief took place at Eastbourne in the early spring of 1835. The new Board of Guardians announced that married paupers would henceforth be separated in the Union workhouses. A coalition of local tradespeople and agricultural labourers quickly formed to resist the new regulations. Mass meetings were organised and protest marches held. The authorities responded in turn by drafting troops and Metropolitan Police into the area. Although the government's tough approach stifled the protests, the campaign of opposition in the Eastbourne Union did not fail completely. The Poor Law Commission told the Guardians that rather than provoke further popular unrest they should, for the time being, relieve married paupers with paid work outside the workhouse.[13]

In other Unions organised protests quickly followed proposals to alter workhouse relief. Not long after it had been elected the Board of Guardians of the Amersham Union, situated on the eastern slopes of the Chilterns in Buckinghamshire, decided to rationalise workhouse accommodation in the Union. The small parish workhouses were to be closed down and paupers transferred to the larger, centralised workhouses in the Union. Separation of male and female inmates was also to be stictly enforced. The first indication of opposition to the proposed changes came with the receipt of a Memorial from three-quarters of the ratepayers of the parish of Chalfont St Giles. The ratepayers objected to the closure of the local parish workhouse and the transfer of its inmates, alleging that it was cruel and unjust to the inmates, most of whom were either aged or inform, to 'be dragged away from their Friends and relations and transported to some Distant dismal Workhouse'. They also thought it cruel and unjust that 'honest industrious labourers' who could not find work were to be 'forced from their cottages', parted from their wives and children, and sent to some distant workhouse. The authorities chose to ignore the memorial. They also took no notice of rumours that terrible cruelties were to be performed on the inmates of the large centralised workhouse at Amersham, and that all those who had ever received poor relief were to have their children taken from them. A few days later, as inmates were in the process of being transferred from the workhouse at Beaconsfield, a large crowd of women gathered and started booing and throwing stones. It was a minor incident, but it did accurately reflect the state of popular feeling in the Union. Once again the authorities ignored the warning.[14]

At Chesham on Friday, 22 May 1835 a much more serious disturbance took place. Paupers were being loaded into a cart prior to their transfer to Amersham, when a large crowd, again mostly women, began to gather in front of the workhouse gates. When it came time for the cart to leave, the crowd refused to let the gates be opened. A magistrate read the Riot Act and for a moment the crowd fell back. The gates were quickly opened and the cart, accompanied by the magistrate, started off towards Amersham. There was not much distance to cover – four miles at the most – but it was nearly all uphill. The crowd followed, catching up to the cart as it lumbered upwards. One by one the paupers were lifted out of the cart, until at the top of the hill it was empty. The crowd now turned their attention on the magistrate, first pelting him with stones and then directly assaulting him. He finally managed to escape by hiding in a hedge. The crowd, well satisfied with their day's work, returned home. As for the paupers, once they were liberated from the cart, they simply made their way back to the old workhouse at Chesham.[15]

Garbled reports that the Chesham workhouse was being attacked reached London that afternoon.[16] The authorities acted immediately: Police were dispatched from London and two days later the Yeomanry was brought in. Ringleaders and known trouble-makers were arrested, and within a few days order was restored. The paupers at Chesham were eventually moved, this time with a military escort and without incident. Following the disturbances Assistant Commissioner Gilbert began to distance himself from the Amersham Guardians' actions, claiming the decision to move the paupers was undertaken without the express order of the Poor Law Commission. To the chagrin of the Amersham Guardians, it was the Union Board, rather than the Poor Law Commission, which therefore had to bear the cost of prosecuting the rioters. At their trial in August the rioters received sentences ranging from two months to three years. That by all accounts was the end of the affair; there were no further incidents and the Amersham Board of Guardians rigorously pressed ahead with enforcing the New Poor Law.[17]

The most serious protest of the year against changes in workhouse relief took place at Ipswich in December 1835. The new Board of Guardians had decided to use the town's two workhouses to separate the male and female paupers. At the St Clements Street workhouse, which was being altered to receive the able-bodied men and boys, the windows overlooking the courtyard were blocked up, the outer wall raised three feet, and a 'shy' erected at the front gate, 'to prevent the egress of the paupers'.[18] The sight of these alterations together with rumours about the cruelties to be practised on the inmates stirred up popular ill-feeling. John Lutton, the Barham workhouse governor, who happened to be in Ipswich on business on the evening of Wednesday, 16 December 1835, describes what happened:

I observed about Two hundred people assembled in front of the [St Clements] Workhouse Wall and about ten or twelve idle and disorderly characters evidently ripe for mischief – In a few minuites *[sic]* three or four lads from sixteen to twenty years of age with the assistance of a few Girls and some mere children commenced destroying the Window shutters which was soon demolished, there were then about Two hundred peop[l]e looking on ... [and] rather exciting the ringleaders by their laughing and shouting at the mischief... [T]he mob was now greatly increasing and about thirty ... men and boys left the scene of destruction ... and went to the common Quay about 300 yards from the Workhouse and returned in a few minutes with a Crome [a large crowbar] with the assistance of which they soon demolished the wall and one of the wings of the building.[19]

A number of the town's constables watched while the destruction was taking place. James Barbridge, relieving officer for the Bossman and Claydon Union, who was also in Ipswich that day, approached one of the constables to ask why he was not attempting to quell the disturbance. The constable replied that 'he was not going to run the chance of hav[in]g his head broke'. Finally the town clerk and junior bailiff arrived and attempted to stop the destruction by reading the Riot Act. Each time the clerk started reading, however, the crowd showered him with stones. It took three attempts before he succeeded in reading the Act. An hour and a half after the alarm had been first given, troops arrived. Several volleys of stones were again thrown, but the military soon succeeded in dispersing the crowd and arresting three of the ringleaders. Soldiers continued to parade the town until eleven o'clock that night.[20]

The following night a noisy crowd gathered outside the other workhouse in Ipswich, St Margaret's, presumably with the intention of destroying the alterations being made there. Although stones and a few other missiles were thrown, the presence of troops stopped any serious damage. Two days later, on Saturday, 19 December 1835, a party of Metropolitan Police arrived in Ipswich and there was no further trouble.

A feature of the Ipswich disturbance was the measure of support the rioters received from the populace at large. The whiggish *Norwich Mercury* pointed out that there were many tradespeople and shopkeepers in the crowd watching the destruction on Wednesday night and that they 'seemed rather to rejoice at this outbreaking of popular indigation'. Dr James Kay, the Assistant Commissioner, informed the Poor Law Commission that Ipswich had for some time been the scene of a bitter struggle between Whigs and Tories. The Tories had attempted to attach all the odium associated with the New Poor Law to the Whigs. According to Kay, it was also noticeable that some of the 'reform party had not been as valiant in defence of the [New Poor] Law' as they might have been, and that the town's Radical journal had 'uttered weekly diatribes against the Boards of Guardians & the Commissioners'. Popular excitement had been further stirred up by parish meetings 'called by Agitators', to oppose the alterations in workhouse relief.[21]

The events at Ipswich heralded similar protests in the region. At Blything, on Monday, 21 December 1835, a large group of labourers descended on the workhouse, armed with 'axe-picks, mattocks, hand spikes, hooks and other instruments', intending to pull the workhouse down. They were only checked by the prompt action of the magistrates and special constables. After a confrontation lasting over an hour the labourers finally dispersed and headed home. In the Cosford Union in Essex, on Tuesday, 22 December 1835, a large crowd attacked the workhouse. And in the Hoxne Union, on the border between Suffolk and Norfolk, the home of one of the Guardians, Mr Pooley, was showered with stones late on the night of Sunday, 28 December 1835. The next day a crowd of two hundred or more, armed with clubs and sticks, marched on the local Board of Guardians' meeting. Unfortunately for the protesters the authorities were prepared for trouble. Seven of the ringleaders were arrested and the rest of the crowd dispersed.[22]

III

Organised protests in the rural areas of southern England invariably met with the same reaction. Special constables were sworn in, the Metropolitan Police were drafted into the area, and (if necessary) the troops were called out. All organised protest met with a firm response. This was not deliberate government policy, at least not at first. Belligerent local authorities were behind the hardline approach. Toughened by their experience of rural violence during the Swing Riots of 1830, the gentry of southern England would brook no opposition from their rural workforce. And the central government, dependent upon the goodwill of the local authorities for the maintenance of law and order, willingly went along with the policy. Throughout the Swing counties of southern England all organised anti-poor law protests were ruthlessly crushed.

The policy did not end popular protest, however; it simply drove it underground. Throughout southern England, traditional forms of rural protest – arson, intimidation and assault – slowly took over from organised public protest. At the Basingstoke Union in Hampshire, a barn belonging to Mr Mundy, an overseer who had 'refused to pay lazy paupers' was burnt down. In the Royston Union on the Hertfordshire-Cambridgeshire border, the relieving officer was physically assaulted when he attempted to take over the payment of poor relief from the overseer. A Mr Wilkinson, who foolishly let it be known that he had identified the attackers, was visited by an incendiary to remind him to keep quiet in future. Whether Wilkinson was sufficiently intimidated is not known; the relieving officer certainly was, because he resigned. At Abington in Cambridgeshire, the workhouse governor was shot at, twice in the one night! One of the newly elected Guardians at Godstone in Surrey had a large stack of peas set alight. In the Swaffham Union in Norfolk, the relieving officer was stabbed by 'a horse dealer' named Henry Riches. In the Freebridge Lynn Union in Norfolk, one parish overseer found that his horse's throat had been cut, another that two of his horses had been stabbed. At South Molton in Devon, an outhouse belonging to a Guardian was deliberately burnt down.[23] And at Henstead in Norfolk, John Cunningham, the relieving officer, was hit over the head, robbed of £12 and his watch, and had his throat cut. He survived to identify the perpetrator as one William Buck. In what is an exceedingly rare piece of evidence from such a case, we learn that Buck had taken his revenge after being refused relief earlier that day.[24]

The events in the Halstead Union in Essex show the difficulty of trying to determine the exact cause of most outbreaks of rural violence. Towards the end of 1836, the clerk of the Halstead Union wrote to the Home Office to inform them that an incendiary was at work in the Union. In the space of just over a week a barn belonging to George De Horne Vaizey had been burnt down; a 'haulin wall' surrounding the hay stacks and a farm building belonging to Joseph Smoothy had been set alight; and buildings, adjacent haystacks and three horses belonging to Robert Burkitt Wyatt destroyed by fire. Both Vaizey and Smoothy were members of the Halstead Board of Guardians. The Union responded by posting a £100 reward and the magistrates wrote asking for the assistance of 'two of the most efficient Metropolitan Police' so they could track the culprit down.[25]

A Mr Sewell wrote to the Home Office on the same subject a few days later. He insisted that the New Poor Law was not the cause of the fires. His reasoning appears rather confused, however, especially when we learn from him that the agricultural labourers in the Union are much annoyed by the fact that under the New Poor Law they were now responsible for paying the parish poor rate. Sewell continued:

> In populous parishes in the country, where the poor are very numerous, parochial rates upon cottages have not usually been demanded; but as the new Poor law bill comes into operation; they are put into the rate book and the change strictly enforced; this has occasioned more disgust and recklessness than any, or all the privations which many of them ... experience.[26]

By late February 1837 there had been three more fires on property in the Union. This time information about the victims is sketchy and it is not clear whether it was property belonging to Guardians or not. Colonel Wade, the Assistant Commissioner, insisted that they were in 'no way connected with the Poor Laws', but were the work of some 'heartless villain'. His insistence is not convincing, however, especially when he directly contradicts Sewell and tells us that there was 'no manifestation of discontent among the labouring classes'.[27]

In October 1837, Wade was again writing to the Poor Law Commission on the subject of fires in the Halstead Union. Again Vaizey was one of the victims. This time all the buildings on a farm he rented from the Hon. Tilney Long Wellesley were burnt down. Again Wade insisted that the fires were not connected with the New Poor Law, but admitted that a Mr Scaley, a magistrate and former Guardian, who was 'intemperate' in his opposition to the New Poor Law, thought otherwise. At the scene of the latest fire, Scaley had apparently told the relieving officer that 'all this is owing to your Poor Law Bill'. Wade went on to mention that Richard Arnall, a widower with two small children and a 'notorious poacher', was strongly suspected of having set the fires, but as yet there was no firm evidence. Finally, in February 1838 a weaver named Abraham Rayner was tried and convicted for setting fire to property in the Halstead Union. He was sentenced to transportation for life.[28]

No reason was given as to why Rayner set the fires. We can however speculate. Halstead was the centre of a decaying woollen area, and Rayner as a weaver would probably have been a recipient of poor relief, possibly under the allowance system. The introduction of the new and restrictive poor relief regulations might well have caused him to seek revenge against the Guardians. Certainly, as Rayner was a weaver and not a farm labourer, it is unlikely that it was a disagreement over wages or employment conditions which inspired him to seek revenge on farmer Guardians.

And what of Assistant Commissioner Wade's continual insistence that the New Poor Law had nothing to do with the fires? The Poor Law Commission and its officers faced a dilemma in explaining the acts of violence which usually accompanied the introduction of the new and restrictive poor relief regulations. It had been assumed that the Old Poor Law had been a major cause of the Swing Riots in 1830 and supporters of poor law reform had argued in Parliament that the New Poor Law would help reduce rural violence. To admit now that the new regulations contributed to rural violence could only give support to the legislation's opponents. With the New Poor Law effectively on probation for the first five years of its operation, the Commission was loath to supply any ammunition to its critics. One solution was to play down the significance of the protests. The officers of the Commission became very adept at either ridiculing or ignoring the opposition they encountered. Assistant Commissioner Charles a'Court, for instance, jokingly wrote to Chadwick on one occasion that he expected to arrive in Petersfield, Hampshire, on the following evening, provided that

the Hambledon paupers will allow me to pass thro' their ill-fated village. I am to harangue them by appointment tomorrow. If they dispatch me let me have Christian burial, at the *expense of the board*.[29]

Light-hearted banter such as this (here concealing a very real fear of violence) characterised many of the early letters from the Assistant Commissioners.

But violence had its uses to the Poor Law Commission as well as its drawbacks. While admitting that reports of riots created an unfavourable impression of the new poor relief regulations in London, Assistant Commissioner W.J. Gilbert pointed out that

in other respects a riot is rather desirable – it opens the eyes of the Guardians – and aids the progress of the new system. In the Torrington and other unions [in Devon] there are many men who would never have been induced to carry out the system as they have done but for the riots in those parishes.[30]

The trick for the officers of the Poor Law Commission was to conceal the level of violence from the government and the Parliament, or deny that it had anything to do with the New Poor Law, while at the same time using such incidents to strengthen the resolve of the local authorities.

Table 3.1: Committals for Rural 'Protest' Crimes in England and Wales, 1828-50

Year	Arson	Stealing sheep	Maiming cattle	Threatening letters
1828	14	201	11	3
1829	37	237	3	4
1830	45	297	6	4
1831	102	253	19	62
1832	111	298	16	6
1833	64	266	33	12
1834	65	237	26	11
1835	76	221	34	15
1836	72	298	35	7
1837	42	371	42	3
1838	39	341	24	3
1839	37	324	25	4
1840	67	375	34	2
1841	25	339	28	1
1842	48	428	37	6
1843	94	403	34	15
1844	232	286	43	14
1845	90	215	28	6
1846	114	211	40	4
1847	115	283	25	7
1848	120	316	27	4
1849	206	356	42	4
1850	167	267	32	4

Sources: 'Returns, Criminal Offenders', *PP*, 1835, vol.XLV; 1841, Session I, vol.XVIII; 1851, vol.XLVI.

Rural 'protest' crimes rose to a peak in the early 1840s and then slowly declined (see Table 3.1). Precisely how many of these 'crimes' were motivated by popular anger over the new poor relief regulations is unclear. Even when the victims were intimately connected with the operation of the New Poor Law – overseers, guardians, relieving officers and the like – we should be wary of concluding that anti-poor law feeling was the sole cause. Overseers and Guardians in rural areas were also likely to have been farmers and landowners, and in this capacity alone could have been subjected to similar acts of violence and mischief. Nevertheless many contemporaries were convinced that the New Poor Law was responsible for the increase in rural crime. In 1838 John M. Cobbett, son of the redoubtable William, informed his patron John Fielden that sheep stealing and other rural crimes had trebled in east Sussex since the New Poor Law was introduced. Similarly *The Times* special correspondent, sent to investigate the dramatic increase in incendiarism in East Anglia in 1844, concluded that the fires were caused by the harsh poor relief system. It is significant that when Chadwick wrote the Report of the 1839 Constabulary Forces Commission he obtained most of his evidence about the growing crime rate through the agency of the Poor Law Commission. Charles Mott, an Assistant Commissioner and friend of Chadwick's, who was shown a draft of the Report, pointed out that 'the statement of the increase of crime ... will cut both ways and will be used by the opponents of the New Poor Law as a powerful argument against the ... statement of the advocates ... that [a] decrease of crime follows the introduction of the New [Poor] Law'. Rather than lessen rural tensions, the New Poor Law had clearly exacerbated them.[31]

IV

There was one type of crime which was clearly caused by the introduction of the New Poor Law: the attempted destruction of the new Union workhouses. It was perhaps inevitable that as existing workhouses were modified to serve harsher functions, and as the new Union workhouses began to spring up in southern England, they should become the object of popular wrath. Stories abounded about the cruelties to be practised in these 'bastiles', the terrible food, the separation of families, the diseases and the lingering death. Initially, as at Ipswich, organised attempts were made to destroy the workhouses. But as the authorities in southern England moved to suppress acts of public protest, the protesters were forced to adopt more clandestine tactics.

The first reported attempt to burn down a Union workhouse took place at Heckingham in Norfolk in April 1836. The Heckingham workhouse had been built in the 1760s, as a House of Industry. Unlike another similar institution at Bulcamp, which was burned to the ground by angry labourers in 1768, it had survived to see the arrival of the New Poor Law. The four hundred and fifty odd paupers in the Heckingham workhouse were, like most East Anglian inmates, an extremely independent and spirited group. Early in 1836 they had assaulted Captain Sir Edward Parry, the Assistant Commissioner, when he visited the workhouse. Parry had had alterations made to the workhouse so that the men and women might at some future date be separated.[32] When Dr James Kay, the new Assistant Commissioner, took over in April 1836, he decided that more restrictive regulations would be gradually put into force in the Heckingham workhouse. He started with the food:

> The inmates are at present provided with a diet of solid food at least one third too great, and with two pints of beer daily, besides vegetable broth &c. I propose gradually to restrict this Diet by orders issued under my own hand.[33]

The next step would be the separation of the male and female inmates. Fearing trouble from the paupers, Kay took the precaution of asking the magistrates to write to the Home Office and request Police assistance. Despite the warning and the preparations, the workhouse was burnt to the ground early on the morning of Saturday, 23 April 1836. Damage was estimated at £3,000 and a reward of £600 plus a free pardon was immediately issued. Later investigations showed that the inmates had been warned to expect a fire that night. '[T]he boys were told by the men to take their shoes up to their bedrooms.' James Barrett, a former inmate, was strongly suspected of setting the fire. But although he was arrested, charged and sent for trial, the case against him was never proceeded with.[34]

Fires at other workhouses followed. An unsuccessful attempt was made to burn down the newly built Union workhouse at Saffron Walden in Essex. At Budbury, in East Suffolk, the attempt was more successful. One wing and half the central section of the new Union workhouse was destroyed. At Rollesby, again in Norfolk, the old House of Industry was set alight and half the building destroyed on the day that the married inmates were to be separated. At Llandovery in Carmarthenshire, and Narberth in Pembrokeshire the workhouses were set on fire. And at Tewkesbury in Gloucestershire a 15-year-old inmate named Ann Ella made four unsuccessful attempts to burn down the workhouse before she was finally detected.[35]

The epidemic of workhouse fires and the obvious hatred that people had for the new workhouses kept Boards of Guardians on edge. As early as September 1835 the Ampthill authorities in Bedfordshire had written to the Home Office expressing fear that 'serious attempts are expected to be made ... to destroy the workhouse' they were building. The Mitford and Launditch Board of Guardians asked for a sergeant and three policemen to be sent to protect the Gressenhall workhouse, as they feared trouble. The request was quickly complied with by the Home Office. At the Depward Union, also in Norfolk, the Guardians were forced to employ watchmen and build a high wall, with corner sentry posts, around the site of the new workhouse. Apparently the building was being demolished at night, just as quickly as it was being built during the day. During the height of the Chartist unrest in 1839 the Boards of Guardians were especially fearful. At Loughborough in Leicestershire, the Guardians thought that their new workhouse would be attacked. In the wake of the Newport rising, the Cardiff authorities swore in special constables and armed the Chelsea pensioners so that they might protect the Union workhouse. And at Belper in Derbyshire, the Guardians feared that their new workhouse would also be the subject of unwelcome attention from the Chartists. As it turned out the Belper workhouse was damaged by fire in suspicious circumstances in October 1841. The large crowd who gathered to look at the blaze not only refused to assist in putting out the flames, but threatened those who did.[36]

The final (and certainly the most bizarre) anti-poor law disturbance in south-east England took place near Faversham, Kent, in May 1838. In the early 1830s a man claiming to be Sir William Courtenay, heir to the Earldom of Devon, appeared in the district. He soon gained a large popular following with his advocacy of the rights of the poor. A gifted mob orator and with a commanding presence, he even stood (unsuccessfully) for election to Parliament. Courtenay's troublesome and increasingly eccentric behaviour also brought him to the attention of the authorities. When it was discovered that his real name was John Nichols Tom, a west country wine merchant and brewer, and that his claim to be heir to the Earldom of Devon was nothing more than a delusion, he was packed off to the Barming Lunatic Asylum. He remained there until late 1837 when his family persuaded the authorities to release him into their care. Instead of returning home with his family, however, Tom resumed his career as a popular agitator. Resentment over the New Poor Law had been simmering in the area for years (the Milton Union, where the first rural protests had taken place, was nearby). Tom, who still persisted in the delusion that he was Sir William Courtenay, helped give that simmering bitterness renewed force and direction. He toured extensively through the agricultural areas of east Kent, making inflamatory speeches against the New Poor Law and winning new followers to his cause. Encouraged by the support he received, Tom's megalomania gradually assumed an even more extreme form. By the Spring of 1838 he had convinced himself and his loyal band of followers that he was the Messiah, come to save them from the New Poor Law. Alarmed by these developments, and by reports that Tom and his followers were arming themselves, the authorities issued a warrant for his arrest. Tom's crusade against the New Poor Law was shortlived. Following the madman's murder of the hapless constable who was charged with arresting him, there was a violent clash between Tom's supporters and troops in Bossenden Wood. Eleven people, including Tom and a Lieutenant Bennett, were killed in the fight. In his report to the Home Office, the Chairman of the Bench at Sittingbourne, the Reverend Dr Poore, justified the local authorities' use of force by arguing that 'unless it was immediately suppressed the scenes of 1835 would [have] be [en] repeated and probably to [a] greater extent'.[37] Throughout south-east England organised opposition to the New Poor Law would continue to be ruthlessly suppressed, driving the protesters underground.

Outside the Swing counties, however (and particularly on the Celtic fringes), organised public opposition to the New Poor Law persisted. In Cambridge the Reverend Mr F.H. Maberly kept the issue of poor relief in the public eye with mass meetings and petitions to Parliament. Even when he was dismissed from his curacy he kept up the agitation. When Maberly was arrested by the police at the declaration of the poll at Cambridge in July 1837, the crowd stormed the police station to rescue him. Further north, on the Isle of Axholme in Lincolnshire, the local farm labourers successfully delayed the introduction of the New Poor Law by the simple expedient of not allowing the new relieving officer to land from the steam packet – the islet's only means of communication with the outside world. And in the town of Stratton in Cornwall the Guardians, while inspecting the site for a new Union workhouse, were confronted by a 'large Body of men in Military array ... armed with Clubs and Bludgeons'. The Guardians, magistrates and relieving officer were bailed up in the Chairman's home by the crowd and demands made that they promise not to build a workhouse. The Chairman was told 'that if such a building was attempted they would destroy it by force'. Shocked by the vehemence of the threat, the officials decided to comply. There were no further disturbances at Stratton, but neither was a Union workhouse built.[38]

But it was in Wales that the most forceful rural opposition to the New Poor Law was displayed. For most of 1837 the Principality was in a state of virtual open revolt against the central authorities in London. Relieving officers were subjected to 'rough music', there were demonstrations with 'red flags', Guardians were stoned, and on more than one occasion Assistant Commissioner Day was forced to flee on foot from an angry crowd.[39] Language difficulties, religious sensibilities and an intense community loyalty added to the authorities' problems in Wales. The regimentation of relief, the Bastardy Clauses and the separation of husbands from wives and parents from children in the new workhouses, were seen as an affront to Welsh non-conformity. Local customs were also threatened. In the iron mining region of north-west Monmouthshire, for instance, iron masters did not pay poor rates on the understanding that they maintained their own poor. George Clive, the Assistant Commissioner for the area, thought that the sooner the 'system is put an end to ... the better'. It was this failure to appreciate the complexity of the situation in Wales and the often high-handed behaviour of the English poor law officials which alienated not only the labouring population of Wales, but also many respectable inhabitants as well. At Cowbridge, Glamorgan, the clergy and magistrates declared the New Poor Law to be contrary to the divine will, and to be cruel, unjust and impolitic.[40] It was no accident that both the Welsh Chartists and the Rebecca Rioters were to make the New Poor Law one of the main targets of their respective campaigns.

VI

Popular animosity towards the 1834 Poor Law in rural Britain was deep-seated and persistent. It was concerned not only with opposing a new and restrictive poor relief system, but also with defending long-established rights and customs. It is true that over the previous half century there had been a gradual but fundamental shift in the relationships which governed life in rural Britain. Certainly James Obelkevich is correct when he claims that the landowning classes' support of the 1834 Poor Law in Parliament 'was only a public and national version of the "abdication" that was an accomplished fact in the village'.[41] But while the gentry denied their responsibilities, the poor in rural Britain had not as yet accepted this abdication'. The process had been a gradual one. First enclosure had denied the rural dweller access to the common land; then their means of obtaining game and wood from the forest was severely restricted; then gleaning rights (the right to collect grain left in the field after harvesting) were challenged; and finally the New Poor Law denied the rural dweller's right to relief. When labourers, tradesmen, small shopkeepers and others in rural Britain protested about changes to the system of poor relief, it was not simply the substitution of relief in kind for cash relief, nor the lowering of the scale of relief, nor the consolidation of workhouse accommodation, nor the changes in the administration of workhouse relief that they objected to. They also objected to the challenge being made to long-established customs and relationships which had existed in their local communities since pre-industrial times. When popular opponents of the 1834 Poor Law in rural England and Wales talked of defending their 'rights' it was the customs and traditional relationships of their own communities that they meant; they were defending the human values of an earlier moral economy against the apparent harshness of a newer political economy.

Notes

1. A. Brundage, *The Making of the New Poor Law* (Hutchinson, London, 1970), pp.75-84.
2. Poore to Lefevre, 30 April 1835, PRO, MH 12/5279; *The Times*, 14 May 1835.
3. Poore to Russell, 3 & 5 May 1835, PRO, HO 52/26.
4. Head to PLC, 7 May 1835, PRO, MH 12/5279.
5. Gledey to PLC, 15 May 1835, and Deposition of C. May, 16 May 1835, PRO, MH 12/1; *Cambridge Chronicle*, 24 July 1835.
6. 'Riot ... Ampthill' (handbill), PRO, MH 12/380.
7. Docking Magistrates to Russell, 2 July 1835, PRO, HO 50/26; *Cambridge Chronicle*, 10 July 1835; *Norwich Mercury*, 18 July 1835.
8. Parry to Lewis, 1 July 1835, PRO, MH 12/8249; *Cambridge Chronicle*, 10 July 1835.
9. *Cambridge Chronicle*, 10 July 1835.
10. Docking Magistrates to Russell, 13 July 1835, PRO, HO 52/26; *Cambridge Chronicle*, 10 July 1835.
11. Docking Magistrates to Russell, 29 July 1835, PRO, HO 52/26; Manly to Docking Magistrates, 31 July 1835, PRO, HO 41/12.
12. Docking Magistrates to Russell, 4 May 1835, PRO, HO 52/26; Hanley to PLC, 8 May 1835, PRO, MH 12/13157, and Gilbert to PLC, 24 May 1835, PRO, MH 12/380; Poore to Russell, 5 May 1835, PRO, HO 52/26.
13. Pilkington to PLC, 30 April 1835; PLC to Thomas, 29 April 1835, PRO, MH 12/12854.
14. Memorial of the Ratepayers of Chalfont St Giles, 18 May 1835; Deposition of Fuller, August 1835; Gilbert to PLC, 24 May 1835, PRO, MH 12/380.

15. Oake *et al* to PLC, 23 May 1835, PRO, MH 12/380.
16. Russell to Rowan, 23 May 1835, PRO, HO 40/12.
17. Gilbert to PLC, 24 May 1835, PRO, MH 12/380; Gilbert to Chadwick, 24 June 1835, Chadwick Papers, UCL, 808.
18. *Norwich Mercury*, 26 December 1835.
19. Lutton to Kay, 17 December 1835, PRO, HO 73/2 (1).
20. Barbridge to Kay, 17 December 1835, PRO, HO 73/2 (1); *Norwich Mercury*, 26 December 1835.
21. Kay to PLC, 5 January 1836, PRO, HO 73/4 (1).
22. *Cambridge Chronicle*, 1 January 1836; *Norwich Mercury*, 26 December 1835; Offord to Russell, 6 January 1836, PRO, HO 52/26.
23. PLC to Russell, 23 June 1835, Power to PLC, 19 August 1835, PRO, HO 73/51; *Cambridge Chronicle*, 4 December 1835; Rose to HO, 20 December 1835, PRO, HO 40/33 (3); A. Digby, *Pauper Palaces* (Routledge & Kegan Paul, London, 1978), p.223; Great Massingham Returns, Q.17, PRO, HO 73/7 (1); 'Second Annual Report PLC', *PP*, 1836, vol.XXIX, p.329.
24. Waters to PLC, 11 June 1836, PRO, MH 12/8415, and *Norwich Mercury*, 2 July 1836.
25. Hustler to Russell, 2 December 1836, Bainester and Cook to Russell, 2 December 1836, PRO, HO 64/6.
26. Sewell to Russell, 8 December 1836, PRO, HO 40/34.
27. Sperling and Gooch to Russell, 24 February 1837, PRO, HO 64/7; Wade Report 1837, PRO, HO 73/53.
28. Wade to PLC, 17 October 1837, PRO, HO 73/52; Hustler to Russell, 13 October 1837, PRO, HO 64/7; *Bell's Life in London*, 18 February 1838.
29. a'Court to Chadwick, 22 January 1835, Chadwick Papers, UCL, 152.
30. Gilbert to Lefevre, 4 May 1836, PRO, MH 32/26.
31. Cobbett to Fielden, 22 October 1838, Fielden Papers, JRULM; *The Times*, 4 July 1844; 'First Report of the Constabulary Forces Commission', *PP*, 1839, vol.XIX; Mott to Chadwick, 21 January 1839, PRO, HO 73/3.
32. 'Second Annual Report PLC', *PP*, 1836, vol.XXIX, p.155.
33. Kay to PLC, 5 April 1836, PRO, MH 12/8455.
34. Kelt to Shaw-Lefevre, 11 April 1836; Kay to PLC, 14 April 1836; 'Reward Poster', Loddon, Norfolk, 26 April 1836; Kay to PLC, 27 April 1836, PRO, MH 12/8455; *Norwich Mercury*, 6 August 1836.
35. *Cambridge Chronicle*, 6 May 1836; *Leeds Times*, 10 December 1836; Kay to PLC, 26 March 1837, PRO, MH 12/8340; *Norwich Mercury*, 25 March 1837; Williams to Russell, 18 August 1838, PRO, HO 64/8; Biddalph to Russell, 21 January 1839, PRO, HO 64/9; *Manchester and Salford Advertiser*, 25 May 1839.
36. Crawley to Russell, 23 September 1835, PRO, HO 52/26; PLC to Russell, 25 May 1836, PRO, HO 73/51; Digby, *Pauper Palaces*, p.220; Brock to PLC, 27 February 1839, PRO, HO 73/55; Cardiff Magistrates to Normandy, 6 November 1839, PRO, HO 40/46; Belper Magistrates to Russell, 30 March 1839, PRO, HO 40/42; *Nottingham Review*, 29 October 1841.
37. Poore to Camden, 31 May 1838, PRO, HO 40/36; for a full account of Sir William Courtenay's career see P.G. Rogers, *Battle in Bossenden Wood* (Readers Union, London, 1962).
38. *Cambridge Chronicle*, 29 July 1837; Brownlow to Russell, 10 June 1837, PRO, HO 52/34; Shearm to Gilbert, 8 February 1837, PRO, HO 73/52.
39. Yates to Chadwick, 22 April 1837, Chadwick Papers, UCL, 2171, and Day to PLC, 22 April 1837, PRO, HO 73/52.
40. Clive to Lewis, 16 March 1836, PRO, MH 32/12; D. Williams, *A History of Modern Wales* (John Murray, London, 1950), p.204.
41. J. Obelkevich, *Religion and Rural Society* (Oxford University Press, London, 1976), p.26.

4 UNFURLING THE BANNER OF RESISTANCE

By the summer of 1836 the Poor Law Commission could be well pleased with its efforts. Most of the Poor Law Unions in the south of England had been established and to all intents and purposes were successfully administering the New Poor Law. True, there had been violent opposition to the new system of poor relief in some areas, but it had been unco-ordinated and was soon subsumed in the general background of bitterness and brutality which characterised class relations in early nineteenth-century rural Britain. Towards the end of 1836 the Assistant Commissioners began moving north of the Trent to perform what they thought would be the relatively easy task of introducing the New Poor Law into the manufacturing districts of the north of England. The *Report* of the 1832 Royal Commission had indicated that the cost of poor relief in the industrial north was much lower than in the agricultural south. It was presumed, therefore, that the Old Poor Law in the north was more strictly administered and free of the abuses present in the south. On this basis the Poor Law Commission confidently assumed that they would have few difficulties in introducing the New Poor Law into the north of England. Their confidence was soon rudely shaken. Not only did the Poor Law Commission encounter the outraged hostility of many local authorities, who had felt themselves to be safe from interference, but also the organised opposition of a militant working class with a long tradition of radical protest.

I

The first inklings of an organised campaign of popular opposition to the New Poor Law in the industrial north of England appeared at Bradford in December 1834. The Reverend George Stringer Bull, vicar of Bierley Parish Church, inflamed public opinion and antagonised local officialdom with his outspoken comments against the 1834 Poor Law. In a series of public lectures, he claimed that the New Poor Law destroyed the 'Poor's right to relief', a right sanctioned 'by Divine Authority' and 'the constitution of the country'.[1] Although Bull's attacks attracted widespread popular support, it soon became evident that the Poor Law Commission had no intention of immediately introducing the New Poor Law into Bradford and the campaign slowly fizzled out.

Because the New Poor Law was not immediately introduced into the north of England, many people came to believe that it had been repealed. Thomas Ainsworth, a manufacturer from Clayton in Dale, Lancashire, wrote to the Poor Law Commission blaming those magistrates 'not friendly to the change' for spreading the rumour. He said that the fall of the Whig government in November 1834 and the subsequent dissolution of Parliament was 'considered conclusive': 'opinion prevails ... that the new Poor law is actually repealed'.[2] Of course not everyone was so gullible. Amongst popular radicals and other groups of well-informed working men the New Poor Law remained a subject for concern throughout 1835-6. A meeting of the Barnsley Radical Association resolved in February 1836:

> That we the Radicals of Barnsley, have minutely discussed the leading features of the Poor Law Amendment Act, and also its cruel operations on the suffering poor; and we have come to the conclusion that a vote of censure and disapprobation be passed upon the said act, and the reformed parliament which enacted it; moreover we express an anxious wish that the aforesaid be repealed, and that of the 43rd Elizabeth be substituted in its place. We also call upon all good men to exert themselves in those encounters with the enemies of popular rights, which we, in union with the surrounding Radical Associations, are determined to enter upon.[3]

While the Poor Law Commission confined its activities to the south of England, the New Poor Law presented no immediate threat to the labouring population in manufacturing districts of the north. It remained a matter for anxious discussion, but with no clear focus for a campaign of agitation it was not yet one for popular action.

Among the first Assistant Commissioners to move north of the river Trent was Richard Digby Neave, who started work in Cheshire in July 1836. It was Neave's first independent assignment for the Poor Law Commission. He had previously spent a couple of months working in Nottinghamshire with Assistant Commissioner Gulson, learning the ropes. Neave adopted the procedure that had worked well in other areas: he met with the respectable inhabitants, examined the parish books, found out which towns acted as commercial and judicial centres, visited existing workhouses, and began dividing up his district into Poor Law Unions. All appeared to go as planned. By September 1836 the majority of Unions in Cheshire had been declared. Only the north-east corner of the county remained to be formed into Poor Law Unions.

The Poor Law Commission's success in Cheshire was to prove shortlived. Soon after being formed, in September 1836, the Macclesfield Board of Guardians decided to build a new Union workhouse. Within a month an architect had been appointed, plans drawn up and the design approved. Shaped in the form of a cross and enclosed by a high wall, the workhouse would offer segregated accommodation for 580 inmates. Estimates put the cost at £5,000.[4] The workhouse was never built. Although a local builder successfully tendered for the job, the project encountered so much local opposition that he was forced to abandon work on it. Macclesfield was the centre of the declining silk-weaving industry and the militant silk weavers were determined to resist any attempt to build the new 'bastile'. Whenever the builder appeared on the streets of Macclesfield, he was 'abused and menaced by the mob'. The Macclesfield, Hurdsfield and Sutton Burial Society, the weavers' burial society, led the campaign. In September 1837 they wrote to the Poor Law Commission claiming that over 11,000 people in the Macclesfield Union had 'unfurled the banner of resistance against that most abominable law' and taunting them with the fact that they had succeeded in preventing the building of a new Union 'bastile'. The Macclesfield Board of Guardians had to be content with modifying the old workhouse and using it as best they could.[5]

Coinciding with the movement of the Assistant Commissioners into the north of England came economic distress. The country's economy had peaked towards the middle of 1836, and thereafter began to decline. By the winter of 1836-7 Britain was facing a severe depression. Effects were not uniform. Some manufacturing industries, such as cotton spinning, would continue to flourish for some time to come, and the boom in railway building did not slacken until well into the 1840s. But the building industry and parts of the textile industry – silk, linen, woollen and worsted – were severely affected. Among the worst-hit occupations were the outwork trades – combers, carders, handloom weavers, croppers, and the like; their already low piece-work rates were cut back even further. It was these people who were to be the mainstay of the anti-poor law movement in the north of England.

The depressed woollen textile town of Huddersfield was the scene of the next major outburst of popular anger against the 1834 Poor Law. Early in December 1836 it became known that the Poor Law Commission intended to introduce the New Poor Law into Huddersfield. In response to this news a crowd of over 8,000 people gathered in the market place to show their opposition. The *Leeds Times* commented that the feeling in Huddersfield was 'so strong' against the New Poor Law, that they feared 'some outbreak if it were attempted to be put in force'. The Huddersfield demonstrators were reported as saying, 'better anything than be starved to death under the hands of the most cold-blooded monsters the world ever saw'. At the climax to the demonstration an effigy of a Poor Law Commissioner was burnt in the market place.[6]

As if to compound the problems they would face in the textile areas of the north of England, the Poor Law Commission appointed Alfred Power to the position of Assistant Commissioner for South Lancashire and the West Riding of Yorkshire. Power, the son of a Lichfield doctor, was only thirty-one years of age. Educated at Cambridge, where he had taken a second-class degree in Classics, he had gone on to study Law and was admitted to the Bar in February 1830. For a while he worked as a barrister on the Midland circuit. In 1833 Power was appointed as an Assistant Commissioner to the 1832 Royal Commission. Here he made the acquaintance of Edwin Chadwick. Like Chadwick he was an ideologue, a disciple of the new political economy, with dogmatic views on the question of poor relief. Perhaps because of his friendship with Chadwick, Power was appointed as an investigator for the 1833 Factory Commission. Together with two other investigators, he was sent north to inquire into the factory conditions in Yorkshire. During their visit the three men were suspected of siding with the factory owners, and were harassed by the supporters of the local Short Time Committees. Power, who was a rigid and arrogant young man, lacking both a sense of humour and a sense of proportion, bridled at the ill-treatment. In November 1834, after assisting in the preparation and drafting of the New Poor Law, he was appointed as one of the nine original Assistant Commissioners to the Poor Law Commission.[7] Until the end of 1836 he worked without incident, establishing the New Poor Law in southern England. When Power returned to the north at the end of 1836 it is unlikely that he had forgotten, let alone forgiven, his earlier treatment; it also soon became clear that the factory operatives of South Lancashire and the West Riding of Yorkshire had in turn neither forgotten nor forgiven him.

At Bury on Friday, 6 January 1837 word of Assistant Commissioner Power's meeting with the select vestry leaked out beforehand. When Power arrived, accompanied by the local Whig MP and one of the magistrates, he found the meeting room crowded with working men. Power told the noisy meeting that it was his business to form a district, centred on Bury, for the purpose of the Registration Act, and that this would later become a Poor Law Union. Asked by the leader of the popular radicals in Bury, the surgeon Matthew Fletcher, whether a Board of Guardians was planned to put the New Poor Law into effect, Power replied that it was. This answer was received with loud groans. Fletcher continued to fire questions at Power about the aims and workings of the New Poor Law. Under the relentless onslaught Power's patience cracked and he angrily left the meeting.[8]

A few days later at Huddersfield, Power received an even more hostile reception. He arrived expecting to meet with the overseers and a small number of the more important ratepayers. Instead he found a town alive with rumour and the meeting room crowded with working men and women. Once again he was closely questioned. Power was told that 'every opposition would be offered to the forming of the Union'. He replied that all opposition 'would be futile', and that the law 'would be put in force'. Told it was 'a bad law', Power said he would not sit and 'hear the law declaimed against'. Christopher Tinker then stood up, announced that he was 'a poor man', and said that if 'all poor men were of his opinion' they would take up a rifle and lodge a ball in the heart of every Commissioner who came into the town. Power lost his temper, said he would not stay to be threatened, bundled up his maps and papers and stormed out of the room. He left town soon afterwards in a post-chaise.[9]

In his correspondence with the Poor Law Commission, Power made light of the affair. He said that it was not true, as reported in the Press, that he had 'left the town in haste'. And as far as the threat to his life was concerned, it had come from 'a very low vagabond, in all probability tipsy', and was not worth bothering with.[10] One has the impression with this and later correspondence from Power, that he was covering up. He had the habit, like most of the other Assistant Commissioners, of initially playing down opposition to the New Poor Law. In October 1837 he was to write, in answer to an Home Office inquiry about whether there had been any outbreaks of incendiarism in his district, that not only had there been no incendiarism, but that 'neither had there been ... any other manifestations of discontent amongst the labouring classes'. Not two months later he exaggerated the extent of popular unrest in his district, telling the Poor Law Commission that he feared an assassination attempt on himself and other poor law officials.[11] Admittedly circumstances can quickly change, but one cannot help suspecting that Power trimmed his reports to preserve self-esteem and suit what he considered to be the political needs of the Poor Law Commission.

Not all of Power's early meetings were marked by confrontation. In a number of towns he was able to meet with the local worthies without attracing the attention of the labouring population at large. In Halifax, for instance, Power spent a number of days in the town making inquiries about the formation of the new Union. At a meeting with 'the vicar, some of the magistrates, the Overseers, and several other gentlemen', Power told them that the Registration Act had necessitated the 'immediate formation of the Unions.[12] He encountered no opposition from the Halifax worthies.

Even if the Poor Law Commission had wished to stay its hand in the north of England until the economic situation improved, they were unable to do so. In 1836 Parliament passed the Births, Deaths and Marriages Registration Act, and placed the administrative responsibility for the legislation in the hands of the new Poor Law Unions. The Registration Act was designed to come into force early in 1837. This created no problems in southern England, where the Poor Law Unions were already established and operating. But in many parts of the north, the work of establishing the new Unions had not even begun. Not only were the Assistant Commissioners to face a well-organised and increasingly militant working class, who were just beginning to feel the effects of depression, but they also had to work with extraordinary haste to establish the new Poor Law Unions before the Registration Act came into operation. One of the consequences of the rush was that most northern Poor Law Unions would be up to ten times the size of unions in the south of England.[13]

Assistant Commission William James Voules warned the Commission as early as January 1837 'that it will be unwise, and unfair to the measure itself [the New Poor Law] to precipitate its application, and risk its cordial and therefore effective reception, at an unseasonable moment, for the sake of introducing a collateral object, namely the Registration Act'. His warning went unheeded. The carefully worked out procedure for establishing Poor Law Unions, which had been used to such good effect in southern England, was abandoned. Union boundaries would be decided long before the constituent townships were examined in any detail.[14] The unseemly haste antagonised not only the labouring population, but also many 'respectable inhabitants' who might otherwise have been friendly towards the New Poor Law.

II

The widespread opposition of 'respectable inhabitants' was something the Poor Law Commission had not really encountered before. And yet they had had plenty of warning. There had been complaints about the New Poor Law from northern parishes while the legislation was still before Parliament.[15] In May 1834, for instance, the Bolton overseers called a series of ratepayers' meetings to consider the Bill. At these meetings, which were attended by large audiences, overseers, ratepayers and poor relief recipients alike roundly condemned the New Poor Law for treating poor people as if they became destitute through their own misconduct. Only one speaker, Charles Darbishire, a quilting manufacturer, spoke in support of the proposed legislation. He later admitted that he got 'out called' for his pains.[16]

Press reaction to the New Poor Law in the north of England was mixed. Newspapers which were later to attack the New Poor Law unmercifully initially supported the Bill. In April 1834 the radical *Leeds Times* thought the Bill was 'calculated to eradicate abominations which have long deserved the abhorrence of the people'. And the Tory *Bolton Chronicle* told its readers that the Bill must strongly recommend itself 'to every person who had paid the least attention to the practical working of the poor laws'. A couple of months later, after the harsher implications of the Bill had become clear, the *Leeds Times* was attacking the New Poor Law as 'bad in principle ... [and] cruel in spirit'. The radical *Manchester and Salford Advertiser* thought a more fitting name for the legislation should be 'An Act for further debasing and degrading English labourers, and for the better encouragement of seduction, and the propagation of bastardy and infanticide'.[17] Of course, support for the New Poor Law was strongest amongst Whig and reformist newspapers. The *Leeds Mercury* described the Bill as 'one of the most important measures that has ever been submitted to Parliament'. The *Manchester Guardian* and *Sheffield Independent* also supported the measure, and attacked *The Times* for, as they saw it, attempting to mislead public opinion over the New Poor Law.[18] Such favourable comments were, however, tempered by two factors which proved enormously important in shaping respectable opposition to the New Poor Law in the north of England. The first was the establishment of the new centralised bureaucracy, the Poor Law Commission. The *Leeds Mercury*, for instance, was doubtful about the wisdom of creating a powerful, independent and costly Commission to administer the new law. Secondly, all northern newspapers agreed that the reforms outlined in the New Poor Law were not applicable to the manufacturing districts of the north of England. As Michael Rose has pointed out, all sections of the northern press had a somewhat 'holier than thou' attitude towards the poor law authorities in southern England. Thus the *Leeds Mercury* 'scarcely ... doubted that the Commission will direct interference chiefly on parishes where great abuses exist and not trouble with vexatious meddling the parishes where the affairs of the poor are well administered.[19] As the Poor Law Commission was to learn, most northern ratepayers and local poor law officials also thought themselves to be outside the scope of 'vexatious meddling'.

Offended local pride, a fear that the New Poor Law would prove more expensive to ratepayers and genuine sympathy for the poor were the cause of deep concern to many influential inhabitants in the north. The Poor Law Commission received a memorial from a number of prominent ratepayers at Hebden Bridge, for instance, asking that the administrative centre of the proposed Todmorden Union be moved to their own township. William Sutcliffe, the worsted manufacturer who forwarded the memorial, said that opinion throughout the neighbourhood was 'favourable to an Union, but decidedly opposed to its being centred at Todmorden'. As the memorialists pointed out, the majority of the townships in the proposed Union were in Yorkshire and produced worsted cloth, whereas Todmorden itself was a cotton-manufacturing town located just across the county border in Lancashire.[20] In the proposed Wigan Union, on the other hand, the respectable inhabitants in several of the smaller townships expressed concern over being swallowed up by their large neighbour. They feared that they would have to pay higher poor rates if joined to Wigan with its large labouring population.[21] Traditionalists objected to the New Poor Law because it offended their perceptions of an organic, harmonious society. The Reverend Patrick Brontë vicar of Haworth, reminded a local meeting that wealth and property had their obligations as well as their rights. 'The working men and labourers trampled on by this bill were the material of the country,' he said; 'remove them and what were Kings, Lords, and Commons worth?' He went on to warn that if the

New Poor Law was put into force, and 'dear times and general distress should come on, starvation, deprived of relief, would break into open rebellion'.[22] There were many people, magistrates, members of the gentry, even some manufacturers, who shared such views. Matthew Thompson, a Bradford worsted manufacturer and magistrate, told an open air public meeting at Bradford in March 1837 that he would 'always be ready ... to assert the rights of the poor, against every attempt to invade them'. Apparently 'always' had rather limited meaning for Thompson, however, because by the end of the year he was calling on the people of Bradford to give the New Poor Law a fair trial.[23]

Not all respectable opponents of the New Poor Law abandoned the opposition cause so easily. There was a significant number of Ultra-Tories and middle-class Radicals who were prepared to ally themselves with the campaign of popular opposition to the New Poor Law. Most had been active in the earlier Factory Reform Movement. Three in particular, Richard Oastler, the Reverend Joseph Rayner Stephens and John Fielden, would become national leaders of the anti-poor law movement.

Richard Oastler was among the most revered of the anti-poor law campaigners. He had earned the title 'King of the Factory Children' together with the trust and support of the Lancashire and Yorkshire factory operatives, for his unflinching efforts on their behalf in the early 1830s. Ostensibly an old-fashioned Church and King Tory, Oastler's background was much more varied than his position as Steward of Fixby Hall, near Huddersfield, would suggest. Oastler had been brought up in a Methodist household to believe in the doctrine of equality of opportunity. He had spent eight years being educated at the celebrated Moravian Settlement at Fulneck near Leeds. The policy of humility, brotherhood and friendship which characterised life in the Moravian Settlement was to leave a lasting impression on Oastler. A chance meeting, in 1830, introduced Oastler to the distress experienced by factory workers in the textile industry. The overthrow of the conditions which caused such suffering henceforth became the abiding passion of Oastler's life. An opponent of political reform, not caring about Trade Unions, and knowing little about the lives of working people, he was still willing to ally himself with working-class radicals and lead a popular movement for Factory Reform. Although in private a mild and gentle man, he had a commanding platform presence. A powerfully built figure, standing over six feet tall, he had 'keen and intelligent blue eyes, a mass of iron grey hair ... and a voice stentorian in its power'. Thomas Trollope, who saw and heard him speak at a crowded meeting in Ashton-under-Lyne in 1838, described him as 'the beau-ideal of a mob orator'.[24] With the arrival of the New Poor Law Oastler once again threw himself into battle against what he saw as yet another blatant attack on the institutions and values he cherished.

The Reverend Joseph Rayner Stephens was also an Ultra-Tory, but unlike Oastler he was no friend to Anglicanism. The son of a Wesleyan Methodist Minister, Stephens had been educated at the Manchester Grammar School and the Methodist School near Leeds. As a schoolboy he had witnessed the Peterloo massacre. At the age of twenty he became a Methodist preacher, serving for a time as a missionary in Sweden. In 1829 he returned home and was ordained as a Methodist Minister. Stephens's strong views on Church Disestablishment led him into conflict with his Wesleyan superiors and in 1834 he was expelled by the Methodist conference for acting as a secretary to an anti-state church association. Separated from his church, Stephens did not give up preaching. He was approached by a group of former Methodists to be the minister of an independent chapel at Ashton-under-Lyne. The sect had other congregations at Oldham, Dukinfield and Bolton. Stephens began his new ministry among men who harboured bitter thoughts about their treatment at the hands of their employers and the government. The failure of the 1832 Reform Act and 1833 Factory Act to relieve their distress and the passage of the 1834 New Poor Law caused deep resentment. Stephens slowly became involved in their struggle. He made his first public speech in favour of Factory Reform in January 1836. Within months he had achieved a following and reputation equal to long-established leaders like Oastler. The explanation for his meteoric rise is to be found in his almost charismatic appeal. A surviving portrait shows a man of average height and build, with a receding hairline, long dark side-burns and a penetrating, even hypnotic, stare. His voice was clear and impressive. He spoke not of abstract rights or ideal improvements, but of pain and privations. His message was apocalyptic: poverty, hunger and suffering were the result of corrupt purposes; to struggle against them was to struggle against evil. His imagery and inspiration came from the Old Testament, and his call to arms to fight the corruption and evil could occasionally sound like a call for revolution. But Stephens was no radical, not even a democrat. In his opinion the existing institutions were sufficient, it merely required that men use them properly.[25] Armed with his apocalyptic vision and inspirational imagery he would do battle with the forces of Mammon which had introduced the New Poor Law and threatened to destroy the traditions he valued.

Oastler and Stephens were Ultra-Tories whose abilities as demagogues gave them a large public following; John Fielden was no demagogue and by all accounts a poor public speaker. Nevertheless as a respected Cobbettite Radical he enjoyed strong popular support. Fielden had grown to wealth with the rise of the Lancashire cotton industry. His father, Joshua Fielden, had been a farmer and woollen weaver, who in the 1780s moved to Todmorden to set up a cotton 'manufactury'. At first all the work was done by hand; but gradually the spinning jenny replaced the wheel and carding machines were introduced. The famous Waterside Mill at Todmorden – the first of many factories owned by the Fieldens – was built to accommodate the new machinery. As soon as they reached the age of ten the sons went to work in the factory. John Fielden was to have bitter memories of these years as a child factory worker in his father's mill and for the rest of his life maintained a deep sympathy and understanding for those subjected to similar, or even worse, suffering. Helped by his five sons, Joshua Fielden's business prospered and expanded. John Fielden, the third son, specialised in the firm's buying and selling. He was made a partner in his early twenties; and on his father's death in 1811, he and his brothers took full control of the concern. Over the next thirty years, the firm of Fielden Brothers, as it was now called, grew to become one of the largest cotton spinning and weaving concerns in South Lancashire. The brothers also had interests in shipping, South American cattle and railway building. In 1846 the firm of Fielden Brothers attained the distinction of being the largest consumer of cotton, as a single company, in the world.

Although Joshua Fielden had been a Quaker and a Tory, all his sons were ardent radicals. As early as 1816 John Fielden and his brothers were supporting calls for the regulation of factories. It was a cause which would occupy Fielden for the rest of his life. On matters of political policy, Fielden was a Cobbettite. He criticised Peel's restoration of the gold standard and favoured an 'equitable adjustment' (a capital tax levy) to help reduce the interest on the National Debt. He was also a strong opponent of 'paper money' and a supporter of universal suffrage. In 1832, following the passage of the Reform Bill, Fielden allowed himself to be nominated in partnership with his mentor, William Cobbett, as a Radical candidate for Oldham. He had no political ambitions himself, but merely hoped that his nomination would help secure Cobbett's election. In the event both Cobbett and

Fielden romped home with enormous majorities. In Parliament Fielden was among the most consistent of Radicals, supporting every democratic proposal. But it was the condition of the northern factory operatives which was his main concern. Both inside and outside Parliament he struggled manfully in their cause. He supported the Ten-Hours Movement and with the advent of the New Poor Law struggled long and hard for its repeal. John Fielden was a quiet, thoughtful, even unassuming man. He was unsuited both with regard to temperament and speaking voice for the role of popular demagogue. Nevertheless, his wealth and influence were to provide invaluable support to the campaign of popular opposition to the 1834 Poor Law.[26]

Oastler, Stephens and Fielden were not the only members of the gentry or middle classes to ally themselves with the campaign of popular opposition to the New Poor Law. There were others, but none (apart from Feargus O'Connor, with whom we shall deal in a later chapter) achieved national status. The Reverend George Stringer Bull had been a popular speaker with the Factory Reformers in Bradford, but although he was one of the first in the north of England to voice public criticism of the New Poor Law, he withdrew from the campaign in 1837 when it took on more radical overtones. Samuel Roberts, a retired cutler and inveterate pamphleteer, was active in the Sheffield campaign, but his domineering style eventually proved too much for the independent-minded workers who made up the vast bulk of the Sheffield protesters. In July 1837 they broke with 'the would-be drill sergeant of Park Grange'. Matthew Fletcher, the radical doctor from Bury, led an enthusiastic campaign in his own area. And there were a handful of radical manufacturers in Manchester who supported the campaign.[27]

Outside Radical and Ultra-Tory circles, however, respectable opposition to the New Poor Law often had a rather brittle quality. The Tory-dominated Blackburn Board of Guardians began by calling for a repeal of the New Poor Law and suggesting that the management of the poor be put back in the hands of the Select Vestry, but within six months they were happy to start implementing the revised regulations put forward by the Poor Law Commission. In the Todmorden Union a number of Guardians, elected because they claimed to be opponents of the New Poor Law, provoked bitter public comment when they began supporting the introduction of the measure.[28] The apparent fickleness of many respectable opponents of the New Poor Law resulted from the fact that they based their opposition on quite different grounds from that of the popular opponents. They were mainly concerned about the cost of poor relief and the loss of local autonomy. A few abandoned the opposition cause for personal gain. James Stansfield, who began as an active opponent of the New Poor Law in the Todmorden Union, lost all his commitment after he had secured the well-paid position of Union clerk.[29] But in most cases the opposition of the gentry and middle class only persisted as long as the New Poor Law was seen to threaten their interests. As soon as they had been assured that poor rates would not increase, and that they would not otherwise be disadvantaged by the New Poor Law, their opposition evaporated.

III

Although leadership was often provided by middling sorts of people, it was ordinary working men and women who provided the most sustained and forceful opposition to the 1834 Poor Law. It was they who mobbed the Assistant Commissioners, signed the flood of petitions, demonstrated and occasionally rioted. And it was working people who would continue to fight a rearguard action against the 'devil's law' until well into the twentieth century.

The opposition of working men and women was based upon both practical and ideological considerations. The Old Poor Law played a crucial role in the domestic economy of most working-class families and provided a bulwark against the threat of utter destitution. Thus the urban factory operative, the struggling outworker in the small textile village and the rural farm labourer all viewed the new and restrictive poor relief regulations as a direct attack on their own security and the well-being of their family. Furthermore, there was something sinister and frighteningly different about the New Poor Law: it was perceived as turning familial values, popular sentiment and existing social relationships on their heads. The paternalism and humanitarianism of the Old Poor Law was to be replaced by the strict economy and harshness of the New.

The working men and women of the northern textile districts had a long and proud tradition of popular radicalism, trade union activity and political agitation. In the immediate post-war years a network of radical clubs and societies had grown up in the northern manufacturing districts. This movement of radical reform reached its climax at Peterloo in 1819. Although popular political activity lay dormant for much of the 1820s, the traditions of popular radicalism established in the immediate post-war years provided an enduring legacy for northern working men and women. There were two aspects of this heritage which were to be of particular importance in shaping the character of northern popular opposition to the New Poor Law. Firstly, it embodied a militant activism. Although popular opponents were happy to initiate discussion, debate, and use propaganda against the New Poor Law, their most concrete expression of opposition took place in the public arena with demonstrations, meetings and (occasionally) riots. Secondly, the spirit of 'Peterloo' embodied a firm and uncompromising assertion of egalitarian and democratic values. Most northern working men and women implicitly rejected the various forms of subordination and deference.[30] They were especially incensed by the way in which their views and opinions were ignored by both the government and the Poor Law Commission.

Assistant Poor Law Commissioners were apparently only too willing to meet with 'the better sort of person', prominent ratepayers, overseers, members of the gentry, magistrates, and the like, to put their minds at rest on matters that might concern them. But the opinions and concerns of ordinary men and women, those most deeply affected by the New Poor Law, were dismissed as being of little consequence. This was the cause of profound resentment and anger amongst many working men and women. Whenever word leaked out that an Assistant Commissioner was to hold a private meeting with some of the local worthies, the popular opponents of the New Poor Law made sure it was interrupted by a noisy demonstration.

One of the most notorious of these demonstrations took place at Keighley in March 1837. News of Assistant Commissioner Power's coming had leaked out in advance and the local opponents of the New Poor Law quickly printed and posted handbills throughout the town, warning the townspeople to make ready for his visit. Whether Power got wind of the preparations is not known, but much to the chagrin of the huge crowd the day passed off without his making an appearance. One of the local officials, himself an opponent of the New Poor Law, sent word to the protesters that Power had delayed his arrival until Wednesday, 22 March 1837. Once again preparations were made. At the last moment on Wednesday morning the authorities decided to switch venues and hold their meeting in the Mechanics' Institute instead of the Courthouse. If the move was intended to forestall any interference from demonstrators, it badly misfired. As soon as the protesters discovered what was happening they descended on the Mechanics' Institute in force. Despite the doors having been locked, the noise and pressure from outside was so great that the officials decided it would be expedient to let the public in. During the course of what was to prove a very rowdy meeting Power was told 'that the people ... will never submit to be bastiled'; that the New Poor Law was 'at direct variance with the comfort and happiness of [the working men's] homes'; and that it would reduce wages – 'which are already low enough'. The crowd shouted their disgust for Power and the New Poor Law, with groans and cries of 'turn him out' and 'we will not have it'. When the demonstrators attempted to take over the meeting completely Power started to leave. No sooner had he risen from his chair, when a cry went up of 'stop him, stop him' and 'no shuffling'. In the ensuing struggle Power had his coat torn off his back as he fought to get out of the hall. Once outside his difficulties continued: he was booed, jeered, hissed and jostled by the boisterous crowd. It was only with great difficulty that he managed to make his way to his hotel. Meanwhile, in the Institute hall, his coat was proudly displayed to the audience – one of the spoils of victory. Power left town shortly afterwards.[31]

A consequence of the Keighley demonstration was that one of the participants, a weaver, was sacked by his employer 'for daring to open his lips to Mr Power'. The radical *Leeds Times* thought the action 'peculiarly mean and arbitrary'. At subsequent meetings organised by the Keighley Radical Association the employer's actions were condemned and money collected for the sacked man. He eventually obtained other employment, but not before his sacking had 'produced a strong feeling of disapprobation amongst the labouring class ... who considered this act of local tyranny as a low attempt to domineer the liberty of speech and thought'.[32]

IV

The traditions of popular radicalism not only helped determine the character and tone of the northern campaign of popular opposition to the 1834 Poor Law, but also provided the organisational base. The Macclesfield, Hurdsfield and Sutton Burial Society co-ordinated the campaign of popular opposition in the Macclesfield Union. At Barnsley the militant Linen Weavers' Union not only provided the organisation but most of the local leaders in the campaign. And at Oldham the local Radical Association provided the infrastructure for a co-ordinated campaign which kept the Oldham Union free from the New Poor Law for over a decade. But foremost amongst all the autonomous working-class institutions which helped organise and lead the campaign of popular opposition to the New Poor Law were the Short Time Committees.

During the Ten-Hours campaign for factory reform in the early 1830s a loose federation of Short Time Committees had been established in the northern textile towns. These local Committees co-ordinated the protests and enabled the movement to press more effectively its demands for shorter working hours for factory children and, by implication, the adult factory workers as well. Although the initiative for the formation of the Short Time Committees had come from working men and women, they were not exclusively working-class organisations. Any sympathiser was welcome to join the Committee provided he or she was willing to support its demands. Nevertheless the vast majority of members were working men, most of whom already knew each other from their involvement in political or trade union activity. The Short Time Committees, like most contemporary working-class organisations, met in local public houses. The meetings were pretty informal affairs and generally consisted of an *ad hoc* gathering of the most active members. Although community-based and informal in structure, the organisation did manage to spawn a Central Committee, based in Bradford, to co-ordinate activities in the West Riding of Yorkshire.[33]

The 1833 Factory Act left the Factory Reform Movement bewildered and confused. The Act, which banned the employment of children in the textile industry until they were 9 years old, and limited the employment of children under 13 to forty-eight hours a week and those under 18 to sixty-nine hours a week, only partially met the Factory Reformers' demands. The Short Time Committees feared that because the 1833 Act placed no restriction on night work for children, the factory owners would operate a double-shift system for the children and work the adult operatives for sixteen hours a day. An attempt was made to transform the Ten-Hours movement into an Eight-Hours campaign for all workers in industry, but a series of disastrous strikes and lockouts destroyed the campaign. A few local Short Time Committees survived, especially in the West Riding of Yorkshire where the Eight-Hours movement had not been as vigourously pursued as it had been in Lancashire. But they were little more than watchdogs. Paradoxically, their main role lay in defending the 1833 Act from the attempts of the factory owners to dismantle it.[34] Early in 1837, faced with the prospect of the rapid introduction of the New Poor Law, the remaining stalwarts of the Factory Reform

Movement and the local Short Time Committees turned against the new threat.

The transformation of the Short Time Committees from factory agitation to anti-poor law agitation was simplest and most complete in the West Riding of Yorkshire. On the evening of Wednesday, 18 January 1837 a meeting was held in the rooms of the Bradford Short Time Committee, to consider what steps should be taken to prevent the establishment of the New Poor Law. According to the whiggish *Bradford Observer*, it was a 'crowded and spirited meeting chiefly of the working classes'. The meeting came to the conclusion that a committee should be formed to spread 'information' about the New Poor Law, and that a 'borough meeting' should be held 'to give expression to public feeling on the subject'. The formation of an anti-poor law committee involved litte more than a name change: the Bradford Short Time Committee suddenly became the Bradford Anti-Poor Law Committee.[35]

Within a week the Bradford Committee had published a pamphlet outlining their opposition to the New Poor Law. A pithy and well-argued critique, the pamphlet begins by expressing concern over the 'most extraordinary powers' entrusted to the Poor Law Commission. The Commission had the power to appoint and dismiss Assistant Commissioners, workhouse masters, assistant overseers and any other paid officer. The Bradford Committee wondered what 'door is here opened for the tyranny over the Parish Officers – and for the *tittle tattle* of certain sneaking fellows, who may creep in as "Guardians", and who may choose to send their tales to the Great Trio in London'? Next, the Poor Law Commission could, with the consent of the majority of Guardians or ratepayers, order the building of workhouses; or, '*without anyone's consent*', order the alteration and enlargement of an existing workhouse. To those who 'fancy that they will "*save* something" ' by this, the Bradford Committee warned: 'let it only be tried in these populous parts, and we shall see what is "saved" '. Furthermore, because the Poor Law Commission had the power to 'regulate all the affairs of workhouses' they could '*separate the sexes ... the man from his wife* – the parent from his child'. The Bradford Committee was also worried by the Commission's power to fix the number and property qualifications of Guardians. By such means the small ratepayers, 'who are the majority', could be excluded from representation on the Board of Guardians. Furthermore, whatever the Guardians might decide in the interests of the ratepayers the Commissioners in London could overrule. The Commissioners could insist, for instance, on all relief being restricted to the workhouse. The Bradford Committee concluded that 'the whole working of the Act is calculated to drive an honest man either to despair or to a workhouse – or to both – in time of pressing need'. The final insult was the clause allowing all poor relief to be 'considered as given, *by way of loan*'. The Poor Law Commission was thereby able to order that the wages of any man who had received relief could be stopped by his master to repay the loan. Relief given to children under 16 years was to be added to the father's account 'as a loan too'. And a widow with relief given to any of her children under 16 years was to suffer the same fate. 'Thus', commented the Bradford Committee, 'is the working man "once down, always down" '. The pamphlet ended with a rousing call to 'all men and all women of any conscience or feeling ... to protest against such a Yoke as this'[36]

Opponents of the New Poor Law in other West Riding Unions were also quick to establish their own anti-Poor Law Committees. Many, like the Bradford Committee, were simply the old Short Time Committees under a new name. William Hill, the Swedenborgian minister and future editor of the *Northern Star*, appears to have played an influential role in the establishment of this informal network of local Anti-Poor Law Committees. The son of a Barnsley handloom weaver, Hill had worked at the loom during his youth. After acquiring some education he had become a schoolteacher and for a time ran his own school near Huddersfield. In the mid-1830s, Hill had become a minister in the New Jerusalem (Swedenborgian) Church. He combined radical political activity with his pastoral duties. It is unclear whether Hill, who at that time was resident in Bradford, was acting in any official capacity for the Bradford Anti-Poor Law Committee, but in February 1837 he visited a number of towns in the West Riding, advocating the formation of local Anti-Poor Law Committees.[37] At a meeting in Huddersfield on Thursday 2 February 1837, Hill told the larger audience that the New Poor Law was 'unconstitutional, and denied the right of the poor to live'. He said that 'people were not bound to obey such a law'. In order effectively to oppose its introduction he recommended the 'formation of associations in every township throughout the Union'. Apparently the popular radicals in Huddersfield accepted his advice because within a fortnight a meeting of delegates had been held to establish a network of Anti-Poor Law Committees in each of the townships in the proposed Huddersfield Union. The meeting passed a series of eleven resolutions condemning the New Poor Law and establishing the local structure. Apart from committees in each township, there was to be a General Committee in Huddersfield 'to watch over the affairs of the whole district'.[38]

Because the Short Time Committees in South Lancashire had been destroyed by the abortive Eight-Hours Movement and the collapse of the National Regeneration Society, South Lancashire was slower to develop a regional organisation to fight the New Poor Law. Nevertheless there was some impressive local activity. In March 1837 there was a meeting of twenty delegates from the eight townships in the proposed Oldham Union. Held under the auspices of the Oldham Radical Association, they met to decide on the 'steps necessary to prevent' the introduction of the New Poor Law. The delegates decided on a total boycott: they would stop anyone from accepting nomination for the office of Guardian. Their organisation held firm and not one Guardian was appointed for any of the eight townships in the Oldham Union.[39] Although attempts were made as early as April 1837 to form a regional organisation in South Lancashire, it was not until November that a South Lancashire Anti-Poor Law Association was actually formed.[40] In the meantime it was the West Riding Committees which provided the leadership for the national campaign of popular opposition to the New Poor Law.

On Wednesday, 8 March 1837 there was a meeting in Bradford of delegates from the Anti-Poor Law Committees of the principal towns of the West Riding. The delegates decided to formalise their organisation with the establishment of a Central Anti-Poor Law Committee based in Bradford. William Stocks, a Huddersfield woollen manufacturer, was to be treasurer, and Samuel Bower, one of the stalwarts of the Bradford factory reform movement, was named secretary. The Central Committee was to promote the formation of 'anti-slavery unions' in every New Poor Law Union. And these local organisations were in turn to extend their influence to every township and village in the Union. The delegates declared that they intended not only to free the 'manufacturing districts' from the operation of the New Poor Law, but also to free the 'agriculturalists' from 'this most unchristian imposition'. The delegates' concern was not merely the result of feelings of Christian brotherhood; they were worried

that the exemption of the manufacturing districts from the operation of the new poor law whilst it was established in the agricultural counties, would ... produce a vast influx of agricultural families ... and ... this would inevitably lead to a general reduction of wages.

The aim of the organisation was thus to be the total repeal of the New Poor Law.[41]

Notes

1. Lupton to PLC, 1 January 1835, PRO, MH 12/14720; G.S. Bull, *The Substance of a Lecture upon the New Poor Law Act* (n.p., Bradford [1835]), p.2.
2. Ainsworth to PLC, 31 January 1835, PRO, MH 12/5529.
3. *Leeds Times*, 5 March 1836.
4. Neave to PLC, 28 September 1836, PRO, MH 12/968 and *North Cheshire Reformer*, 2 December 1836.
5. Davenport to PLC, 31 May 1837, PRO, MH 12/968; *The Times*, 28 September 1837; *Manchester and Salford Advertiser*, 6 January 1837.
6. *Leeds Times,* 17, December 1836; S. Chadwick, *The Factory King* (n.p., Kirkburton, 1944), p.9.
7. F. Boase, *Modern English Biography,* vol.II (Frank Cass, London, 1965), p.1611; C. Driver, *Tory Radical* (Oxford University Press, New York, 1946), pp.228-36; A. Brundage, *Making of the New Poor Law* (Hutchinson, London, 1978), pp.29-33, 83.
8. *Bolton Chronicle,* 14 January 1837; *Manchester and Salford Advertiser,* 14 January 1837; and Power to PLC, 8 January 1837, PRO, MH 32/63.
9. *Halifax Express,* 18 January 1837, and *Halifax Guardian,* 14 January 1837.
10. Power to PLC, 15 January 1837, PRO, MH 32/63.
11. Power to PLC, 22 October 1837, PRO, HO 73/53; Power to PLC, 2 December 1837, PRO, MH 12/14720.
12. *Halifax Express,* 11 January 1837.
13. M. Rose, 'Administration of Poor Relief in the West Riding of Yorkshire c.1820-1855, unpublished D.Phil thesis, Oxford, 1965, p.115.
14. Voules to Lefevre, 21 January 1837, PRO, MH 32/73; Power to PLC, 25 November 1836, PRO, MH 32/63.
15. *Manchester Chronicle,* 31 May 1834.
16. *Bolton Chronicle,* 17 & 24 May 1834; Darbishire to Heywood, 27 May 1834, Heywood Papers, BMBA, 2HE/30/6.
17. *Leeds Times,* 26 April and 5 July 1834; *Bolton Chronicle,* 26 April 1834; *Manchester and Salford Advertiser,* 14 June 1834.
18. *Leeds Mercury,* 26 April 1834; *Manchester Guardian,* 17 May 1834; *Sheffield Independent,* 10 May 1834.
19. *Leeds Mercury,* 17 and 31 May 1834; M. Rose, 'The Anti-Poor Law Movement in the north of England', *Northern History*, vol.1, 1966, p.72.
20. Sutcliffe to PLC, 28 Janaury 1837, PRO, MH 12/6272.
21. *Blackburn Gazette,* 22 February 1837.
22. *The Times,* 27 February 1837.
23. *The Times,* 14 March 1837; *Bradford Observer,* 2 November 1837.
24. W.H.G. Armytage, *Heavens Below* (Routledge & Kegan Paul, London, 1961), pp.56-7; Driver, *Tory Radical,* pp.36-42; T.A. Trollope, *What I Remember,* vol.II (Bentley, London, 1887-9), pp.11-12.
25. M.S. Edwards, *Joseph Rayner Stephens, 1805-1879* (Wesley Historical Society, Manchester, 1968), pp.1-7; F.H.A. Micklewright, 'Joseph Rayner Stephens', *London Quarterly and Holborn Review,* January 1943, p.52; an oil painting of Stephens (unknown artist, *c.*1840) survives in the Astley Cheetham Art Gallery, Stalybridge. [R. Lowery], 'Passages in the Life of a Temperance Lecturer' in B. Harrison and P. Hollis (eds.), *Robert Lowery* (Europa, London, 1979), pp.110-2,

describes how Stephens was able to hold an audience spellbound.

26. G.D.H. Cole, *Chartist Portraits* (Macmillan, London, 1965), pp.218-38; A reproduction of a contemporary painting of Fielden is to be found in H. McLachlan, *The Methodist Utilitarian Movement* (Manchester University Press, Manchester, 1919), p.122.

27. 'Report from the Select Committee on the Poor Law Amendment Act', *PP*, 1837-8, vol.XVIII, Q.6258; *Sheffield Iris*, 25 July 1837. Little is known of the Manchester manufacturers who opposed the New Poor Law: William Clegg was a business associate of the Fieldens; Joseph W. Hodgetts was a manufacturing chemist and a former Salford Vestryman; and G.W. Seed was a small cotton manufacturer. Only the radical pill-box maker, Elijah Dixon, has left any record; see W.E.A. Axon (ed.), *Annals of Manchester* (A. Heywood, Manchester, 1886), p.358, and J. Johnson, *People I have met* (n.p., Manchester, n.d.), pp.135-40.

28. *Blackburn Standard*, 25 January 1837; 'To the Rate-Payers of the Todmorden Union', 16 March 1839, (Broadside), PRO, HO 40/37.

29. Sutcliffe to PLC, 21 February 1837, and Power to PLC, 16 March 1837, PRO, MH 12/6272.

30. T.R. Tholfsen, *Working Class Radicalism in Mid-Victorian England* (Croom Helm, London, 1976), pp.50-2.

31. *The Times*, 28 March 1837; *Leeds Intelligencer*, 25 March 1837.

32. *Leeds Times*, 8 April 1837.

33. Driver, *Tory Radical*, p.82; J.T. Ward, *The Factory Movement 1830-1855* (Macmillan, London, 1962), p.167.

34. 3 & 4 Will.IV, c.103; Driver, *Tory Radical*, pp.167, 238, 261-7.

35. *Bradford Observer*, 26 January 1837.

36. [Anon.], *The Poor Law Act. To the People of the 30 Townships, which the Poor Law Commissioners propose to form into the Bradford Union* (n.p., Bradford, [1837]).

37. E. Hoyle, 'History of Barnsley and the Surrounding District', vol.II, article 151, bound newspaper cuttings, BML. Hill appears to have been responsible for the establishment of Anti-Poor Law Committees in Huddersfield, Dewsbury, Keighley, Halifax and Barnsley – all centres of proposed Poor Law Unions.

38. *Halifax Express*, 8 February 1837; 'New Poor Law Act', 15 February 1837 (handbill), Brougham Papers, UCL 17802.

39. *Manchester Chronicle*, 11 March 1837; *Blackburn Gazette*, 29 March 1837; *The Times*, 3 April 1837.

40. *Manchester and Salford Advertiser*, 11, 25 November, and 2 December 1837.

41. *Leeds Intelligencer*, 11 March 1837.

5 DEMONSTRATIONS AND PETITIONS

The campaign of popular opposition to the 1834 Poor Law began with the object of securing a total repeal of the legislation. The means to be used were the traditional ones of popular agitation – meetings, demonstrations and petitions. Such methods were of course legal, but perhaps more importantly they were also well known to the northern opponents of the New Poor Law. Northern working men and women were heirs to the traditions of popular radicalism, and they were already familiar with the techniques of demonstrating and petitioning. This new campaign of popular agitation would help arouse and sustain the opposition movement and force Parliament into repealing the New Poor Law.

I

Petitioning was the customary means by which aggrieved citizens protested injustice and the repentant sought mercy for their misdeeds. At some stage this highly legal and perfectly respectable form of complaint was converted for use as a means of political protest. In the seventeenth century a variety of political groups resorted to petitioning to promote their aims. The Levellers, in particular, were assiduous petitioners: they considered the mass petition central to their strategy of informing public opinion and arousing popular support.[1] Following the 'Glorious Revolution' of 1688 the use of petitions as weapons of political protest appears to have temporarily declined. It is not until the appearance of the County Association Movement during the American War of Independence that petitioning was once again used to support the cause of political reform.[2] Whether the popular radicals in early nineteenth-century Britain were taught the use of petitioning by respectable reform groups like Wyvill's Yorkshire Association, or borrowed the tactic from seventeenth-century radical movements, is not known. What we do know is that during the years of bitter struggle which followed the Napoleonic Wars, the petition was firmly established as a weapon in the arsenal of popular radicalism.

Petitions were both the plea of the powerless and proof of their powerlessness. Occasionally the petitioners had their powerlessness brought home to them. When the working men and women of South Lancashire gathered at St Peter's Field, Manchester, on 16 August 1819, to 'petition' for reform, they were cut down by the sabres of an enraged Yeomanry.[3] Eleven protesters were killed and over four hundred wounded at 'Peterloo'. In the light of such experiences it is not surprising that the petition became one of the 'sacred' weapons of popular radicalism.

Throughout 1834 and 1835 a flood of petitions protesting against the New Poor Law descended upon Parliament. Most of these petitions came from meetings of concerned overseers and ratepayers. For the most part the government remained unmoved. Of all these early petitions, only one appears to have caused them any concern. This petition, asking that the parish of Stoke Poges not be included in a New Poor Law Union and protesting against the splitting up of married couples in workhouses, was presented to the House of Lords by the Duke of Buckingham. The Home Secretary, Lord John Russell, wrote to the Poor Law Commission emphasising the 'great importance' of this petition. The Duke of Buckingham and his heir, the Marquis of Chandos, were very influential in their county and the government was concerned to see that they did not become enemies of the New Poor Law. The Commission advised the government that the parish of Stoke Poges must remain in its Union, but that the aged and infirm 'should be treated with care and tenderness and not necessarily be forced into the Workhouse'.[4]

The Commission's low-key advice led Lord Brougham to claim in his speech in reply to the petition that it was not the intention of the Poor Law Commissioners to separate husband and wife in the workhouse. Brougham's astonishing claim might have helped mollify the Duke of Buckingham, but it upset most of the Assistant Commissioners. Colonel Charles a'Court wrote to the Poor Law Commission wanting to know how Brougham could say that separation of the sexes was not intended when his instructions explicitly stated 'that such separation must be *entire* and *absolute*'. The Commission feebly replied that although separation of the sexes was still official policy, 'the pressure of public opinion or the will of parliament may oblige us to modify our plans in this respect'. They therefore suggested to a'Court that the subject be as 'little agitated as possible at present'. Alfred Power summed up the views of most poor law officials, when he told Chadwick that 'Ld. Brougham's defences [of the New Poor Law] will be the death of us'.[5]

Although the flood of petitions did not change government policy, we should be wary of viewing them as failures. Petitions function at two levels. First, and most obviously, a petition is an attempt to obtain a particular demand, or set of demands. But because petitions are totally dependent upon the authorities' willingness to accede to their prayers, they are rarely successful at this level. (Although it has to be noted that two contemporaneous petitioning campaigns on behalf of the Tolpuddle Martyrs and Glasgow Cotton-Spinners did achieve their aims.) What is more important is the role of petitions in rousing and sustaining popular agitation. The anti-poor law petitions gave a focus for the activities of local protest organisations and were an effective way of publicising their demands.

With the arrival of the Assistant Commissioners in the north of England in late 1836, the petitioning campaign took on a new lease of life. Initially most of the petitions again came from meetings of concerned ratepayers, overseers and the like. Once again they had little effect on government policy. The fate of the petition from the ratepayers of the township of West Derby, near Liverpool, was typical of most. At a meeting of the West Derby ratepayers, held at the local workhouse on Wednesday, 11 January 1837, it was decided to memorialise the Poor Law Commission against the inclusion of the township in a New Poor Law Union. The ratepayers passed resolutions defending the way the Old Poor Law had been administered and expressing regret at the proposed formation of a Poor Law Union. The memorial was duly drawn up and a subcommittee appointed to present it to the Assistant Commissioner and to arrange for copies to be sent to the Home Secretary and the local Member of Parliament. The Poor Law Commission's reply to the memorial was brief and to the point. The Commission said that an order 'declaring the West Derby Union' had already been issued when the memorial was received, and that as the memorial did not contain any new grounds which would have affected their decision, the order would stay in force. The letter ended with the curt comment that the Poor Law Commissioners did not doubt that the New Poor Law would 'be found practically beneficial in the district ... as it had been elsewhere'. The West Derby ratepayers were far from satisfied with the reply. At a subsequent meeting they decided to petition the Home Secretary and if that failed to petition both Houses of Parliament. In the meantime they would publicise their complaint by having the original memorial and correspondence printed in the press.[6]

II

A co-ordinated campaign of petitioning and demonstrating against the New Poor Law began with the formation of Anti-Poor Law Committees in the West Riding of Yorkshire. At its inaugural meeting on Wednesday, 18 January 1837, the Bradford Anti-Poor Law Committee resolved to hold protest meetings in every township in the proposed Union, and to get up 'a Petition to Parliament for ... [the New Poor Law's] "Amendment" '. The Huddersfield Anti-Poor Law Committee adopted a similar proposal, recommending that 'remonstrances or petitions ... be sent to Parliament from every township, hamlet, or division in the district as early as possible'.[7] As the campaign gained momentum, meetings and demonstrations were held and petitions began to flood into Parliament from the north of England.

Details of how this campaign was organised are somewhat murky. Lacking (at this stage) a Central Committee to oversee the campaign, it fell to local Anti-Poor Law Committees to hold their own demonstrations and organise their own petitions. While some Committees attempted to obtain signatures from all the inhabitants in their area, others only obtained signatures from those who attended their meetings; still others thought it sufficient if the chairman of a meeting signed the petition on behalf of those present.

The meeting held at Almondbury, a weaving village near Huddersfield, in late February 1837, was perhaps typical. Held on the Poorhouse Green, the meeting was ostensibly called to 'take into consideration the merits of the Poor Law Amendment Bill'. In fact, it was called by local popular radicals to promote the campaign of popular opposition to the 1834 Poor Law in the Huddersfield Union. The meeting began by appointing a chairman, Hiram Harling, and then presented a series of resolutions to the crowd of some 1,500 for their support. The first resolution reiterated popular criticisms of the New Poor Law: it denied 'the right of the poor to live in the land of their birth', 'an inalienable right'; it denied 'the rate-payers the right to dispose of their own property', and it was 'calculated to wring out of the very vitals of the homeless, helpless poor, means sufficient to keep a set of hirelings in luxury and affluence'. The second resolution was a vote of confidence in the administration of the Old Poor Law and a call to stop paying any rates that would be distributed 'by order of the Commissioners'. The third resolution called on the meeting to 'petition the House of Lords for its total repeal' and called on 'every man who has any regard either for himself, his family, or his species, to join in the same'. The fourth and final resolution approved of all the motions passed at the recent meeting of delegates from the townships in the Huddersfield Union. All the resolutions were passed unanimously.[8]

The sheer volume of petitions from the north of England slowly began to have some effect in Parliament. In February 1837, John Walter, proprietor of *The Times* and Tory MP for Berkshire, moved the appointment of a Select Committee to investigate the operation of the New Poor Law. Many backbenchers, uneasy at the constant stream of petitions, were predisposed to favour an inquiry. The government therefore reluctantly agreed to set up a Select Committee. Walter's original motion was amended, however, so that only the orders and regulations issued by the Poor Law Commission were to be subject to investigation. If the opponents of the New Poor Law had been expecting an impartial inquiry they were to be sadly disappointed. When the membership of the Select Committee was announced, 17 of the 21 members were known supporters of the New Poor Law. Perhaps even more to the point, Walter complained that 'there was not a single member who was personally connected with the manufacturers of the country' and not one representative from the north of England, the region whose vociferous opposition had led to the creation of the Select Committee.[9]

The West Riding Central Committee quickly came to the conclusion that their cause would not be assisted by participating in such a one-sided investigation. They therefore decided to ignore the activities of the Select Committee entirely. In a handbill outlining the reasons for their decision the West Riding Central Committee sarcastically commented that it would be a pity 'to spoil the mess by mixing truth and honesty with what alone can be expected from men whose business it is to punish poverty as a criminal offence'.[10] Not surprisingly the Select Committee Report when it finally appeared praised the operation of the New Poor Law. There was some mention of cases of hardship and the need for greater vigilance if cruelties were to be prevented, but neither the Boards of Guardians nor the Poor Law Commission were criticised.[11]

III

The West Riding campaign reached its climax with the massive demonstration on Peep Green on Whit Tuesday, 16 May 1837. The decision to hold the demonstration had been taken at the inaugural meeting of delegates to the West Riding Anti-Poor Law Central Committee in Bradford on Wednesday, 8 March 1837. The delegates had drawn up a requisition to the Earl of Harewood, the Lord Lieutenant of the West Riding, asking him to call a 'county meeting' to discuss the New Poor Law. Although 4,000 signatures were collected in support of the requisition, Harewood refused to call the meeting. He said the subject had already been 'much agitated'. Undaunted, the Central Committee decided to hold the meeting on their own authority.[12]

The task of organising the demonstration was shared between the Central and local Committees. The Central Committee was responsible for co-ordinating matters. It chose the meeting site and date, provided the platform for the speakers, drew up the resolutions which would be presented to the meeting for its support, and invited the speakers. In keeping with the original intention of holding a 'county meeting', called on the authority of the Lord Lieutenant, invitations were issued to representatives of all the political parties. Most of the parliamentarians who were invited – the Home Secretary, Lord John Russell, the Tory leader, Sir Robert Peel, the radical Joseph Hume, and the hated Whig member for the county, Lord Morpeth – chose to decline. These invitations were undoubtedly extended in good faith and were not intended merely to embarrass the recipients. The organisers took great pains to invite speakers representing the full range of social and political opinion: there were working men, radical agitators, newspaper owners, paternalist factory owners, Ultra-Tories, an erstwhile Methodist preacher, Utopian Socialists and a farmer. Such a range of speakers could only emphasise that the New Poor Law question was above party or sectional interest: it concerned the country squire and factory owner as much as the handloom weaver and farm labourer.

The local Committees and informal village groups were responsible for drumming up support and ensuring that as many people as possible attended the demonstration. The processions, which were such an important part of the day's events, were organised with meticulous care. Flags and banners were prepared, suitable slogans and mottos chosen, arrangements made for bands to accompany the processions, music selected, the order of march decided upon and arrangements made for the provision of refreshment for the thirsty marchers. Each person was to march behind their respective Trade Union, Friendly Society or Radical Association banner. These groups would form up into local processions which would march into a central town where they would, in turn, become part of a larger divisional procession. The divisional processions, led 'by the officers and members of the local Committees', would then march to the meeting site at Peep Green. It was a system of organisation which had been used to great effect by the West Riding Short Time Committees in the early 1830s.[14] The long columns of disciplined marching men, each behind his respective Trade Union, Friendly Society or Radical Association banner, not only celebrated 'mutuality', but also served to remind their opponents of the size and strength of the opposition movement.

From early morning the towns and villages of the West Riding of Yorkshire echoed to the sounds of bands parading the streets, calling together the marchers. By first light the processions from the outlying townships were already on the road. With flags and banners flying, and music playing, they presented an impressive sight, attracting considerable attention as they passed through the rural villages. The reporter from *The Times*, observing the progress of the processions, thought their appearance 'striking'. 'The people', he wrote, 'were of the most respectable class of operatives; their demeanour sober, decent and determined.' This quiet determination was echoed in the mottos and slogans emblazoned on the marchers' flags and banners. Some were in doggerel:

Remember Heaven has an avenging rod.
To smite the poor is treason against God.

A banner carried by a group of marchers from Kirkburton was emblazoned with the Biblical quotation:

What mean ye that ye beat my people to pieces, and grind the faces of the poor, saith the Lord God of Hosts. Ye are cursed with a curse, for ye have robbed me, even this whole nation.[15]

One quotation was especially popular: 'The poor have a claim of the soil, and verily they shall be fed'. Others were more threatening:

We will not be commissioned by three infernal lickspittles. The poor have a right to a subsistence from the land. Woe unto him that grindeth the faces of the poor.

On a flag carried by the men from Lepton, three figures were shown hanging from a gibbet. Below was the inscription: 'The three Poor Law Commissioners drawing their wages'. The banner leading the

Huddersfield procession was equally forthright: 'The Huddersfield division swears destruction to all Malthusian bastiles'. Another banner boldly declared:

> The working men of Lockwood will not be separated in a bastile, nor will our children be made emigrant slaves. Before that we will die on the field.[16]

By early morning the processions from Huddersfield, Dewsbury, Halifax, Bradford, Meltham and Cleckheaton had arrived on the ground. They were followed by crowds of onlookers, many of whom had been attracted by the music and brilliant flags and banners. Throughout the morning a steady stream of processions and groups of people kept arriving at the ground. Not all arrived on foot. Those who could afford it hired carriages for the day. A compositor from Halifax arrived in 'most gallant style', driving a 'profusely decorated' phaeton and accompanied by a number of 'fair companions'.[17] By the time the meeting was due to start, the crowd was estimated at between 200,000 and 260,000; far in excess of the organisers' expectations.[18]

The demonstration at Peep Green was not simply a 'protest' meeting – albeit one heavy in ritual. There was also humour, entertainment and festivity. The processions, with their bands playing and their brilliant flags and banners, attracted large crowds of excited onlookers. And while the organisation of the march echoed the methods used by Short Time Committees, they were also suggestive of the traditional Whitsuntide 'club walk' or Friendly Society outing. The festive atmosphere was further accentuated by the sight of Peep Green itself: 'beer barrels and nut stalls ... were scattered over the ground'.[19]

Drink and other such entertainments were the very essence of popular recreation in early-Victorian Britain. The story of how these popular leisure pursuits were attacked by moral reformers and slowly eroded by urbanisation and the imposition of industrial work discipline, is well known. What is not so often recognised is the tenacity with which many working people clung to their traditional leisure pursuits, integrating them into other, more recent, working-class activities. Thus, under the cloak of the 'club walk', the Friendly Society outing, the Trade Union dinner, or even a 'political' demonstration, many traditional amusements survived until late in the nineteenth century. Certainly any public gathering of a plebeian nature could, in the 1830s and 40s, still be relied upon to attract its share of publicans, who would set up their beer tents on the outskirts of the assembly and do a roaring trade. It is not surprising therefore to learn that the anti-poor law demonstration at Peep Green had its share of beer tents and stalls.[20]

Furthermore, this particular demonstration was held during Whitsuntide, a traditional holiday period and a time when Peep Green might well have served as the venue for a local fair. There was no contradiction in the organisers choosing such a site or time to hold their demonstration. Such amusements were certainly consistent with their supporters' values. In fact the conjunction of festivity and protest might well have won new working-class converts to the anti-poor law cause. Unfortunately, it also earned the scorn of the 'respectable' Whig Press. The *Leeds Mercury* commented:

> it was quite evident to any impartial observer that the motives which had influenced a vast proportion of the people to come to the meeting were either those of curiosity or to seek occasion for enjoyment.

Such imputations aside, the presence of beer tents and other amusements at the meeting had important practical functions. It not only helped quench the thirst of the marchers, it also assisted in entertaining those who could not hear the speakers. Estimates of the attendance at Peep Green ranged from 60,000 to 200,000. And yet although the hustings were specially constructed at the lowest point on the green, so as to form a natural amphitheatre, it is unlikely that more than a small proportion of those in attendance (perhaps 15,000) could have heard the speeches. The *Leeds Mercury* thought that perhaps 12,000 to 14,000 'were paying any attention to the proceedings'. For those who could not hear the speeches, amusement was therefore to be the order of the day: some people enjoyed themselves at the beer tents, others were to be seen engaged in sporting activities; 'and those who had a relish for less active pursuits engaged in a tete-a-tete with the fair sex'. Still others were to be seen 'parading the spacious moor with the several bands of music', which spent the day playing popular tunes and airs.[21]

And what of the meeting proper, the speakers and the audience of 12,000 to 14,000 who could actually hear what was being said? Obviously with so many people unable to hear the speeches there was a tendency at large demonstrations for the focus of the meeting to move away from the speakers' platform. Certainly there is no doubt that for the majority of people at Peep Green the speeches were somewhat secondary to the day's other events (at least until the following week when they were able to read them in great detail in the local press). Nevertheless, in both form and content the speeches provide a valuable insight into some of the tensions present in the campaign of popular opposition to the New Poor Law. Once again it is clear that the structure of the meeting followed the highly legalistic form of 'respectable' political demonstrations as well as the traditions of popular radicalism. There was the formal nominating and electing of a chairman by the meeting. There was the reading of the requisition which had been presented to the Lord Lieutenant of the Riding, asking him to call the meeting. (Although the fact that the Lord Lieutenant had refused to call the meeting does not appear to have been mentioned.) The emphasis is constantly placed on the meeting's 'constitutional' character. The secretary read the letters from those parliamentarians who declined their invitation to attend. And the chairman in his opening remarks alluded to a mass meeting held at Wakefield in 1776, the last time the House of Commons had proposed to amend the poor laws on similar principles. In 1776, he said, the people had 'boldly declared they would not have such a law'.[22] A precedent established and their right to hold the meeting asserted, the speeches could get under way.

The presentation of the speakers was no haphazard affair. There were a number of set resolutions which the speakers had to present to the meeting for their approval. Each speaker was either to move, second, or simply speak in support of a particular resolution. All in all it was an extremely complicated business for the organisers; with twenty-five different speakers, presenting six resolutions, every speaker had to be allotted his place with great care. It was important to start off with a good speaker, someone who could rouse the audience and help bond it together. The most popular speakers, on the other hand, had to be saved until near the end of the programme. This was important because if they spoke too early those people who had only come to hear them might leave, or the speeches of those who came afterwards could prove an anticlimax.

Members of the audience were not passive spectators to these events: they were an integral part of the process, responding to and interacting with the speakers. As Brian Harrison and Patricia Hollis have pointed out with reference to Robert Lowery, the character of the speeches given, whether violent or moderate, was to a large extent determined by the type and mood of the audience being addressed.[23] Robert Lowery himself admitted that the speeches made at anti-poor law meetings

> consisted of that kind which is ever the most eloquent and impressive to the feelings of the multitude, where speaker and audience are one in feelings and desire. The speaker only gives vent to the hearers' emotions. His words at once find a response in their wishes. The speech may not be elegant in phraseology nor select in its words, nor composed of nicely-balanced sentences, but the souls of all being in accord, the ideas and words flow in one earnest, rapid torrent from the heart of the speaker to the hearts of all.[24]

We can see something of this interaction between the speaker and the audience in the first speech of the day, that of the Barnsley linen weaver, Joseph Crabtree. He began by establishing his credentials; he said that it might appear strange 'that an humble individual like himself' should have moved the first resolution at so important a meeting, but, as Crabtree explained, he was 'one of those Yorkshiremen who had laboured, ever since God gave him power, to maintain that class of people who had passed a law to prevent him and his family having a subsistence when labour was denied him'. The working class he regarded as 'the most important of all others', and he thought they 'ought to be consulted in all matters by the ... Government'. Warming to his subject, Crabtree said he had recently told the same things to 'noble personages' in London. When asked by Lord John Russell 'how do the people of Yorkshire . . . like the New Poor Law Bill?, Crabtree had replied, 'Not at all'. This produced loud cheers from the crowd. Crabtree then began to draw in the crowd by criticising them. He said that working people wrong to have waited until the pressure of the New Poor Law came upon them before they protested and that it was 'much better to prevent a disease than to cure it'. The crowd responded with cries of 'we won't have it'. Crabtree said he was proud to hear them say that, 'but what would they do'? 'We will fight against it', cried the audience. Aware that the crowd's responses were leading him into dangerous water, Crabtree chose his words carefully. 'Yes they must fight', he said , but 'fight morally'; they had to prove to their governors that they possessed the wisdom and experience to govern themselves.[25]

If Crabtree avoided being provoked into advocating violence, or at least threatening violence, other speakers were not so reticent. The radical journalist and popular agitator, Bronterre O'Brien, told the crowd that if he petitioned Parliament for a repeal of the New Poor Law, he would want to do it like the petitioner spoken of in *Gil Blas*, who had one hand 'upon the trigger of a blunderbuss'. The audience broke into loud laughter and cheers at this remark. O'Brien continued: of course he was not advocating that the audience arm themselves with blunderbusses – 'they were dangerous weapons' (more laughter), but when they petitioned, they ought to do so with all the force and determination that 'the law and constitution of the country would allow them'.[26] O'Brien's threat was hyperbole. The audience and the speakers at the anti-poor law demonstrations were heirs to the traditions of popular radicalism and the Romantic Era. As Kitson Clark has indicated, many early-Victorian public speakers commonly assumed the posture of romantic figures and played out predetermined roles in front of their audience.[27] O'Brien had adopted the role of a firebrand revolutionary; it does not necessarily follow that either he or his audience believed he actually was one.

The influence of the romantic tradition, exaggerated imagery, grotesque humour and emotional resonance, can be seen most clearly in the speech of the Reverend Joseph Rayner Stephens. Stephens began by denying the government's right to separate husband and wife in a workhouse. They had 'as much right to chop off his hand or foot, to behead, draw and quarter him, as to take away his wife from him'. He said that rather than see his wife and children taken from him, 'he would plunge a dagger into the breast of him who ... attempted it'. This brought loud cheers from the audience. Stephens was well into his stride now. He said they had assembled together 'to declare they would not have this atrocious bill either in whole or in part, either in principle or in practice, either in its head or in its tail'. The crowd burst into cheers and loud laughter. Stephens built on the imagery he had created: 'they would neither have the sting in its tail, nor the teeth in its jaws'. More loud cheers, and Stephens was in full flight: 'they would plunge the sword of truth into its entrails, and dig a pit deep as hell in their imaginations in which to entomb all the Whig filth and rottenness'. With the crowd enthusiastically applauding, Stephens now offered a picture of hope, an image of where their struggle could lead. '[T]hey would sheath their bloodless sword, and come once more to Hartshead Moor [Peep Green] to keep with gladness the jubilee of renovated and regenerated England (cheers) – of England the brave, the happy, the free – of England the bold and the fearless.'

Stephens said he supported the object of the meeting 'heartily, zealously, and unflinchingly'. He said he would never pay any rates or acknowledge any authority of the Poor Law Commissioners. 'If their command were law', he said, 'he would be outlawed.' This brought renewed cheering. 'If that was the law for the poor, there should ... be no law for the rich.' Alluding to the notion that the rich and the poor shared in the wealth of the nation, Stephens now raised the question of the security of the property-owning classes if the New Poor Law was introduced. 'If that were the law', said Stephens, 'they would do what Lord Brougham recommended them to do – fall back on their resources.' 'They would give up benefits and sick clubs – all burial societies' and they would 'go to Woburn Abbey and ask Lord John Russell whether it [the Abbey] was not part and parcel of the property belonging to the working classes of England.' The crowd cheered enthusiastically. Again the speech was hyperbole. Stephens was merely telling the crowd what they expected to hear – he was merely conforming to popular notions of a violent revolutionary. He did not seriously suggest that violence was an option available to them. Stephens' threats were intended as rhetoric and his joking references to seizing property were the means, both for himself and his audience, of giving vent to political frustrations which could not safely be channelled into more positive action.[28]

The tensions and apparent contradictions in the campaign of popular opposition to the New Poor Law are nowhere better illustrated than in disagreement over the issue of universal suffrage. During the course of his speech, O'Brien said he considered petitioning a 'paltry and ridiculous thing'. He said that he 'heartily' agreed with the importance of the resolution condemning the New Poor Law, but 'he candidly confessed' that he did not believe 'to merely petition' was enough. 'Even if that act was repealed, the people would still be in no better condition than before it passed.' O'Brien concluded his speech by asking the audience to remain after the end of the meeting, 'with the view of passing resolutions he intended to move in favour of universal suffrage'. O'Brien was supported in his call by Feargus O'Connor. But not all the speakers were so enthusiastic. John Fielden chastised O'Brien and O'Connor for mixing up the anti-poor law agitation with demands for universal suffrage. He said no one wished for an introduction of universal manhood suffrage more than he did, but that he thought they could 'best promote' the repeal of the New Poor Law by confining themselves for the time being to that question.[29]

In all events a large proportion of the audience did stay at the close of the anti-poor law meeting to discuss the question of universal suffrage. After a long and at times heated debate, the resolutions in favour of universal suffrage were withdrawn in deference to the opinions of those who thought they would prejudice the main object of the meeting.[30] For the time being the different elements of the anti-poor law movement, the populist expressives with their organic view of society and the instrumentalists who saw the struggle in terms of differing class interests, agreed to bury their differences. But the tensions over the different tactics and methods to be used to oppose the New Poor Law remained. Here were the beginnings of the schism which would carry the popular radical and working-class opponents of the New Poor Law into the ranks of militant Chartism.

After nearly six hours of speeches the meeting began to draw to a close. It was moved that a petition, embodying the six resolutions unanimously passed by the meeting, be drawn up, signed by the chairman and presented to both Houses of Parliament. This was unanimously agreed to. Thanks were voted to the speakers, the Central Committee and the chairman. And the meeting then closed. Those who had spent the day either listening to the speeches or amusing themselves at the various entertainments on the moor again formed themselves up into their respective processions and with the music playing and flags flying began the long march home.

IV

As a spectacle and as a means of arousing popular support the Peep Green demonstration was a resounding success. The radical *Leeds Times* called it a 'momentous meeting ... the most important ever seen in England', and one which 'marks an era in the history of the people'. The demonstration had not only signalled that the working people were 'now determined to struggle for their own interest', but it also served as 'a warning ... to the oppressing Aristocracies, that their day of power, and cruelty and misrule , is nearly passed'. 'The avowed object of the meeting', continued the *Leeds Times*, 'was to express the opinion of the population of the West Riding on the New Poor Law, and their opinions *have* been expressed in a way which can neither be doubted nor disregarded.'[31]

But others both doubted and disregarded the success of the meeting. Assistant Commissioner Power informed his superiors in London that 'a very large meeting' had been held, but he was of the opinion that 'after this demonstration, the excitement will have a tendency to subside – and that our Rules & Regulations will ... [do] better after than before it'. The Whiggish *Leeds Mercury* was scathing in its comments: 'there had never been in Yorkshire a meeting displaying less of wisdom and more of intemperance'. '[T]he orators were the most violent, perverse, and wrong-headed men that could be collected together in England.' It concluded: 'The Petition and Resolutions of such a meeting will have very small weight in the House of Commons'.[32]

If Edward Baines, junior, the proprietor and chief editor of the *Leeds Mercury*, had intended to provoke the opponents of the New Poor Law with his outspoken comments, he succeeded completely. In the days following publication of the report, effigies of Baines, bearing Cobbett's famous epithet, 'the Great Liar of the North', were ceremonially burned in more than a dozen West Riding towns, At York an effigy of Baines was paraded around town on a donkey (Baines was popularly known as 'Neddy' Baines) and then shot; at Huddersfield an effigy of him was burnt at a stake in the market place; and at Heckmondwike his effigy was cremated outside the home of the local agent for the *Leeds Mercury*. At Dewsbury, after parading his effigy around town on a donkey and then setting it alight, the crowd held an impromptu meeting in the centre of the town and resolved that in future they would not visit any public houses or beer shops which took in the *Leeds Mercury*.[33]

The campaign of effigy burning testified to the growing frustration and bitterness of the opposition movement in the West Riding. For nearly six months they had demonstrated and petitioned for an immediate and total repeal of the New Poor Law. They were still as far away from this goal as they had been when the Assistant Poor Law Commissioners had first moved into the area at the end of 1836. The popular opponents of the New Poor Law had hoped that just as popular agitation during the 1831 Reform Crisis had helped force the conservative forces to capitulate, so popular agitation over the New Poor Law would succeed. But the two campaigns were different. During the Reform Crisis there had been an effective majority in the Houses of Commons favouring reform, and it had been supported and encouraged by the middle classes. But there was no significant parliamentary support for the repeal of the New Poor Law and, apart from some concern over its cost, there was no large-scale support for repeal from the middle classes. But most importantly, Parliament was sufficiently isolated from the centre of anti-poor law agitation in the north of England not to feel threatened by it. In 1831 the Reform agitation and the Swing uprising had combined to raise the spectre of violent revolution. Although undoubtedly concerned, the government in London perceived no such threat from the demonstrations or petitions against the New Poor Law.

V

Although failing to convince the government, the demonstrations and petitions assisted the growth and development of an opposition movement. This was emphasised again late in 1837 with the campaign of mass petitioning sponsored by the South Lancashire Anti-Poor Law Association. Although an attempt had been made to form a regional association for South Lancashire in April 1837, it had met with little response and was dropped. With the backing and support of John Fielden and the influential Oldham Radical Association, another attempt in November 1837 was more successful. A meeting of delegates was held at the Commercial Inn, Manchester, on Wednesday, 8 November 1837. Chaired by the Oldham radical, John Knight, the meeting decided that 'an organised system of opposition to the New Poor Law' was 'desirable'. A Central Committee would be formed in Manchester, and local committees established in 'every town, village and hamlet in South Lancashire'.[34] Because the Central Committee was formed first, the South Lancashire organisation would possess a more centralised leadership structure than its West Riding equivalent. Backed by Fielden's money the South Lancashire Anti-Poor Law Association set about organising itself in a most businesslike manner. The old Palace Inn in Market Street, Manchester, was taken over as an office for the Central Committee. The Salford stationer and radical bookseller, Reginald John Richardson, was appointed full-time secretary, and a small staff was recruited to help run the office. To help finance the office the local committees were asked to start raising subscriptions and forward the money to the Central Committee. William Clegg, a spinning-mill owner and business associate of John Fielden's, was named treasurer.[35]

In order to arouse popular support and promote the establishment of local committees the Manchester Central Committee adopted two tactics. The first was to send out missionaries to hold meetings and drum up support. The second was to sponsor a mass petition calling for the repeal of the New Poor Law. Unlike earlier petitioning campaigns there was to be only one petition and it was to be co-ordinated by the Central Committee. The campaign had a specific aim and deadline: the Central Committee had arranged with John Fielden and Lord Stanhope that they would move motions in the two Houses of Parliament on 20 February 1838 calling for a repeal of the New Poor Law. The mass petition was then to be presented to lend support to the motion. Both the missionaries and the petition succeeded admirably in mobilising support for the new organisation. Within a month meetings had been held and committees established in New Poor Law Unions throughout South Lancashire. Enthusiasm for the petition was especially marked. It was felt that with a massive petition the legislature would at last be forced to take note of popular views.

Once again a clear and detailed picture of how the signatures were amassed is not available. What little information we do have comes from official sources and is slanted towards discrediting the petition. Nevertheless, it does provide a valuable insight into the way in which some of the signatures were collected. In Leigh, for instance, two men were said to have gone from door to door gathering the signatures. Apparently they had a copy of the parish rate books with them because the Home Office informant claimed that 'when a house was locked up they forthwith put down on the sheet the name of the occupier as his signature'. The anonymous informant went on to claim that the two men also 'signed the names of Paupers receiving outdoor relief from the Parish who they had never asked to sign, and those of Boys from 8 to 12 years of age'.[36] Undoubtedly there was the occasional falsifying of signatures, but that still should not distract our attention from the large number who willingly signed the petition. The Leigh petition contained signatures from 5,585 ratepayers. Leigh's share of the 1842 Chartist Petition, with a national total of three million signatures, was 8,400 (see Table 5.1).

Table 5.1: Number of Signatures on Petitions in the South Lancashire Area, 1838 and 1842

Township	1838 anti-poor law petition	1842 Chartist petition
Ashton-under-Lyne	16,368	14,200
Leigh	5,585	8,400
Manchester	30,000	92,280
Middleton	1,600	3,200
Oldham	6,590	9,970
Rochdale	48,800	19,600

Sources: *The Times*, 7 February 1838; *Northern Star*, 10 February 1838; D. Jones, *Chartism and the Chartists* (Allen Lane, London, 1975), p.87.

Not all areas were able to conduct a door-knock campaign. In Manchester, Richard Muggeridge, the Poor Law Commission's immigration agent, saw 'Tables ... placed in the Streets in low neighbourhoods, with sheets of Petitions for signature'. Apparently the local activists did not want to waste an opportunity for supporting another worthy cause either, because there were two tables together, 'one with a Petition in favour of the Glasgow Spinners the other against the Poor Law Amendment Act'. Eager to cast doubt on the petitions, Muggeridge commented: 'There was nothing to prevent the same person writing a different name every time he passed the table,' but he offered no evidence that this happened.[37]

The South Lancashire Anti-Poor Law Association's petitioning campaign built to a climax with a meeting of delegates at Manchester on 5 February 1838. All the petitions were brought together at this meeting ready to be sent off to London. The smallest petition came from the village of Eton, near Macclesfield, with 79 signatures; the largest was from Manchester with over 30,000. While most of the petitions contained only the signatures of male adult ratepayers, a number of townships included signatures from women on their petitions. There were also three petitions signed exclusively by women. In all a hundred and seven townships sent petitions to the meeting and delegates attended from as far afield as Clitheroe in the north to Macclesfield in the south. When added together the petitions contained 122,847 signatures.[38] The petition was not nearly as large as the later Chartist petitions (see Table 5.1), but considering the restricted geographical area, the problems of creating an organisational structure and the relatively short collection period of just two months, it was still an impressive achievement.

Despite this, Parliament remained unmoved. Fielden's motions for a repeal of the New Poor Law, supported by the South Lancashire petition, was soundly defeated, 307 votes to 17. The rejection shook the South Lancashire Anti-Poor Law Association. After a delegates' meeting on 12 March 1838, William Clegg wrote to Fielden that of the twenty or so delegates who attended 'all said they were quite sick of petitioning and did not believe that they could induce their constituents to send any more *prayers* to Parliament'. 'They were', he said, 'for trying some other plan now.' Two weeks later Clegg was again writing to Fielden, this time with news of a visit by the Birmingham radical John Collins. Collins had been sent north by the Birmingham Political Union to see if he could induce other radical organisations to co-operate in a new national campaign to obtain universal suffrage. Members of the South Lancashire Anti-Poor Law Association were strongly in favour of the proposal. They reasoned that a parliament elected by universal suffrage would have no choice but to repeal the 1834 Poor Law. Increasingly popular radicals in the north of England turned their attention towards other means of fighting the New Poor Law, a demand for universal suffrage and the fight for the People's Charter.[39]

Notes

1. J. Frank, *The Levellers* (Harvard University Press, Cambridge, Mass., 1955), pp.148-9, H.N. Brailsford, *The Levellers and the English Revolution* (Cresset, London, 1961), p.189.
2. I.R. Christie, *Wilkes, Wyrill and Reform* (Macmillan, London, 1962), pp.166-74.
3. Strictly speaking the meeting was held to support a remonstrance, not a petition. See S. Bamford, *Autobiography, Vol.II: Passages in the Life of a Radical* (first published 1841; Frank Cass, London, 1967), p.270.
4. A. Brundage, *The Making of the New Poor Law* (Hutchinson, London, 1978), pp.156-7; PLC Minutes, 17 March 1835, PRO, MH 1/2.
5. *Hansard*, 3rd Series, vol.XXVI, 17 March 1835, cols 1061-73; a'Court to Lefevre, 19 March 1835, and Lefevre to a'Court, 20 March 1835, PRO, MH 32/2; Power to Chadwick, 19 March 1835, PRO, MH 32/62.
6. *The Times*, 15 April 1837.
7. [Anon.], *The Poor Law Act* (n.p., Bradford, [1837]); 'New Poor Law Act', 15 February 1837 (handbill), Brougham Papers, UCL 17802.
8. *The Times*, 6 March 1837; *Leeds Intelligencer*, 4 March 1837.
9. *Hansard*, 3rd Series, vol.XXXVI, 24 February 1837, cols 1032-4, and 6 March 1837, col.1280.
10. *Leeds Intelligencer*, 25 March 1837.
11. 'Reports from the Select Committee on the Poor Law Amendment Act', *PP*, 1837, vol.XVII Part 1, pp.11-12.
12. *Leeds Intelligencer*, 11 March 1837; *Leeds Times*, 20 May 1837.
13. *Bradford Observer*, 18 May 1937.
14. C. Driver, *Tory Radical* (Oxford University Press, New York, 1946), pp.155-6.
15. Isaiah, 3:15 and Malachi, 3:9.
16. The best coverage of the slogans on the flags and banners was provided by *The Times*, 18 May 1837, and *Halifax Guardian*, 23 May 1837.
17. *Halifax Express*, 20 May 1837.
18. The estimate of numbers attending anti-poor law meetings was a source of continual dispute between the pro- and anti-poor law factions. The anti-poor law press gave the attendance as follows: *Leeds Intelligencer*, 20 May 1837, estimated 120,000; *Leeds Times*, 20 May 1837, thought somewhere between 100,000 and 200,000; and *The Times*, 18 May 1837, estimated 150,000. The estimates from the pro-poor law Press were significantly lower: *Bradford Observer*, 18 May 1837, said 'competent judges' thought 100,000; *Leeds Mercury*, 20 May 1837, estimated between 60,000 and 70,000; and *Manchester Guardian*, 20 May 1837, thought 75,000. The anti-poor law *Halifax Guardian*, 20 May 1837, discussed the different newspaper estimates in some detail before adopting the *Leeds Intelligencer*'s figure of 120,000. They called the *Leeds Mercury* 'an old trickster in such things – uniformly exaggerating on one side and depreciating on the other'.
19. L. Whistler, *The English Festivals* (Heinemann, London, 1947), p.163; *Leeds Mercury*, 20 May 1837.
20. R.W. Malcolmson, *Popular Recreation in English Society, 1700-1850* (Cambridge University Press, Cambridge, 1973), pp.89-171; D.A. Reid, 'The Decline

of Saint Monday, 1766-1876', *Past and Present*, 71 (May 1976), pp.72-4; B. Harrison, *Drink and the Victorians* (Faber, London, 1971), pp.48-55; W. Vamplew, *The Turf* (Allen Lane, London, 1976), p.18.

21. *Leeds Mercury*, 20 May 1837; *Leeds Times*, 20 May 1837.

22. *The Times*, 18 May 1837. The *Leeds Mercury*, 6 February 1776, carries a report of the Wakefield meeting.

23. B. Harrison and P. Hollis, 'Chartism, Liberalism, and the Life of Robert Lowery', *English Historical Review*, vol.132 (1967), pp.513-14. See also E. Canetti, *Crowds and Power* (Victor Gollancz, London, 1962), pp.15-90, and W. Kornhauser, *The Politics of Mass Society* (Free Press, New York, 1965), p. 39.

24. [R. Lowery], 'Passages in the Life of a Temperance Lecturer' in B. Harrison and P. Hollis (eds), *Robert Lowery* (Europa, London, 1979), p.96. For the opinions of other Chartist orators see: T. Cooper, *The Life of Thomas Cooper* (first published 1872; Leicester University Press, Leicester 1971), p.180, and Feargus O'Connor quoted by A. Briggs, 'The Local Background of Chartism' in A. Briggs (ed.), *Chartist Studies* (Macmillan, London, 1977), p.10.

25. *The Times*, 18 May 1837.

26. Ibid.

27. G. Kitson Clark, 'The Romantic Element, 1830-1850' in J.H. Plumb (ed.), *Studies in Social History* (Longman, London, 1955), pp.109-31.

28. *The Times*, 18 May 1837; M. Vicinus, 'To Live Free or Die: The Relationship between Strategy and Style in Chartist Speeches, 1838-9', *Style*, vol.X, no.4 (Fall 1976), p.483.

29. *Halifax Guardian*, 23 May 1837; *The Times*, 18 May 1837.

30. *Halifax Guardian*, 23 May 1837.

31. *Leeds Times*, 20 May 1837.

32. Power to PLC, 20 May 1837, PRO, MH 32/63; *Leeds Mercury*, 20 May 1837.

33. The epithet first appeared in *Cobbett's Two-Penny Trash*, vol.1, no.1, July 1830; *Leeds Times*, 27 May 1837, and *Leeds Intelligencer*, 27 May 1837.

34. *Manchester and Salford Advertiser*, 11 November 1837.

35. Ibid., 2 December 1837; *The Times*, 16 December 1837.

36. Unsigned letter to HO, 7 February 1838, PRO, HO 40/40, f.463.

37. R.M. Muggeridge, Report on the South Lancashire Anti-Poor Law Association, n.d., PRO, HO 40/40, f.471.

38. *The Times*, 7 February 1838, and *Northern Star*, 10 February 1838.

39. *Hansard*, 3rd series, vol.XXXX, 20 February 1838, col.1416; Clegg to Fielden, 13 & 26 March 1838, Fielden Papers, JRULM.

6   CHARTISM

Conventional wisdom has it that Chartism 'swallowed up' the anti-poor law movement in the north of England.[1] Such a view is misleading because it ignores the fact that many Chartists perceived the demand for the People's Charter merely as an extension of the campaign of popular opposition to the New Poor Law; and because it takes no account of the influential role which the anti-poor law movement played in shaping the character of northern Chartism. Rather than being 'swallowed up', the campaign of popular opposition to the 1834 New Poor Law actually helped spawn that particular brand of militant and robustly working-class Chartism which developed in the north of England. Contemporaries were convinced that the New Poor Law had spawned Chartism. Samuel Roberts claimed there was only one thing about which both he and Lord John Russell agreed: the New Poor Law was 'the parent of the Chartists'. Sir George Crewe also agreed, writing 'that of all the various causes ... operating to promote strife and division [between classes], the New Poor Law has been the most powerful'. And A.A. Young observed that 'hostility to [the 1834 Poor Law's] operation is now made the groundwork for one of the most formidable combinations that have ever existed in England'. Even the military commander for the north of England, General Sir Charles James Napier, was convinced that the New Poor Law lay behind the Chartist disturbances. '[T]he Whigs and Tories', he wrote, 'are the real authors of these troubles, by their national debt, corn laws, and new poor law.' But perhaps the last word should go to that keen student of working-class politics in England, Frederick Engels. 'From Newcastle to Dover', he wrote,

> there is but one voice among the workers – the voice of hatred against the new [Poor] Law. The bourgeoisie has formulated so clearly in this law its conception of its duties towards the proletariat, that it has been appreciated even by the dullest . . . Hence it is that this new Poor Law has contributed so greatly to accelerate the labour movement, and especially to spread Chartism...[2]

I

The Chartists' demands for democratic reform were not new. The 'six points' of the People's Charter had been included in the Radical programme for parliamentary reform since the 1780s. Notions of short parliaments, equal-sized constituencies and universal manhood suffrage could be traced back to the seventeenth century, while demands for the ballot, the ending of property qualifications and the payment of members, had been around since the middle of the eighteenth century. The outbreak of the French Revolution saw most upper-class English Radicals forsake this programme of democratic reform. It was only the popular radicals who remained committed to the full programme. In the immediate post-war years, as respectable Radicals pursued a less ambitious programme of reform, the popular radicals became sole heirs to the old Radical programme of democratic reform.

The traditions of popular radicalism ensured that even during the height of the anti-poor law agitation the cause of democratic reform would never be entirely forgotten. It was not unusual to find speakers at early anti-poor law meetings advocating universal suffrage, nor was it unusual to find such meetings passing resolutions in favour of political reform. Thus at Stockport, in March 1837, a meeting of working men called to discuss the New Poor Law decided that their best course of action was to petition Parliament in favour of political reform. Their six-point demand was for equal representation, annual parliaments, the removal of property qualifications, vote by ballot, the payment of members and universal suffrage.[3] The same demands would be published fourteen months later in *The People's Charter*.

When two missionaries from the London Working Men's Association, Henry Vincent and John Cleave, visited the manufacturing districts of the north of England in the later half of 1837, they were astonished by the intensity of popular radical opinion. At the village of Almondbury, near Huddersfield, they witnessed a 'mock election' between an Ultra-Tory and an Ultra-Radical based on the principle of universal suffrage and using the ballot. The Ultra-Radical won easily. Vincent enthused to his friends back in London: 'What would the suffrage do? Eh!' Radicalism, as Vincent was to remark a year later, was an integral part of popular culture in the industrial north of England.

Ever since the year 1818 the Yorkshire and Lancashire people have been peacefully struggling for Universal Suffrage. They were the only two counties in which the principle existed to any extent, and the choicest spirits have become almost worn-out by their continuous exertions. However they will nobly do their duty now –

They see now, for the *first time*, a corresponding energy in other parts of the nation. You have no idea of the intensity of radical opinion here.|You have an index from the numerous public house signs – full length portraits of Hunt – holding in his hand scrowls containing the words Universal Suffrage, Annual Parliaments, and the Ballot. – Paine and Cobbett also figure occasionally.

In such a climate it is not surprising that some popular radicals were obsessed by the need for political reform. During the campaign to boycott the Guardians' election at Middleton, in March 1837, a petition was circulated calling for a repeal of the New Poor Law. Twenty townspeople refused to sign the petition and at a later public meeting a strong vote of censure was passed against them. It would be wrong, however to presume that those who refused to sign the petition were all supporters of the New Poor Law. John Wrigley told the meeting he 'would sign for nothing but universal suffrage'. Wrigley worked himself up so much talking about 'poor Hunt' and his fight for their rights that he eventually burst into tears.[4]

Political reform meant more than the realisation of some abstract democratic theory: it was the means by which a fiercely proud and independent working class sought to have their voice heard and their opinions given the weight they deserved. Trade Unionists in particular were notoriously independent. The radical stationer and former joiner, R.J. Richardson, once made the mistake of inviting one of William Cobbett's sons, the lawyer James Paul Cobbett, to a meeting of Manchester Trade Unionists. The meeting, which had been called to support a petition for a total repeal of the New Poor Law, had heard a succession of Trade Unionists say how it 'now became the working man entirely to depend on themselves and one another'. Cobbett's presence was therefore viewed as something of an insult. A delegate from the powerloom weavers, a Mr Douglas, told the meeting that he was glad to see men of ability and talent advocating the rights of labouring men, but he would rather see labouring men themselves taking a more active part. Douglas concluded by saying that he thought the opinions of working men were as important as anybody's, and that they had the right to be heard.[5] Such sentiments lay near the heart of the popular demand for political reform.

Nor was it merely tradition or sentiment which suggested that the labouring population should be granted full political rights. Common sense indicated that the 1834 Poor Law would only be repealed after the system of political representation had been radically transformed.

Bronterre O'Brien argued, as early as January 1837, that the only way to defeat the New Poor Law was for the working population of Britain to obtain the right to vote. Nor was the 'schoolmaster' the only popular radical to see the logic of such a claim. At an anti-poor law meeting held at the Manchester Corn Exchange in March 1837, a member of the audience had sought leave to move a resolution in favour of political reform. He said that to petition Parliament for a repeal of the New Poor Law was futile, and 'that no effectual remedy [of the New Poor Law] would be obtained, until there was a reform of the House of Commons on the principal [sic] of universal suffrage'. Although the chairman of the meeting, George Condy, the editor of the radical *Manchester and Salford Advertiser*, objected strongly to the resolution – claiming it was a 'firebrand act' which would 'do the work of the enemy' – the largely working-class audience insisted that the motion be put to a vote. It was carried overwhelmingly.[6]

Such occurrences were quite common. As we have already seen, at the massive Peep Green demonstration held in May 1837, Bronterre O'Brien and Feargus O'Connor had shocked some of the other speakers on the platform by suggesting that petitioning the existing Parliament was a 'paltry and ridiculous thing'. Instead they proposed demanding universal suffrage. It was only after a long and heated discussion that the resolution in favour of universal suffrage was withdrawn in deference to those who thought it would prejudice the main object of the meeting. From early 1838 onwards, however, supporters of political reform were increasingly loath to back down. At an anti-poor law meeting at Almondbury, near Huddersfield, in January 1838, it was agreed to send two petitions to Parliament: one seeking the total repeal of the New Poor Law; the other the immediate introduction of universal suffrage, short parliaments, vote by ballot and the ending of property qualifications. At Halifax, a couple of weeks later, the demand for political reform actually took precedence over a call for the repeal of the New Poor Law. Robert Sutcliffe, a Halifax handloom weaver, told the meeting that if the great mass of people had had a voice in electing their parliamentary representatives, the New Poor Law 'would never have been passed'. Abraham Hanson, a handloom weaver from Elland, agreed with him. He told the meeting that petitioning for a repeal of the New Poor Law to the existing Parliament was 'a farce'. Hanson went on to say that society was now divided into two classes – 'that which preyed and that which was preyed upon'.[7] The growing anger and frustration of popular radicals in the north of England over the New Poor Law provided fertile soil for the growth of Chartism.

II

The leader who most accurately sensed the changing mood of popular opponents of the New Poor Law in the north of England was Feargus O'Connor. O'Connor was an Irishman, a romantic adventurer and a boastful egotist; he was also a mob orator of outstanding ability and a deeply committed radical who had a passionate concern for the poor and downtrodden on both sides of the Irish Sea. Despite his own privileged background, O'Connor had an affinity for the life of the common people: he shared their taste for spectacle and boisterous amusement, he was witty, had a lively sense of humour and peppered his speeches with what seemed like an inexhaustible supply of comic anecdotes. But most importantly of all, O'Connor was no proselytiser: unlike many other popular radical leaders, he viewed the life of the common people as something which was morally valuable and not as something to be changed. In this respect he was perhaps closer to the previous generation of popular radical leaders like Henry Hunt and William Cobbett than to the intellectually inclined artisans of the London Working Men's Association or the moderate leaders of the Birmingham Political Union. O'Connor's affinity with the labouring population and their adulation of him was one of the most characteristic features of northern Chartism.

The story of O'Connor's adventurous adolescence, his involvement in Irish politics, his squabbling with his erstwhile party leader, Daniel O'Connell, and his eventual disqualification from serving as MP for Co. Cork because he did not meet the required property qualifications, is well known.[8] It is worth emphasising however, that O'Connor's introduction to political agitation took place in the rowdy and often violent theatre of Irish popular politics and that this influenced his own approach to politics. O' Connor was both a demagogue and a committed Radical. At Westminster he had shown himself to be a consistent supporter of Radical policies. His clash with O'Connell did not merely result from his leader's favouring a moderate approach to achieving a repeal of the Irish Act of Union; the two men also differed over their attitude to poor law reform. O'Connell had been infuenced by the ideas of political economy to believe that a statutory right to poor relief demoralised the poor; O'Connor favoured a much more generous and humane policy.[9]

Following his disqualification from Parliament in 1835, O'Connor began to establish a reputation for himself within popular radical circles in England. As early as 1833 he had addressed a meeting of Lovett's National Union of the Working Classes and during 1834 he was active both inside and outside Parliament in defence of the Tolpuddle Martyrs. Now the pace of his activities increased: he stood unsuccessfully for the late William Cobbett's seat at Oldham; formed his own Radical Association at Marylebone in London; and made numerous tours of the Midlands and the north to win popular support. His break with Lovett and the London Working Men's Association early in 1837 convinced O'Connor that his future lay with the depressed factory operatives and outworkers in the industrial north of England, rather than with the more intellectually-inclined skilled tradesmen in the metropolis.

O'Connor addressed his first anti-poor law demonstration at Huddersfield on Saturday, 14 January 1837. In what was to be a preview of the personality cult which later grew up around him, he was drawn into town in an open carriage by four horses, accompanied by a procession led by torchbearers, bands and banners. Welcoming him to the platform, Richard Oastler said that he was 'proud to find that a Tory and a Radical [could] ... meet together to advocate the Christian and natural rights of poverty and labour'. O'Connor told the meeting that no honest man could support the present government – a government whose power was 'only upheld by a pitiful majority in the House of Commons', but which should have been 'based upon the love of the people'. He said that the government had 'put asunder whom God hath joined together in holy wedlock ... and instead of being the protectors of infancy, they tear them from their parents, and put them into prison-houses and bastiles'. Over the following months O'Connor increasingly frequently came north to address anti-poor law meetings and demonstrations, and built up his personal following.[10]

Much of O'Connor's popular appeal rested on his ability as an orator. He had a striking physical appearance. R.G. Gammage, the first Chartist historian, said of him that 'compared to the generality of men he was a giant indeed'. He stood over six feet tall with a powerfully built, even 'athletic' body. This, together with his 'aristocratic bearing', meant that 'the sight of his person was calculated to inspire the masses with a solemn awe'. But it was his voice which moved the crowds. Thomas Cooper, himself no mean public speaker, described it as a 'powerful baritone voice'. At an indoors meeting Gammage thought that Henry Vincent was perhaps his superior, but in the open air 'O'Connor was the ... universal idol, for the thunder of his voice would reach the ears of the most careless, and put to silence the most noisy of his audience'. With his rich Irish humour and rhetorical breadth, O'Connor was regarded as the most effective mob orator of his day.[11]

Luck also played its part in O'Connor's rise to prominence. By nature he was a gambler and in the autumn of 1837 he gambled on the establishment of a new radical provincial newspaper aimed specifically at the disaffected working class. O'Connor had first raised the possibility of such a paper at the anti-poor law meeting at Peep Green in May 1937. The idea for the newspaper was not his alone; and nor was the money he gambled on its establishment. But it has to be recognised that it is unlikely that the projected paper would have got off the ground without O'Connor's enthusiasm and backing. It is easy with the benefit of hindsight to condemn O'Connor for claiming all the glory that came with the success of the *Northern Star*, but equally had the newspaper been a failure it would have been his reputation which would have suffered. To O'Connor's credit he took the gamble and when it paid off it was he who reaped the financial and political rewards.[12]

The first edition of the *Northern Star and Leeds General Advertiser*, to give the paper its full title, appeared on 18 November 1837. The paper was an instant success. Despite the relatively high price for working men and women (it cost 4½d, the normal price for provincial newspapers at the time) the first week's print run of 3,000 copies sold out immediately. The printer, Joshua Hobson, later told how they could have sold three times that number, but that their financial position was so precarious that they could not afford the stamps to print any more. Within months the *Northern Star* was outselling every other provincial newspaper in Britain. Eventually its national weekly sales would rise to 50,000, rivalling even that of *The Times*.[13]

From the beginning the *Northern Star* was a severe critic of the 1834 Poor Law. It reported anti-poor law meetings, demonstrations and clashes with the authorities. Its reporting of the disturbances at Bradford in November 1837 not only helped to establish its reputation as an outspoken critic of government policy but also earned the attention of the Crown Law officers. It was only the fear that an acquittal would harm the government's reputation which saved the *Northern Star* and its proprietor from immediate prosecution. Even when, in late July 1838, O'Connor swung the paper behind the campaign for the recently published *People's Charter*, it maintained its strong coverage of the anti-poor law agitation. Each week there were reports on the latest clashes at Boards of Guardians' meetings and lurid stories of the cruelties practised on inmates by sadistic workhouse masters. One of these sensational reports eventually led to O'Connor being charged with publishing a false and malicious libel. Although found guilty he was never actually sentenced. By the time sentence was due to be handed down, in March 1840, O'Connor was again facing trial, this time on the more serious charge of seditious libel. He was eventually found guilty and sentenced to eighteen months in York Castle.[14]

III

There was a close, even intimate, relationship between Chartism and popular opposition to the 1834 Poor Law in the north of England. To start with, most of the leading Chartists in the north were active in the anti-poor law movement. Of the twenty northern delegates who attended the 1838 Chartist Convention, fourteen had taken a leading role in the anti-poor law agitation (see Table 6.1). In fact they do not

Table 6.1: Delegates to the 1838 Chartist Convention from the North of England

Active opponents of the New Poor Law	Unconnected with anti-poor law agitation
Peter Bussey (Bradford)	William Carpenter (Bolton)
John Deegan (Stalybridge)	Robert Knox (Durham)
James Fenny (Wigan)	Peter McDouall (Ashton)
Matthew Fletcher (Bury)	William Ryder (Leeds)
Robert Lowery (Newcastle)	Joe Taylor (Carlisle)
Richard Marsden (Preston)	Joseph Wood (Bolton)
James Mills (Oldham)	
Bronterre O'Brien (Stockport)	
Feargus O'Connor (Leeds)	
Lawrence Pitkethly (Huddersfield)	
R. J. Richardson (Salford)	
James Taylor (Rochdale)	
James Whittle (Liverpool)	
James Wroe (Manchester)	

Source: J.W. Knott, 'The Devil's Law. Aspects of Popular Opposition to the 1834 New Poor Law', PhD thesis, Australian National University, 1981.

appear to have distinguished greatly between their anti-poor law and their Chartist activities. While secretary of the South Lancashire Anti-

Poor Law Association, Reginald John Richardson was able to serve as the Manchester delegate to the huge demonstration at Birmingham on 6 August 1838 which adopted the national petition. He then immediately threw himself into organising the massive Chartist demonstration at Kersal Moor, Manchester, on 24 September 1838. It was not until the end of 1838 that Richardson finally resigned from his position with the South Lancashire Anti-Poor Law Association, declaring that there was no hope for effecting a repeal of the New Poor Law until the Charter had been obtained.[15]

The claim that the New Poor Law would not be repealed until the Charter had been obtained was a theme returned to again and again by speakers at Chartist meetings. O'Connor told the audience at Halifax in late July 1838 that the 'only means that remained in the hands of freemen [to fight the New Poor Law] was to join together in the bonds of indissoluble union till they fairly obtained Universal Suffrage'. He said he had just returned from a tour of Scotland and that 'when the people of Scotland found that they could not shut the toll bar against Whig oppression, they would join with the people of England in their crusade against this infernal Poor Law Bill'.[16] O'Connor was exaggerating, of course, the Scots had never enjoyed a legal right to poor relief and popular attitudes to the New Poor Law were therefore quite different north of the Tweed. But it was an English audience he was addressing and he knew it gratified his listeners to think of themselves as part of a homogeneous national movement whose first aim would be to repeal the hated New Poor Law.

It was the continued predominance of anti-poor law feeling which probably best explains the role of the Reverend Joseph Rayner Stephens in the Chartist movement. Stephens was no radical and his attitude towards political reform was at best ambivalent. But it was he, rather than the radical Feargus O'Connor, who often received the most enthusiastic response and drew the largest crowds at the Chartist demonstrations and meetings in late 1838 and early 1839. One of the most often used quotations in Chartist historiography is Stephens's remark that Chartism was 'a knife and fork question'. This quotation, which comes from a speech Stephens made at the massive Kersal Moor demonstration at Manchester, on 24 September 1838, is invariably interpreted as meaning that Chartism was motivated by 'economic issues'.[17] While in a very broad sense this is perfectly true, it does miss the point Stephens was specifically making. The phrases 'a knife and fork question' and a 'bread and cheese question' were metaphors frequently used by speakers to refer to the near-starvation diet served up in the new Union workhouses. Stephens, quite simply, was saying that Chartism was a poor-law question. Let us look again at what he said in greater detail.

> This question of Universal Suffrage was a knife and fork question . . . this question was a bread and cheese question ... and if any man asked him what he [Stephens] meant by Universal Suffrage, he would answer, that every working man in the land had a right to have a good coat to his back, a comfortable abode in which to shelter himself and his family, a good dinner upon his table, and no more work than was necessary for keeping him in health, and as much wages for that work as would keep him in plenty, and afford him the enjoyment of all the blessings of life which a reasonable man could desire. (Tremendous cheers).

This is more than a catalogue of economic demands; there are echoes here of popular expectations concerning poor relief – the provision of clothing, housing, food and work. In a later but rarely quoted passage from the same speech, Stephens again referred to the New Poor Law.

> the repeal of the New Poor Law would be far from hindering this [Chartist] movement; on the contrary, it would greatly accelerate its progress. (Continued cheering.) The people of Lancashire and of Yorkshire, and of England, would never allow their feelings for the repeal of the New Poor Law to step in between their race with the rest of their countrymen ... but they were determined to ... obtain that power which, when once possessed, would enable them immediately to repeal it, and every other bad law in existence.[18]

IV

Although popular opposition to the 1834 Poor Law was slowly subsumed into the background of Chartist agitation, it continued to influence the direction and the character of the movement for much longer than is often recognised. Certainly, as almost every Chartist orator was aware, the New Poor Law was the one topic which was guaranteed to arouse Chartist audiences throughout the country. Assistant Commissioner a'Court reported from Wiltshire in September 1838 that the speakers at Chartist meetings were receiving an enthusiastic response when they promised 'destruction of all the New Workhouses, instant repeal of the Poor Laws and *condign punishment of those who passed them*'. Henry Vincent, one of the speakers a'Court was undoubtedly referring to, told friends that he was able to move a meeting of Bath women to tears when he spoke of the New Poor Law. At a Chartist meeting at Blackburn in July 1838, the most enthusiastic applause came when James Holden, a young factory operative, threatened 'vengeance' on the Whigs for having introduced the New Poor Law.[19]

The hated New Poor Law had a central place in Chartist demonology. There was rarely a Chartist meeting or demonstration without the presence of at least one flag or banner referring to the New Poor Law. Some of them were quite elaborate. At Carlisle in October 1838 the Women's Political Union carried a beautiful silk banner showing a 'representation of the atrocious New Poor Law ... a painting of a Guardian tearing a Child from its mother's breast'. On the reverse was a picture of a 'Guardian separating man and wife', and the motto 'who God has joined together let no man put asunder'. Others were much simpler, both in construction and message. At a demonstration at Colne in October 1838 there was a plain calico flag in the procession. It bore the simple slogan: 'No New Poor Law – no Bastile Punishment'. Still others showed evidence of a black humour. In the same procession at Colne one of the marchers had a skeletal-like effigy suspended from a pole. It carried the words, 'just escaped from the Bastile'. Occasionally there were attempts at crude verse. The banner carried by the men from Bashall's Factory in the procession at Preston in November 1838 was in doggerel: 'No Bastile for Me,/I intend to be free.' And at other times the slogan was right up to date. A banner carried at the Peep Green demonstration in May 1839 drew attention to the recently published pamphlet which purported to advocate infanticide by showing 'a representation of Marcus destroying a babe in a Union Workhouse'. But more often than not the old stand-by slogans, 'Down with the Bastiles', and the biblical 'woe unto him that oppresses the Poor', were deemed sufficient.[20]

It was hatred of the New Poor Law which determined Chartist strategy during the 1841 General Election. In the north of England the Whigs were viewed as the authors of the New Poor Law, whereas the Tories were seen as opponents – albeit often luke-warm opponents – of the legislation. Feargus O'Connor therefore advised his supporters to campaign for a Tory victory in the General Election. Not all Chartists agreed. Bronterre O'Brien denounced O'Connor's advice as madness.

He said it would mean the annihilation of Chartism if the Tories were returned. O'Brien suggested that the Chartists should support neither of the major political parties unless an alliance with one or the other could lead to the return of a Chartist candidate.[21] But it was O'Connor who was once again most closely attuned to popular opinion on the subject. In the north of England most Chartists campaigned actively against the Whigs and their hated New Poor Law.

In Huddersfield the local Chartists campaigned with wit and style. They paraded the town in a small procession, displaying emblems attacking the New Poor Law. The procession was led by a man carrying a pole bearing a large lump of cheese, a large loaf and a piece of roast meat. It bore the slogan 'Chartist fare for all working men'. Next came a pole with the slogan 'American loaf, Republicanism and a cheap government'. Then there was a pole bearing a red herring and a split potato with the slogan, 'Whig fare for able-bodied labourers'. And then another pole, with a small black loaf and the slogan 'Neddy Baines's coarse sort of bread for the poor'. Next came a cart with a tub labelled 'red herring soup' and a jar labelled 'skilly-go-lee' on the front. 'Skilly' was the slang term for the gruel, or oatmeal soup, which was rumoured to be served in the new bastiles. Much to the amusement of bystanders, the 'skilly' was raised up every now and again in a ladle and one of the Chartists would shout, 'soup, four quarts a penny'. But the most conspicuous article in the cart was a 'poor old donkey', dressed in the Whig colours of red and yellow, and with a copy of the *Leeds Mercury* tied to its tail. Placards on the donkey and on the side of the cart proclaimed 'behold the great liar of the north, old Neddy', a reference to Edward 'Neddy' Baines, MP for Leeds and owner of the *Leeds Mercury*. From the back of the cart the Chartists handed small red cards to bystanders. The cards read, 'free tickets for the bastile'.[22]

Nationally the Tories won the election. What effect the Chartists' campaign had upon the result is unclear. In Huddersfield there was no Tory candidate, and Stansfield, the sitting Whig member, was returned unopposed. Where the Chartists' anti-poor law campaign did appear to have had some impact was in the election of the two members for the West Riding. The Tory *Halifax Guardian* had claimed that the fate of the New Poor Law hung on the election result. It warned that if the two sitting Whigs, Morpeth and Milton, were returned 'the New Poor Law [would] ... become *permanently* the law of the land, and the chains of the already oppressed poor be rivetted on their pining limbs'. Both Whigs were defeated and replaced by the two

Tories. But if the Chartists had hoped that a change of government would mean a change of policy with regard to the New Poor Law they were to be sadly disappointed. Soon after gaining office Sir Robert Peel, the Prime Minister, and Sir James Graham, the Home Secretary, declared that they would continue the New Poor Law.[23]

V

Because Chartism was such a heterogeneous movement it is impossible to talk of a uniform Chartist policy towards the 1834 Poor Law. There were, for instance, a number of Chartists who had been influenced by the ideas of philosophical radicalism and claimed that the ancient rights and privileges they had enjoyed under the Old Poor Law were incompatible with their demands for political equality. Equally some hardline Chartists believed that nothing should be done to ameliorate the effects of the New Poor Law. They argued that the new system of poor relief provided a useful source of popular resentment which could be channelled into political agitation. But the proponents of such views were never very influential.[24] The vast majority of Chartist supporters remained opposed to the New Poor Law and fearful of its impact on themselves and others.

What would Chartists replace the 1834 Poor Law with, had they been successful in forcing its repeal? Again there was no single answer. Most Chartists probably began by advocating a return to the Old Poor Law. Gradually this changed, however, as people began to question whether the 43rd of Elizabeth was all it could have been. Modifications to the Old Poor Law began to be suggested. There was even a move towards centralism. Feargus O'Connor told an audience at Sheffield in September 1839:

> there ought not to be any poor in the land. If society was properly constituted [as it presumably would be under the Charter], all the sick and infirm would be provided for by the government.

Bronterre O'Brien outlined in some detail the policy he thought should be introduced. In place of the 'degrading' New Poor Law he would establish

> a just and efficient poor-law (based upon the original Act of Elizabeth), which would centralize the rates, and dispense them equitably and economically for the beneficial employment and relief

of the destitute poor . . . The employment to be of a healthy, useful, and reproductive kind. Till such employment be procured, the relief of the poor to be, in all cases, promptly and liberally administered as a right, and not grudgingly doled out as a boon...

Who was to provide the money which would fund such a system? O'Brien suggested 'the owners of *realised* property', those who had profited by the labour of the poor and 'whose enormous revenues ... are the main cause of so many labourers falling into pauperism'.[25]

Ultimately, however, the Chartist movement remained powerless to effect any alteration of the New Poor Law, Chartists were intent on attacking the hated legislation at its source, they were intent on attacking Parliament and the system of parliamentary representation. The flaw in such an approach was that they were attacking the New Poor Law where it had the greatest amount of support and where they were politically the weakest. It was perhaps inevitable that the Chartists would adopt such a means of procedure. Chartism, after all, was a national movement aiming at national reform. This was part of Chartism's great appeal to working men and women throughout the British Isles. It was also part of the explanation of why Chartism increasingly became irrelevant to the real campaign of popular opposition to the 1834 Poor Law. The operation of the New Poor Law was most vulnerable at the local level and it was here that the most effective campaign of opposition was being fought.

Notes

1. M. Hovell, *The Chartist Movement* (Manchester University Press, Manchester, 1970), p.98. See also: A. Briggs, 'The Local Background to Chartism' in A. Briggs (ed.), *Chartist Studies* (Macmillan, London, 1965), p.11; C. Driver, *Tory Radical* (Oxford University Press, New York, 1946), p.393; N.C. Edsall, *The anti-Poor Law Movement, 1834-44* (Manchester University Press, Manchester, 1971), p.167.

2. S. Roberts, *Chartism its Causes and Cure* (n.p., Sheffield, 1839), p.3; G. Crewe, *A Word for the Poor and Against the Present Poor Law* (Rowbottom, Derby, 1843), p.20, (original in italics); A.A. Young, *The Poor Law* (Hatchard, London, 1834), p.3; W. Napier, *The Life and Opinions of General Sir Charles James Napier* (Murray, London, 1857), vol.II, p.6; F. Engels, *The Condition of the Working Class in England* (first published in German 1845; Panther, London, 1972), p.316.

3. *Manchester and Salford Advertiser*, 25 March 1837.

4. Vincent to Minikin, 4 September 1837 and September 1838, Vincent-Minikin Correspondence, TH, VIN 1/1/3 & 10; *Manchester Chronicle*, 11 March 1837.

5. *Manchester and Salford Advertiser*, 15 April 1837; *Manchester Chronicle*, 11 March 1837.

6. *Bronterre's National Reformer*, 7 January 1837; *Manchester Chronicle*, 4 March 1837.

7. *Halifax Guardian*, 23 May 1837; *Leeds Times*, 6 January 1838; *Halifax Express*, 27 January 1838.

8. D. Read and E. Glasgow, *Feargus O'Connor* (Edward Arnold, London, 1961), pp.9-39; G.D.H. Cole, *Chartist Portraits* (Macmillan, London, 1965), pp.300-10; J. Epstein, *The Lion of Freedom* (Croom Helm, London, 1982), pp.7-53.

9. *Hansard*, 3rd series, vol.XXVI, cols 1214-8.

10. R. Oastler, *Damnation! Eternal Damnation to the Fiend-Begotten, 'Coarser Food' New Poor Law* (Hetherington, London, 1837), p.4; *Leeds Times*, 21 January 1837.

11. R.G. Gammage, *History of the Chartist Movement, 1837-54* (first published 1854; Merlin, London, 1969), p.45; T. Cooper, *Life* (first published 1872; Leicester University Press, Leicester, 1971), p.179; J. McCarthy, *A History of Our Own Times* (Chatto & Windus, London, 1904), vol.1, p.81. See also M. Vicinus, 'To Live Free or Die: the Relationship between Strategy and Style in Chartist Speeches, 1838-9', *Style*, vol.10, no.4 (Fall 1976), p.500.

12. Epstein, *The Lion of Freedom*, pp.61-8. E.L.H. Glasgow, 'The Establishment of the *Northern Star* Newspaper', *History*, vol.XXXIX (1954), pp.54-67, presents a very unflattering picture of O'Connor's involvement by drawing on the opinions of his enemies and critics. To be fair to O'Connor, however, it is worth noting that the *Northern Star* was not the only provincial radical working-class newspaper launched that year. Augustus Hardin Beaumont's *Northern Liberator* started publication in Newcastle-upon-Tyne four weeks earlier in October 1838. The standard of journalism in the *Northern Liberator* was in certain respects higher than that of the *Northern Star*, and yet it was O'Connor's paper which attracted the greater readership. There are strong grounds for claiming that O'Connor's popularity made the difference, ensuring the success of the *Northern Star*.

13. Only a fragment of the first issue is preserved in Britain in the Place Newspaper Collection, set 56, vol.1, f. 155, BL. *Manchester Examiner*, 6 November 1847. Read and Glasgow, *Feargus O'Connor*, p.60, estimate the maximum sales of the *Northern Star* at 50,000 in the first half of 1839. *The Times* was published three times a week and just outsold the *Star* on a weekly basis.

14. Power to PLC, 2 December 1837, PRO, MH 12/14720; Phillipps to PLC, 29 December 1837, PRO, MH 19/63; Chadwick to Maule, 29 January 1839, PRO, HO 73/55; *Northern Star*, 27 July 1839; *Manchester and Salford Advertiser*, 27 July 1839; Epstein, *The Lion of Freedom*, pp.211-2 and Read and Glasgow, *Feargus O'Connor*, pp.88-9.

15. *Northern Star*, 11 August, 22 & 29 September 1838; Clegg to Fielden, 22 September 1838, Fielden Papers, JRULM; Driver, *Tory Radical*, pp.395-6.

16. *Northern Star*, 4 August 1838.

17. J.F.C. Harrison, 'A Knife and Fork Question', *Victorian Studies*, vol.XVIII, no.2 (December 1974), p.100. See also Hovell, *The Chartist Movement*, p.118; Driver, *Tory Radical*, p.397; D. Read, 'Chartism in Manchester' in Briggs, *Chartist Studies*, p.34; J.T. Ward, *Chartism* (Batsford, London, 1973), p.100.

18. *Northern Star*, 29 September 1938.

19. a'Court to Lefevre, 13 September 1838, PRO, HO 73/54; Vincent to Minikin, 20 October 1838, Vincent-Minikin Correspondence, TH, VIN 1/1/12; *Blackburn Standard*, 10 July 1839.

20. *Northern Star*, 27 October and 10 November 1838.

21. Ibid, 29 May and 19 June 1841.

22. *Halifax Guardian*, 19 June 1841.

23. Ibid, 26 June 1841; Driver, *Tory Radical*, p.437.

24. *Manchester and Salford Advertiser*, 14 November 1840, 28 May 1842, and *Blackburn Standard*, 1 June 1842.

25. *Sheffield Iris*, 24 September 1839; J.B. O'Brien, *The Rise, Progress, and Phases of Human Slavery* (first published 1849; Reeves, London, 1885), pp.112-13. N.C. Edsall, *The anti-Poor Law Movement* (Manchester University Press, Manchester, 1971), p.121, claims that popular opponents of the 1834 Poor Law never put forward their own proposals for a system of poor relief, they merely opposed. Obviously he never looked at the schemes proposed by Chartist leaders.

7 GUARDIANS AND CROWDS

Early in January 1837 the Poor Law Commission had issued orders for the election of Boards of Guardians in a number of the northern Poor Law Unions. Although most working-class opponents of the 1834 Poor Law were denied the right to elect Members of Parliament, they could (in their capacity as ratepayers) vote in local Board of Guardians' elections. Here was an opportunity to defeat the New Poor Law locally. Opponents of the New Poor Law had two choices open to them: enforce a boycott of the elections, or attempt to get anti-poor law candidates elected. A total boycott was the ideal solution. But could it be achieved? For a boycott to be effective all the ratepayers, in all the townships in a Union, had to be dissuaded from nominating Guardians. The danger was that if the opposition failed, the supporters of the New Poor Law would be left in control of the Union Board. With little time to organise there was disagreement over which tactic to adopt. The popular radicals and other hardline opponents of the New Poor Law tended to favour a total boycott; they claimed that even if anti-poor law Guardians were elected they would be powerless to refuse the directions and orders of the Poor Law Commission. 'Respectable' opponents, and especially the Tories, were more circumspect; they favoured the election of anti-poor law candidates.

I

Meetings of parish ratepayers had traditionally appointed officials under the Old Poor Law, and (initially at least) this practice was continued under the New Poor Law. Township meetings were held to nominate people for the office of Guardian. They were to be the scene of some bitter clashes. At Stockport on 23 January 1837 a meeting was held to consider the propriety of nominating 'fit and proper' persons to hold the office of Guardian. The chairman of the meeting, Mr Rawlinson, began by saying that although he was opposed to many of the clauses of the New Poor Law he hoped the speakers confine their remarks to the appointment of Guardians. This did not meet with general approval, and several of the operatives who were present said that the bill was 'unchristian and unconstitutional' and that the ratepayers could do no better than recommend that no Guardians be nominated. The meeting was exceedingly lively and at one stage the chairman was accused of being a supporter of the New Poor Law. Eventually, the meeting broke up in disarray, with the chairman storming out of the room.[1]

At Halifax the Whigs called a meeting of the ratepayers to nominate 'proper persons' to serve as poor law Guardians for the town. Much to the Whigs' chagrin, a large number of working people also attended. The chairman, Mr P.K. Holden, told the meeting that the Guardians would be expected to put the Registration Act into effect, but that the New Poor Law was 'not likely to come into operation ... for some time to come'. This provoked an interjection from a member of the audience, that 'he hoped never'. During the course of what was to prove a rather acrimonious meeting the Whig candidate for the office of Guardian, Jonathan Ackroyd, was called 'the greatest tyrant in the town' and soundly rejected by the votes of the working-class ratepayers. One of the working men, Robert Wilkinson, then moved 'that the new poor law is inimical to the best interests of society, at variance with the principles of the Christian religion; and derogatory to the human character'. Although the resolution was loudly applauded, the chairman initially refused to put the motion. After a good deal of confusion and loud booing he was forced to give way. The motion was passed by an overwhelming majority. A large section of the audience was obviously opposed to the nomination of anyone for the position of Guardian and it was only after a good deal of discussion that they finally agreed to nominate the Owenite, Joseph Nicholson, for the position of Guardian. Nicholson had argued that it was better to have 'friends' administering the New Poor Law than 'enemies'. As the meeting closed, those who had supported the New Poor Law were hissed, and three groans given for the measure itself.[2]

The first elections for the Board of Guardians were conducted against a background of confusion and indecision. Party loyalty and personal interest combined to ruin all attempts at a co-ordinated election policy amongst the different groups opposing the New Poor Law. Most Tories, for instance, realising that the new Boards of Guardians could be an important source of future patronage, refused to support the policy of boycott. While some isolated townships refused to return Guardians, enough Guardians were returned in every Union where elections were held to constitute Boards. The Oldham Union put up the stiffest resistance. Oldham itself and three of the seven townships in the Union failed to return Guardians.³ In Huddersfield the opponents of the New Poor Law did manage to get a majority of their candidates elected to the Board, but it was a near run thing; most of the working-class ratepayers refused to register a formal vote and instead returned their voting papers with a 'strong protest against the [New Poor] law written thereon'.⁴

Despite their apparent success, the Poor Law Commission could take little comfort from the election results. Not only had several townships failed to return Guardians, but the election results in a number of Unions were being contested because of alleged irregularities. At Leeds, which was the first Union in the manufacturing districts of the north to hold a Board of Guardians' election, the disputed election result turned into a nightmare for the Commission. The Leeds ratebooks had not been kept up to date and many ratepayers failed to receive their voting papers. The plural voting system caused still further confusion. Some of those entitled to extra votes failed to receive the additional voting papers; while others not entitled to the extra votes received papers. In the middle of the voting, which was held over three days, the leading Tories in Leeds complained to Assistant Commissioner Power of 'gross partiality' on the part of the overseers. They stated that Whig friends of the overseers had been served with additonal voting papers while many Tories had been denied votes. Realising the danger inherent in such charges, Power immediately set off for London to consult with the Poor Law Commission. In the meantime the Leeds election results were held over. Eventually the Commission determined that there had been gross irregularities and that, rather than offend the Tories and risk making them permanent enemies of the New Poor Law, the Guardians' election should be declared 'null and void'. It was another seven years before the Poor Law Commission felt confident enough to hold the next Board of Guardians' election in Leeds. In the meantime the overseers continued to administer the Old Poor Law.⁵

The Poor Law Commission's biggest problem, however, was that the terms for the Boards of Guardians elected in January and February 1837 extended only until March. This not only aggravated those respectable inhabitants who had exerted themselves in the face of sometimes bitter opposition to elect 'suitable' Guardians, but it also allowed opponents of the New Poor Law time to agree upon a workable policy and regain the ground they had lost in the first election.⁶ Despite the difficulties in achieving a total boycott, opponents in a number of Unions (Oldham, Ashton-under-Lyne,

Rochdale, Bury, Burnley and Todmorden) persisted with the policy. And there were a few isolated townships in other Unions which again insisted on not returning Guardians. In most Unions, however, the opposition forces turned their attention to electing anti-poor law candidates.

Once again Oldham showed itself to be most firmly in the hands of opponents of the New Poor Law. Protest meetings were held, petitions raised and delegates elected to attend conferences to discuss tactics. A meeting of delegates from the eight townships in the Union decided that the best strategy to adopt would be for no one to serve as a Guardian.[7] The campaign culminated with a large public demonstration in Oldham itself. Processions from each township marched into Oldham where they were addressed by John Fielden, Richard Oastler, and the future Radical member of the borough, General Johnston. The Reverend John Hart, minister of the Ebenezer Chapel in Middleton, led the procession. He carried a copy of the 1834 Poor Law which he later publicly burnt.[8]

Oldham was especially well placed to wage an effective boycott. Although a populous Union it was confined to a relatively small geographical area, the eight townships in the Union had a strong radical tradition, and the working class were both organised and had a long history of involvement in local affairs.[9] All the townships were placed under tight control, and popular pressure mobilised against would-be supporters of the New Poor Law. In Middleton, for instance, the twenty people who had refused to sign the petition against the New Poor Law had their names read out at a town meeting. The townspeople were also advised that they should not deal with the four shopkeepers who had not signed the petition. Similar pressure was brought to bear on those foolish enough to nominate as Guardians – most withdrew their nominations before the election. The Oldham campaign was a resounding success for the opposition forces. Only one Guardian was elected, but he was an opponent of the New Poor Law and immediately resigned his office.[10] Oldham was to remain without a Board of Guardians until 1847.

None of the other Unions which attempted a boycott was as successful as Oldham. Nevertheless some came quite close. In the Bury Union, the opponents of the New Poor Law fought a vigorous and at times violent campaign of boycott. As a result over half of the Union's twelve townships refused to nominate Guardians, and many of those nominated and elected refused to serve. Although the boycott was incomplete, the bitterness of the campaign and the threat of continued violence effectively barred the introduction of the New Poor Law into the Union until 1840. The only Union in the West Riding to attempt a total boycott was Todmorden. Although it was a relatively small Union with only six townships, there was a good deal of variation between the Lancashire cotton townships around Todmorden and the worsted townships further up the Calder valley in Yorkshire. Todmorden itself and the adjacent township of Walsden refused to return Guardians, but the four worsted townships all did so. Nevertheless, the Poor Law Commission could take little comfort from the result, the Guardians who had been elected all claimed to be opposed to the New Poor Law and said that they would implement only the Registration Act – nothing else.[11]

In a number of South Lancashire Poor Law Unions the opposition forces attempted to use existing parish institutions to delay the holding of Board of Guardians' elections. Salford had the greatest success. When Assistant Commissioner Power asked that the town's ratebooks be made available so that an electoral roll could be compiled, the Salford Select Vestry and overseers refused. He was told that the Vestry were willing to call a public meeting to take advice from the ratepayers, but that they could not supply him with the information he required without the ratepayers' consent. Power rejected such a mode of procedure as unacceptable. Eventually, after more than a year's delay (and the success of pro-poor law candidates in the annual election of overseers), the ratebooks were made available to the Poor Law Commission and the Guardians' election held.[12] Despite this a valuable lesson was learnt from the tactics adopted by the opposition forces in Salford: long-established parish institutions such as the Vestry, workhouse committee and the office of overseer could be used to frustrate the implementation of the 1834 Poor Law. Such tactics would later be used by opposition forces on other Poor Law Unions.

II

If Oldham was the most painful thorn in the side of the Poor Law Commission in South Lancashire, Huddersfield easily assumed that role in the West Riding. The second largest Poor Law Union in the country, the Huddersfield Union stretched from the Lancashire-Yorkshire border in the west to the proposed Barnsley Union in the east. It was 20 miles long and over 15 miles wide and contained no fewer than thirty-four townships. It was also claimed to be the fourth most populous Union in Britain. The Union was as diverse socially and economically as it was large. Some of the townships were almost entirely agricultural, there were prosperous woollen milltowns, and there were depressed outwork villages where the population eked out a precarious existence in the woollen and worsted trades. Perhaps in recognition of the difficulties of obtaining a total boycott in such a varied Union, it was not attempted in Huddersfield. Instead, the opposition forces directed their energies to electing anti-poor law Guardians.

At the first election for the Huddersfield Board of Guardians, in January 1837, a small majority of anti-poor law Guardians had been returned. At the first and only meeting of this Board they had decided to adjourn without even appointing a Union clerk.[13] This left the Poor Law Commission in a quandary. The Union clerk was essentially a paid secretary to the Board of Guardians. He handled correspondence and general inquiries but had little to do with the actual administration of the New Poor Law. In fact his main duties were to act as the registrar for births, deaths and marriages under the Registration Act. Thus the non-appointment of a clerk appeared to be more an attack on the Registration Act than one on the New Poor Law. The Poor Law Commission decided to adopt an attitude of wait and see; there would be another election in March and perhaps then a clerk would be appointed.

The March Board of Guardians' election confirmed that a majority of anti-poor law Guardians controlled the Huddersfield Board. The Huddersfield Anti-Poor Law Committee reasoned that the Poor Law Commission could do little to advance the New Poor Law as long as no clerk was appointed. They therefore decided to continue to resist the appointment of a clerk. The first meeting of the new Board of Guardians was held in the George Inn on 3 April 1837. Assistant Commissioner Power was in attendance, and so was a large body of popular radicals who insisted on their right to be present during the discussions. Apparently the opposition Guardians, many of whom were Tories elected by the rural townships in the Union, could not be entirely trusted and the popular radicals were there to keep an eye on them. Following an adjournment for lunch the Board was expected to reassemble in the same room, but instead special constables were found guarding the stairs and the Guardians were ushered into a private room upstairs. Supporters of the New Poor Law obviously thought the opposition guardians would be more likely to appoint a clerk if they met in private. Angered by their exclusion from the meeting, the popular opponents made a number of unsuccessful attempts to force their way upstairs. With the crowd yelling abuse in the street, the Guardians voted to defeat a motion appointing a clerk and adjourned their meeting for two months.[14]

To add to the Poor Law Commission's difficulties in the Huddersfield Union, the campaign of demonstrations and petitions organised by the West Riding Anti-Poor Law Committee was reaching its climax with the massive Peep Green demonstration held on 16 May 1837. The failure of the campaign and demonstration to change government policy left popular opponents of the New Poor Law frustrated and bitter. Nor was popular opinion eased by the growing trade depression. In the spring of 1837 the woollen and worsted industries in the West Riding underwent a dramatic slump. The outwork trades were hardest hit. The *Leeds Times* reported that in the Huddersfield area alone, close to 8,000 handloom weavers engaged in 'fancy weaving' were without work. They calculated, taking into account the workers and their dependants, that over 30,000 people around Huddersfield were suffering severe distress. The figure was significant: it represented over a third of the population of the Huddersfield Union. 'The sufferings of the weavers are unprecedented', commented the *Leeds Times,* 'and not a hand was held out to their relief'.[15]

It was against this background of growing frustration, unemployment and hunger that the next Huddersfield Board of Guardians' meeting was held. The Poor Law Commission, eager to secure the appointment of a clerk, began to put pressure on the Guardians. The Poor Law Commission warned the Guardians by letter that '[a]ny further postponement ... will be in direct contravention not only of the Order of the Union but of ... the Registration Act'. And that 'if the provisions of the Registration Act should fail of being carried to effect through their [the Guardians'] default, they alone will become responsible for defeating the intentions of the legislature'.[16] The Huddersfield Anti-Poor Law Committee decided to counter the Commission's increased pressure with a little popular pressure of their own. They would hold a demonstration in Huddersfield on the same day as the Board of Guardians was to meet.

A crowd estimated at 10,000 assembled in front of the Druids Hotel on 5 June 1837, the morning of the Guardians' meeting. They were accompanied by a band and several banners, 'some of which were borne by women'. One of the banners carried the slogan, 'For God, the King, and the People; we will oppose to the utmost that law and that faction which deprives us of our liberty, as Englishmen, and that party whose liberality is tyranny.' Another proclaimed: 'England, home and Liberty; local rights, wholesome food, and no separation in bastiles'. A large black flag showed a picture of three men hanging from a gibbet with the inscription 'The Kings of the bastiles drawing their wages'. On the reverse side was a figure intended to represent the Devil and the slogan 'I have him' and 'stone him'. There were also a number of protesters who carried placards proclaiming: 'We are all constables; no friend of the poor will break the peace; hurrah for the magistrates.' These slogans referred to the magistrates' decision to turn down the Whigs' request for military protection, and Richard Oastler's promise to them that there would be no violence.[17]

Before setting off to the workhouse where the Guardians were meeting, the crowd heard a rousing speech from Oastler in which he attacked the pro-poor law chairman of the Huddersfield Board of Guardians, William Swain, and his 'bloody committee' for wanting to introduce the military into Huddersfield. Oastler referred to Swain, a prominent factory owner, as 'a Luddite' – a taunting reference to Swain's participation in the bloody defence of Rawfold's Mill against a Luddite attack in 1812.[18] Oastler commended the magistrates for having nothing to do with their evil schemes. 'I feel', he said, 'exceedingly obliged to the magistrates that through their confidence in your peaceable disposition, we are this day allowed to exercise our constitutional privileges without having the bayonets and the sabres of the soldiers with us'.[19]

The organisers intended to form the crowd into a procession, march the mile or so to the workhouse and then return to Huddersfield. The crowd, however, had other things in mind. A rumour had been put about that Assistant Commissioner Power would attend the Board meeting, and the protesters were eager to give him a rowdy reception. When the procession arrived at the workhouse, they found the gates locked and the Guardians already in session. Oastler sent a note to the chairman of the Board of Guardians asking that a deputation be allowed in as observers. Swain sent a curt refusal. The mounting frustration and anger of the past few months now boiled over. The crowd stormed the gates and forced their way into the workhouse yard. Some began battering down the doors, while others forced the windows and began climbing in. Oastler and the other leaders were powerless to stop the crowd. The Guardians quickly adjourned their meeting amidst threats that the protesters would 'pull down the buildings if the Guardians did not immediately break up their meeting'. Several members of the crowd, 'principally women', began a thorough search of the workhouse to see if they could unearth Assistant Commissioner Power. They 'explored the cellars, searched all the closets, beds, and bed-rooms in the house ... all the while vowing vengeance upon the commissioner'. Thwarted in their purpose (a couple of newspapers wrongly reported that Power made his escape through the back door) the searchers were supposed to have 'cleaned the paupers' trenchers of their dinners, [and] distributed them among themselves, saying it was their own, and [that] they had a right to it'.[20]

In the meantime the Guardians, escorted by a number of special constables and Oastler, began walking back to Huddersfield. They were heading for the Albion Inn where they hoped to be able to resume their adjourned meeting. They were followed in turn by the band and most of the protesters. The Guardians were hooted and jeered at by spectators along the road.

> Groups of men and women stood waiting their reception on the road, and as they passed ... called out for Mr Power, saying they had determined to do him his job, to make a potato pie of him... [O]ne man said, 'd[am]n him, I made a vow when I left home this morning, that I would have his heart back with me tonight'.[21]

The threats were not all verbal either. As the Guardians passed through Newtown,

> Mary Fernside, came out of the crowd with a large table knife in her hand, and called out to Mr Swain ... 'D[am]n thee, I'll run this knife into thy guts'.

She started to move towards Swain, 'but seeing that Mr John North, whom she knew, noticed her, she went back'.[22]

As the Guardians got within sight of the Albion Inn the crowd began pressing in on their hapless victims. '[T]he Guardians who were known to be favourable to the [New Poor] Law were repeatedly surrounded by the mob, and their lives threatened if they attempted to carry it into effect.' Swain, the chairman, was singled out for particular attention. '[S]everal attempts were made to assault and injure Mr Swaine [sic] ... and had it not been for the interference of Mr Oastler, there is great reason to fear that fatal violence would have been done.' As the Guardians arrived outside the Albion Inn an attempt was made to force Swain past the entrance 'with the intention of taking him to the river which runs a little below'. Oastler and the special constables had great difficulty getting Swain safely into the inn.²³

It is clear that the leaders of the anti-poor law movement in Huddersfield had lost control of the crowd by this stage. In trying to protect Swain, Oastler had himself been subjected to the same rough treatment that was meted out to the pro-poor law Guardians. According to the reporter from the *Halifax Express*, 'the mob not only took no notice of his efforts, but knocked him about as much as the rest'. Later, when Oastler presented himself from an upstairs window in the Albion Inn to calm the crowd, they taunted him and refused to follow his advice. It is worth following Oastler's futile attempt to control the crowd in detail, as it gives the lie to the view that popular opposition to the New Poor Law was an unconscious response, stirred up by 'mob orators' and 'a handful of demagogues'.²⁴ Oastler told the crowd that if there was 'the slightest disturbance', the faith of the people of Huddersfield would be broken with the magistrates. 'I would rather die than be one of the people who would break the peace', he said. 'Are we to come in [to the Board of Guardians' meeting]?', asked the crowd. 'No you can't,' answered Oastler. Hooting and booing followed. Oastler then said he was going to go to the Druids Arms to continue the meeting they had started that morning, and that he hoped they would follow him. This brought loud cries of 'No' from the crowd. 'I know that a great many of you will go with me,' said Oastler. The crowd reponded: 'Nay, we won't.' 'I know you will,' pressed Oastler, and the crowd responded with more loud hooting. 'I can tell you, that if you break the peace, it will forward the [New] poor law very much,' said Oastler. Again he repeated that he was going to the Druids Arms and that he knew 'some of my lads will go with me'. Oastler then left the window and went down into the street, presumably with the intention of leading the crowd away to the Druids Arms. But he only met with cries of 'let him go by his sen', 'Nay, it won't do', 'King, you're betraying us now', and 'This is quere *[sic]* sort of advice.' The crowd were to remain in front of the Albion Inn as long as the resumed Board of Guardians' meeting remained in session.²⁵

Inside the Albion Inn, the shaken Guardians tried to continue their meeting. George Tinker, an outspoken pro-poor law Guardian, immediately moved that none but Guardians be allowed in the room. The motion was put and carried, and the strangers who were present were asked to withdraw. One of them, a Mr Earnshaw, threw open a window and yelled to the crowd below that 'all but the Guardians were ordered out of the room'. The crowd roared their disapproval. The

special constables then escorted Earnshaw and the other strangers out
of the room and the meeting recommenced. As a forceful reminder of
the crowd's presence below, a stone came crashing through one of the
windows. A few minutes later the chief constable came rushing into the
room to warn that the crowd were getting out of hand and requesting
that the Riot Act be read. Mr B.N.R. Battye, the chairman of the
bench, said he thought that they should consider the situation carefully
before rushing to read the Riot Act. '[T]he people were under very
great excitement,' he said, 'and he was very much against provoking,
without occasion, this greatly excited people'. The pro-poor law Vice-
Chairman, Sidney Morehouse, said that 'if protection was not given,
he would take measures to represent Mr Battye's conduct in high
quarters'. Battye then went to one of the windows and addressed the
crowd below. He told them that

> their great friend, Mr Oastler had pledged that they should keep the
> peace...He had been requested to read the Riot Act, and he said he
> would read no Riot Act. (Cheers). He wished them to understand
> him; ... he would read no Riot Act ... until he saw a very different
> disposition pervade that assembly... The magistrates were not
> wishful to have the sabres of the soldiers amongst them, and he
> called upon them to be peaceable and quiet, and shift the blame
> from the shoulders of the magistrates.[26]

A number of pro-poor law Guardians later wrote to the Poor Law
Commission complaining about the magistrate's behaviour. Battye
eventually received a letter from the Home Office, asking why he had
not read the Riot Act that day.[27]

With the crowd shouting abuse outside, the Guardians tried to
settle down and discuss the question of appointing a clerk. Swain, the
Chairman, read a letter from Assistant Commissioner Power, pointing
out that the Registration Act was due to go into force on 1 July 1837
and that a clerk would need to have been appointed by then. Samuel
Midgley, one of the leading anti-poor law Guardians, said that he
thought they could go ahead with the Registration Act without
appointing a clerk. He spoke for most opponents of the New Poor Law
when he said that he was concerned that by appointing a clerk they
would also get the New Poor Law. Eventually, after a good deal of
debate, the motion to appoint a clerk was defeated, eleven votes to
nineteen. Battye said he thought that that ended their meeting and that

they should all go about their business. He got up and left the room. Midgley threw open the window and told the crowd below that the motion had been defeated. This was greeted by loud cheers. In order to be able to put the Registration Act into force the Guardians voted to divide the Union into registration districts. It was decided that the existing assistant overseers would act as registrars for births, deaths and marriages in these districts. Fearful of the crowd's vengeance, the Guardians and newspaper reporters who were present 'mutually pledged' not to reveal how individual Guardians had voted on the motion to appoint a clerk. The meeting was then adjourned for one week.

With the meeting adjourned and the Guardians dispersing, the crowd slowly made their way back to the Druids Inn, where their own meeting was due to recommence. When the reporters arrived they found an unnamed operative addressing the gathering from an upstairs window. The speaker told the crowd that the rich and powerful were

> not better than other people. Those who sat down under the new poor law deserved scouting from society. He argued that the rich had an interest opposed to that of the poor and could not feel for them, and that they, the people, were the great bulk, the source of wealth and of political power.

Another speaker, the radical draper and leading member of the local Anti-Poor Law Committee, Lawrence Pitkethly, told the crowd that the principal object of the New Poor Law 'was to lower their wages'. He said it was 'a very bad omen that they [the Guardians] would not tell them how they voted as to the election of a clerk. They were not so bad as that in the House of Commons'. Towards the end of his speech Pitkethly turned to the reporter from the *Halifax Express*, a Mr Clarkson, and demanded an apology from him for the biased report his newspaper had carried of the Peep Green demonstration. Clarkson refused to apologise or express his opinions to the meeting on the subject. The meeting therefore voted to eject him. Several people 'took him by his coat and dragged him out of the room'. He was taken to the landing on the stairs, lifted over the banisters and dropped. Luckily for Clarkson, he was caught by those below and did not sustain any serious injury. Still his ordeal had not finished. The man who had lifted him over the banister — 'a brute, about 30 years of age and . . . pitted with the small pox' – continued to push and kick him down the stairs. It was only the interference of a couple of bystanders which saved Clarkson from serious injury.[28]

The leaders of the anti-poor law movement in Huddersfield must have had mixed feelings about the day's events. It was true that there had been no real violence and that the crowd's threatening behaviour had so intimidated the pro-poor law Guardians that the motion to appoint a clerk had been easily defeated. But they must have been concerned by the crowd's refusal to acknowledge their leadership at crucial stages during the day. It was a worrying development for the leading opponents of the New Poor Law. The day closed with the crowd celebrating their triumph: there was a bonfire in the market place and effigies of Assistant Commissioner Power and Chairman Swain were consigned to the flames.[29]

The Poor Law Commission responded quickly to their defeat in Huddersfield. Finally recognising the reality of an opposition majority on the Huddersfield Board of Guardians, they decided to resort to legal subterfuge. In a letter to the Guardians the Commission pointed out that the adjournment of their meeting without having appointed a clerk was 'a direct contravention of the law'. This being the case (and here was their sleight of hand) no such illegal act could be binding 'on such portion of the Board as may be willing to act in execution of the law'. What they were proposing was that a minority of the Guardians (provided they constituted the required quorum of three) could push through the appointment of a clerk against a majority vote.[30]

The Poor Law Commission's manoeuvring went completely astray. With troops stationed near the town, the Huddersfield Board of Guardians met a week later on 12 June 1837. Again a crowd collected outside the meeting, but this time there was no disturbance. There was no need for one. The previous week's events were still firmly in the Guardians' minds and the mere presence of the crowd was warning enough. A number of the pro-poor law Guardians did not even turn up for the meeting. The Chairman, Swain, sent a letter saying he declined to have anything further to do with the Board. Others sent their resignations to the Poor Law Commission. When the letter from the Poor Law Commission was read, stating that only three Guardians were required to appoint a clerk, there was uproar. A number of Guardians said that they would rather resign than be mere tools of the Commission. A petition pointing out that the New Poor Law was unsuited to the Huddersfield Union was then read out and adopted by the Board. The meeting closed with the Guardians adjourning their business until three months hence.[31]

Despite the opposition forces' victory, popular pressure on the supporters of the New Poor Law continued. Threats and intimidation appeared to be almost daily events. The burning of effigies, which had been going on since the Peep Green demonstration, was especially popular. Anyone who had publicly offended popular values found themselves the subject of the crowd's displeasure. On Tuesday, 13 June 1837, the day after the Board of Guardians' meeting, effigies of Thomas Day and his wife were cremated in front of their home. Mrs Day had been reported as saying that 'nettles and coarse bread were quite good enough for the labouring classes'. Benjamin Haigh of Paddock, and George Dyson, a butcher of Huddersfield, were also burnt in effigy outside their homes. Their outspoken comments in support of the New Poor Law had given offence.[32]

In an attempt to contain the growing campaign of intimidation, the Huddersfield magistrates issued a handbill warning against effigy burning. They said that the burning of effigies had put 'Individuals in great bodily fear' and they therefore gave notice that in future all persons participating in such activities would 'be taken into custody, and dealt with according to Law, as Rioters and Disturbers of the Public Peace'. Effigy burning in the Huddersfield area petered out following the warning. For the leaders of the anti-poor law movement in Huddersfield it might well have been a blessing in disguise. The campaign of effigy burning had been undertaken on the crowd's own initiative and there had always been the possiblity that the protests could get out of hand and that acts of physical violence could result which would see Huddersfield flooded with troops. On the day after the issuing of the warning by the magistrates, a public meeting was held to express confidence in them. They were thanked for resisting the introduction of troops into the town.[33]

III

The success of the campaign of popular opposition to the 1834 Poor Law in Huddersfield affected other Poor Law Unions as well. In Barnsley the Poor Law Commissioners decided that because of the town's own militant opposition and its proximity to Huddersfield, it had better remain under the Old Poor Law for the time being. A notable feature of the opposition in Barnsley was the strong leadership provided by the Linen Weavers' Union and the militancy of the unemployed. At a meeting of unemployed linen weavers held on

Market Hill, Barnsley, on 26 June 1837, it was claimed that relief from the poor rates was a matter of right, not of privilege. Joseph Crabtree, secretary of the Linen Weavers' Union, advised the crowd that they

> should make a claim in terms which cannot be misunderstood; the collector of the [Parish] poor's rates hesitates not to tell you that unless you pay, he will summon you before the magistrates, and make you pay. Now then with the same authority, do you go to the overseers and tell them that if they do not relieve you, you will summon them before the magistrates...

Crabtree proposed that 'all those who are in a state of destitution, assemble together tomorrow morning, and proceed in a body to the public offices, and remain there till relief be granted them'. The resolution was passed unanimously. The next morning a large crowd of unemployed marched *en masse* to the parish office, demanding relief. The beleaguered overseers, fearful of the consequences should they refuse, immediately complied with the request and began distributing money to the crowd.[34]

The growing militancy and confidence of the opposition forces in the West Riding of Yorkshire began to concern the government as well as the Poor Law Commission. Huddersfield was seen as the key to the unrest. London decided to make another attempt at forcing the Huddersfield Guardians to appoint a clerk. The Poor Law Commission issued orders commanding the Guardians to meet at the 'Albion Hotel' in Huddersfield on 17 July 1837 and to 'proceed to the election of a clerk' without adjourning their meeting. To isolate the Guardians from popular pressure and the threat of violence, the Commissioners arranged with the Home Office for a force of Metropolitan Police to be on hand to protect the Guadians and for a detachment of cavalry to be on stand-by outside town. The Home Office extracted a high price for its assistance. 'It is obvious', wrote Lord John Russell, the Home Secretary, 'that if you shall endeavour to compel unwilling Guardians to assume the administration of relief among an excited community, you run the risk of strengthening prejudice against the [New Poor] law.' Russell therefore recommended to the Commission that 'an interval of twelve months should be allowed to elapse ... before you issue any further Orders for the administration of the Relief of the Poor in the Huddersfield Union'. Assistant Commissioner Power saw Russell's remarks as 'a mistake'. He claimed that Oastler 'will now take advantage of it to proclaim a triumph and I fear mischief will arise in the neighbouring Unions'.[35]

As directed, the Huddersfield Board met on 17 July 1837 to try once again to appoint a clerk. If the display of police and special constables was intended to reassure the Guardians that they could proceed without fear of violence, it badly misfired. The very fact that the police and troops were deemed necessary only emphasised the Guardians' vulnerability and the Poor Law Commission's weakness in the face of popular pressure. It was one thing to appoint a clerk while under police protection, but all of the Guardians knew that the police and troops would soon depart and that they would again be at the mercy of the labouring population. To remind them of their helplessness, some of the pro-poor law Guardians were threatened during the days before the meeting. Sidney Morehouse, the pro-poor law Vice-Chairman, told how he had found 'Sidney Moorhouse *[sic]* shall die today' chalked on the gates of his factory. He also spoke of having seen 'people about his premises at midnight, so cloaked that he could not see who they were'.[36]

Although two nominations were made for the position of clerk, no seconders could be found. Eventually after nearly seven hours of stalemate the meeting broke up. The anti-poor law Guardians argued that as there was no such place as the 'Albion Hotel', only the Albion Inn, the order calling the Board of Guardians meeting was invalid. Their argument eventually carried the day. The Chairman and Vice-Chairman found themselves alone in the room and with no quorum present were forced to abandon the meeting.[37]

As a reminder of what could happen, there were two further disturbances that month involving Huddersfield opponents of the New Poor Law. Although they occurred in connection with the General Election, there is no doubt that popular anger over the New Poor Law contributed to the outbreaks. The first disturbance occurred in Huddersfield where Oastler was a candidate in the election and the New Poor Law a leading issue. In a close contest Oastler went ahead of his Whig opponent William Rooks Crompton Stansfield in the early voting. But gradually his lead was cut and when at last Oastler fell behind on the poll his supporters began stoning those known to be Whig sympathisers. The Metropolitan Police who were on hand could not contain the crowd and eventually the Riot Act had to be read and a detachment of cavalry brought in. Even so it was some time before the town was again calm.[38]

Three days later another disturbance took place in nearby

Wakefield. On nomination day for the election of the county members, Oastler led a march of opponents of the New Poor Law from Huddersfield to Wakefield. They were determined to raise the issue of the New Poor Law during the nomination speeches. The actions of a group of drunken Whig supporters trying to push their way through the crowd appears to have sparked the violence. Within minutes Tories and popular radicals were battling with Whigs. Eventually the fighting petered out and when the troops arrived they found that the nomination speeches had resumed and the town was peaceful again.[39] Nevertheless it served as yet another reminder of what could happen when popular feelings were ignored.

There was one further attempt to appoint a clerk to the Huddersfield Union that year. On 11 September 1837 the meeting of the Board of Guardians voted eight to two against the appointment of Cookson Stephen Floyd. Apparently the pro-poor law Guardians were so dispirited that they could not even muster three votes in favour of the candidate.[40] Once again the threats of the Huddersfield crowd had successfully defeated the combined forces of the government and the Poor Law Commission.

IV

The Poor Law Commission's preoccupation with the events in Huddersfield meant that for most of 1837 the New Poor Law remained a dead letter in the manufacturing districts of the north of England. Against Assistant Commissioner Power's advice, the Poor Law Commission determined that a cautious approach to the introduction of the New Poor Law was warranted. Rather than try to bring all the Poor Law Unions under the New Poor Law, only a few would be given control of poor relief in their respective areas. As a further concession it was decided to leave Boards of Guardians free to grant any form of poor relief that they wished. This was an extraordinary concession. The Poor Law Commission's previous practice had been to issue orders prohibiting a Board of Guardians from giving cash relief in aid of wages, rent relief, and relief to paupers resident outside the Union. The Commission had also previously insisted that at least half of all relief given to widows or able-bodied paupers should be given in kind. Throughout southern England and the Midlands these regulations had been included as a matter of course in the orders issued to Boards of Guardians. Now the Commission had suddenly decided to omit them entirely. Instead it was to be 'left ... to the discretion of the several Boards of Guardians to realize the objects of these rules in such a manner and to such an extent as they might find compatible with the circumstances of the ... Union'. The Commission wrote of 'peculiarities' and the 'depressed state of trade' in the manufacturing districts weighing 'strongly against the issue of the usual regulations'. Popular opposition to the 1834 Poor Law in the north of England was not mentioned.[41]

Towards the end of 1837 the Poor Law Commission chose six Unions in which to introduce their new watered-down regulations. Four were in South Lancashire, Chorlton-upon-Medlock, Leigh, Blackburn and Warrington; and two were in the West Riding, Wakefield and Bradford. Assistant Commissioner Power unveiled the Poor Law Commission's new regulations at a meeting with the Guardians of the Chorlton Union, just south of Manchester, in August 1837. They were favourably received. The *Manchester Times* 'congratulate[d] the public', whom they presumably thought responsible, 'on some important alterations in the system of granting out poor relief which have been adopted by the New Poor Law Commissioners'. The *Manchester Chronicle* was equally enthusiastic:

> It would seem that the Poor-Law Commissioners have at length discovered that the rules and regulations which they have laid down for the government of the various Unions are not at all calculated for the manufacturing districts, and that, to enable them to carry the new law into effect in this neighbourhood, they must submit to such a relaxation of their code as will leave the principle upon which relief is to be administered pretty much as they found it.

The *Chronicle* overstated the case. The watered-down regulations were a major concession, but they did not constitute anything like a return to the Old Poor Law. More especially, they did nothing to reassert the rights of human nature which the Old Poor Law had embodied. The bastardy clause, the new settlement law, and the workhouse were not removed. What the concessions did do was to meet many of the objections which had been made by 'respectable' opponents of the New Poor Law. The local authorities, the Guardians, were to retain some of their freedom for autonomous action and presumably ensure that the cost of poor relief did not escalate for the local ratepayers.[42]

In five of the six Unions in which the Poor Law Commission had chosen to try out the revised regulations they encountered little or no resistance. The Tory-controlled Boards of Guardians in Chorlton, Leigh, Blackburn, Warrington and Wakefield were willing to take over the control of poor relief and the popular opposition in those Unions was muted and disorganised. In the sixth Union, Bradford, the Poor Law Commission miscalculated. Superficially Bradford appeared to be a reasonable choice for a test of the revised regulations. Although it had originally been one of the main centres of opposition, there had been nothing to match the vigorous resistance staged at Huddersfield. Furthermore the Bradford Board of Guardians, despite attempts by opponents to elect anti-poor law candidates, were firmly in favour of introducing the New Poor Law. A leading opponent of the law, the Tory magistrate and worsted manufacturer Matthew Thompson, had undergone a change of heart and now favoured giving the New Poor Law a fair trial. Even the Reverend Mr Bull, who had been such a vociferous opponent of the New Poor Law in its early days, had fallen quiet and virtually withdrawn from the opposition movement. Assistant Commissioner Power was privately assured that Bull would no longer take 'any part in encouraging violence ... before [the Bradford Union] was brought into operation'. Power's information was correct and Bull took no further part in the campaign; but his conclusion was wrong and there was violence.[43]

Trouble came at the meeting of the Bradford Board of Guardians on Monday 30 October 1837. On the Saturday before the meeting a 'bell man' had been employed by Peter Bussey, the radical publican and a leading member of the Bradford Anti-Poor Law Committee, to perambulate the town with the following message:

I am to give Notice to the working class of this town that the Assistant Poor Law Commissioner will be at the court house in this town on Monday next at 10 o'clock in the morning when the People of Bradford are invited to attend at ½ 9 o'clock at the Court house.
By order of Peter Bussey.

Despite torrential rain a large crowd of operatives gathered outside the Courthouse on the Monday morning, demanding admittance. Power and the Guardians forcibly resisted their attempts to enter. The town constables refused to assist them, however, saying that they could not see why the people should not be allowed in. After half an hour of struggle, and fearing the door would give way, the Guardians adjourned to the Swan Hotel where Power was staying. No sooner had they arrived at the hotel than Power was informed that Matthew Thompson favoured holding the Guardians meeting in open session. Power immediately set off to convince Thompson that the meeting should be a closed one. Thompson remained unpersuaded and declared that the existing public excitement would be allayed if the public were admitted to the first Board meeting. He also warned that there could be a disturbance if the Guardians stayed at the Swan. Against Power's vehement opposition Thompson's argument was accepted by the majority of the Guardians.[44]

The Guardians reassembled in the Courthouse that afternoon. The room was crowded to capacity with working men and women. Thompson and the town's reformer MP, Ellis Cunliffe Lister, told the meeting that although they had both originally been opposed to the New Poor Law, they supported it now that they had seen the new regulations which the Poor Law Commission intended to introduce. This brought loud boos and jeers. Lister said he was willing to answer questions from the audience and several were put to him. During one exchange he was asked by an operative: 'Are the Guardians the servants of the ratepayers or of the Commissions?'

Mr Lister.	Of the ratepayers.
Operative.	Then the ratepayers say the poor shall be relieved as they have been hitherto, and ... do not want the New Act.
Mr Lister.	The Guardians have to go by the Act of Parliament.
Operative.	The people of Huddersfield have prevented the introduction of the Poor-Law into their town – why cannot the people of Bradford do the same?
Mr Lister.	I always thought that the people of Bradford had more good sense than the Huddersfield people, they did not kick up a row at the elections as they did at Huddersfield...
Operative.	So then, because the Bradford people are quiet and peaceable they are to be imposed upon, I think that just the reason their wishes should be attended to.[45]

At one stage Peter Bussey's brother unsuccessfully tried to move a motion from the floor adjourning the Guardians' meeting for twelve months. Despite the noise and confusion which reigned throughout the meeting, Power was able to get the Guardians to pass all the resolutions he had proposed.

Assistant Commissioner Power was attacked as he left the building at the close of the meeting. He informed the Poor Law Commission that

> I was violently assaulted by some of the persons assembled outside, and by others who immediately issued from the Court House for that purpose. They were fortunately not provided with any heavy weapons for attack, or I believe, from the disposition shown, I should not have escaped with my life. The first blow I received was upon my head from a tin can [a wool comber's oil can], which was given with great violence, but being without weight made only a slight contusion. Umbrellas, stones and mud were applied very freely, and after receiving many blows I extricated myself with great difficulty from the crowd, and reached the Inn by dint of great exertion, being pursued almost to the door.

Power went on to say that during the attack not a single constable came to his assistance. He said that as his work required him to remain in Bradford for the next two weeks, he needed 'personal protection'; and in view of what had hapened he could place 'no reliance ... on the ordinary civil force'. Furthermore, he was concerned that the Bradford Board of Guardians 'may become intimidated unless a vigorous show of support is made by the Government'. Power therefore recommended 'that application be made forwith ... for a sufficient force of Metropolitan Policemen to be [sent] down here in plain clothes as soon as possible'. He thought that 'six will probably be sufficient' and asked that they 'remain until the next meeting of the [Board of] Guardians and possibly be reinforced before that time'. Power added that the government might also like to consider 'whether in order to assure the Guardians and the public of the determination of the Government to enforce the law, some military force should not be quartered in this place until the Guardians ... have made some considerable advance in carrying [the law] ... into execution'.[46]

The police were slow in arriving. Although Power had requested that they be on hand for the workhouse inspection the following Friday, they did not arrive in time. Nevertheless Power and the Guardian subcommittee decided that as there was 'no appearance of excitement' they could proceed with the inspection anyway. Their entrance into the Bradford workhouse was observed, however, and they had scarcely been inside the building for ten minutes when a large crowd began forcing their way in. According to Power, the workhouse master made no attempt to stop the crowd. Rather than risk injury Power returned to his room at the inn. Meanwhile the Committee proceeded with their examination of the other workhouses in the Union.[47]

In his correspondence with the Poor Law Commission Power now began to reveal second thoughts about his request for police assistance. He said that the use of the police was 'as much as possible to be avoided ... as likely to extend the unpopularity of the new law, and particularly of the ... Guardians'. On the other hand the Guardians were divided over the possible use of the police. 'From some of the Guardians', continued Power, 'I have heard an intimation that they will resign, if any extraordinary aid is called in to enforce the peaceable execution of the law, whilst others have said they will not attend [the Board of Guardians] if such scenes as occurred on Monday are allowed to take place.' Power concluded: 'On the whole I think there is far more risk of a falling off in the Guardians on the employment of a police force from London, than from the dread of future disturbance.' After discussing the matter with Thompson, it was decided that the police should be sent away to Leeds as soon as they arrived. By such means it was hoped that their presence would not become public knowledge and the cause of popular unrest.[48]

On the following morning, 4 November 1837, a sergeant and six policemen arrived from London. Before they had even reported to Thompson the town was alive with stories of their presence. The police were quickly sent off to Leeds to await instructions. Thompson informed Power that he planned to use them as spies. Two or three of the policemen would come back to Bradford in 'coloured cloths *[sic]* ... and endeavour to obtain information as to the feelings of the people'. Meanwhile some of the newspapers carried sensational reports of the police presence in Bradford; they were described as 'being very muscular and ... armed with cutlasses'. The fact that there were only six policemen appears to have caused some ridicule. The Bradford Union clerk, John Reid Wagstaff, informed Power that persons had been heard to say that it would be seen 'whether any Poor Law Comm[issione]r and six London Police can control a countryside'. He warned Power that it might not be safe for him to attend any meetings, 'where you are expected, during the present excitement'. Wagstaff said that the notices explaining the New Poor Law which he had posted on the walls about the town were 'for the most part covered with mud'.[49]

During the following week Sergeant Wray and one or two other policemen returned to Bradford dressed in plain clothes. In the light of what was to happen, Wray's report on the state of popular feelings in Bradford is worth quoting in detail:

> The feeling is generally against the [New Poor Law] measure more than I have ever saw before in any other part of the country and I have been in many. The feeling is particularly against Mr Power they call him the Poor Law Bugger and they say if he comes into this place we will do for him . . .
>
> This matter is the general conversation every evening in all the [Public] Houses we have gone into and the Company make no secret of it [,] not the slightest. They say it is their intention to put a stop to it 'as they say in Cornwall one and all' we have never met with one person who attempted to say it is the law and must by obey'd[.] I should think it dangerous for anyone to appear to be an advocate of it[.] I for one should not like to appear an advocate of it in any company we have been in[;] I should expect to be well thrashed if I did... I should say that no civil force ... would be able to preserve the peace and nothing but a military force to assist the Constables special or otherwise could preserve the peace...

Wray ended by claiming that their true identities had been kept secret from the townspeople. A few days later, placards appeared asking if there was 'a body of the London Police lurking about in Bradford' and whether they were 'acting as spies – changing their dresses – speaking and listening in the public houses – and ever watching the residences of private individuals ...?' So much for secrecy.[50]

On the Sunday evening, before the Board of Guardians were due to hold their next meeting, Power held an informal gathering in the Sun Inn with two of the magistrates and Henry Leah, the chairman of the Board of Guardians. It was decided that because of the excited state of the town the Board of Guardians meeting should be postponed for a week. As soon as they heard of the gathering the popular opponents of the New Poor Law denounced what they saw as yet another example of the Assistant Commissioner holding 'secret meetings', and on a Sunday too! A placard immediately appeared pointedly asking if the Poor Law Commissioners had 'issued a "written order" to allow business to be done on the Lord's Day?' The *Halifax Guardian* commented:

We are informed that a very angry and deep ... feeling prevails at Bradford on the unwise conduct of the Board of Guardians; and we much fear that, if an attempt be made to force the obnoxious regulations of the Somerset House Potentates down the throats of the Poor of Bradford, lamentable consequences will ensue.

The government was also starting to fear 'lamentable consequences'. The Home Secretary ordered the immediate withdrawal of the Metropolitan Police from Bradford and their replacement with a detachment of cavalry. After reading Power's reports, Lord John Russell also advised the Poor Law Commission that it would be best if Power did not return to Bradford at present.[52]

The order to move troops to Bradford was received at Leeds barracks early on Saturday morning, 18 November 1837. Within hours Leeds was alive with rumour that an outbreak had taken place in Bradford. There were stories that 'mills had been set on fire' and 'owners of the mills attacked' for being 'favourable to the new law'.[53] Nothing of the sort had happened, of course. The situation in Bradford was tense, but it also has to be remembered that the Bradford authorities themselves had not requested either police or military assistance. All such requests and decisions had been made by Assistant Commissioner Power and the Home Office in London. The Metropolitan Police had exacerbated tensions in the town; now the presence of troops would strain them to breaking point.

The troop of Hussars arrived in Bradford late on Saturday night. They found the streets crowded with people, watchful, silent and apprehensive. The whole population of Bradford, it seemed, had turned out to observe them. It was an ominous welcome. But for the time being there was no disturbance. The Guardians met at the Courthouse in closed session on Monday morning, 20 November 1837. Extensive preparations had been made to make sure the Guardians were not disturbed. All the doors to the Courthouse were barred and there was a barricade erected across the steps at the front of the building. Twenty special constables had been sworn in to guard the building. The troops were to remain stationed at their billet until needed. When the meeting started there were no more than one to two hundred people in the immediate vicinity of the Courthouse. Towards twelve o'clock, however, the number began to grow dramatically. Within twenty minutes the crowd had grown to five or six thousand. *The Times* was later to claim that the disturbance was sparked off by the appearance of a number of pro-poor law Guardians at the

Courthouse windows. The sight of the Guardians brought a volley of stones from the crowd and some windows were broken.

One of the magistrates set off to call out the troops. Upon their arrival, the troops were greeted with loud yelling and 'every effort was made to frighten the horses and throw the riders'. The troops formed up in front of the Courthouse facing the crowd and for a while there was no hostile activity. The initial shock soon subsided, however, and 'One daring fellow' climbed up the outside of the balcony with the aim of dismantling the barricade which blocked the Courthouse steps. Before the special constables could stop him 'a large body of men ... rushed up the steps and attacked the folding doors [trying] to force a passage to the Guardians'. At the same time, the stoning recommenced. Mr J.G. Paley, one of the magistrates, now began to read the Riot Act, but in the noise and confusion his action went all but unnoticed. 'He then ordered the military to clear the Court House Yard and the steps.' Some of the troops galloped into the crowd to force them away, others dismounted and with swords in hand drove the crowd off the steps and the balcony. The crowd fought back with renewed stoning. There was a plentiful supply of material; fresh stones had recently been laid on the New Leeds Road which ran in front of the Courthouse. Several of the soldiers received quite serious wounds from the stoning. Captain Murray, their commander, was lucky to escape with only minor injuries when a man sneaked up behind him and 'hurled a great stone at his head'.[54]

The tactics of the crowd were to allow the soldiers to ride through their ranks before forming up again behind them and stoning them from the rear. Boys and young men were said to have been the most active combatants. Although the crowd had fallen back from the Courthouse steps they showed little inclination to abandon the field of battle entirely. At about this stage a large group of young men made their way to the rear of the Courthouse and 'began very deliberately and industriously to smash the windows'. It was only after they had succeeded in breaking all the windows that the cavalry were able to disperse them.[55]

At the end of their meeting, the Guardians in the company of the magistrates and special constables left the Courthouse on foot. A large section of the crowd followed and as they neared Brook Street began stoning the Guardians, who were forced to take shelter in Schuster's warehouse. The Guardians were eventually rescued by a party of troops. With the Board meeting over the crowd in front of the Courthouse slowly began to disperse and shortly afterwards the troops themselves were ordered back to their billet. No sooner had the troops left, however, than a large crowd again began to form in front of the Courthouse. In a very deliberate manner they began stoning the building. Within minutes every pane of glass in the building had been broken. The troops were again called out. They were greeted by 'derisive shouts' and more stones from the crowd. Again the crowd showed a marked reluctance to depart the scene and in the growing darkness found it much easier to sneak up and stone the troopers. Up until now the troops had been content to use only the flat side of their sabres to clear away the crowd, but as fatigue increased and their tempers rose they began to employ harsher means. One rioter was hit by a rifle ball. Another shot hit a bystander in the arm. The wound was so serious that it was eventually found necessary to amputate the young man's arm. Apart from a few sabre cuts, there were no other serious injuries. Although the soldiers used firearms and the cutting edge of their sabres the crowd obstinately refused to retire from the scene and continued to skirmish with the troops until late in the evening. It was only after fresh troops had arrived from Leeds and heavy rain had begun to fall that the crowd at last began to move off to their homes.[56]

V

There can be no doubt that the drafting of the troops into Bradford exacerbated an already tense situation. The authorities might have succeeded in ensuring that the Bradford Board of Guardians meeting was not interrupted, but by the use of troops they enabled the opponents of the New Poor Law to win a moral victory. Even the whiggish *Bradford Observer*, which had assiduously supported the New Poor Law, admitted that the presence of the military had 'provoked ... hostile feeling'.

> While we blame the populace for acts of outrage, and the wanton destruction of property, we cannot deny that they had gross provocation, in being menaced with soldiery ... It is an insult to Englishmen to overawe them by the military; and for our part we confess our indignation was not a little roused, when we heard ... that the soldiers were to be brought into the town.

The owner and editor of the paper, William Byles, commented in a separate editorial that as far as he could ascertain neither the magistrates nor the Guardians had asked for troops to be sent. He concluded: 'until we know who advised the Secretary of State to send troops we don't know who is to blame'.[57]

Within days the Bradford Riots had become the talking point of popular radicals and opponents of the New Poor Law throughout the country. Meetings were held in Huddersfield, Halifax, Keighley and other places to consider what response should be made. A cartoon in *Cleaves's London Satirist* aptly summed up popular feeling. It showed Brougham, Russell and Melbourne, dressed in soldiers' uniforms, forcing the New Poor Law down the throat of a working man, tied to a chair. In a thundering letter to the editor of the *Northern Star*, Oastler charged the local authorities with being the real authors of the disturbances in Bradford. He alleged that Assistant Commissioner Power, Union Clerk Wagstaff and Chairman Leah had met and conspired together to postpone the Board of Guardians meeting for an extra week, the aim being 'to give time for Mr *Conspirator* POWER to write to the THREE KINGS for HER Majesty's troops to be sent to BRADFORD, to force the damnable New Poor Law down the throats of the people with bullets and sabres'.[58]

One immediate consequence of the disturbance at Bradford was to leave the supporters of the New Poor Law fearful and worried. Henry Leah, the burly iron founder who was chairman of the Board of Guardians, informed Wagstaff, the Union clerk, that 'in consequence of what had transpired he felt convinced that the [New] Poor Law Act could not be carried into force in this District and therefore he should attend no more meetings of the Guardians to risk his life'. Wagstaff said that one of the factors which had brought Leah to this decision was the report in the neighbourhood 'that if only the Chairman and Clerk were got rid of then there would be an end of the Poor Law Act as no other person would be found to take either of the situations'. Wagstaff added that 'during the week threats of no very mild description have been during the nights written on the steps of my House'. Power immediately wrote to Leah asking him not to resign, but only to 'desist from attending the meetings of the Guardians for the present'.[59] So intimidated in fact were the Guardians that hardly any of them turned up for the next Board meeting on 27 November 1837. Once again crowds gathered in the street outside the Courthouse, but this time there was no disturbance. There was no need for any: the Guardians adjourned their meeting without transacting any business.[60]

On 2 December 1837, the *Northern Star* carried a report of a speech made by Oastler at Huddersfield in which he had intimated that Assistant Commissioner Power, Chairman Leah, Clerk Wagstaff and others were marked men and would do well to be in fear of their lives. Power took the remarks as a personal threat. He immediately wrote to the Poor Law Commission, drawing their attention to the report and claiming that Oastler 'appears plainly to state his wish for my assassination'! Power's brother Henry wrote to the Poor Law Commission saying that his family were extremely apprehensive for Alfred's safety. The Poor Law Commission replied that 'nothing would induce them to expose Mr Power's valuable life to any unnecessary hazard'.[61]

Needless to say the authorities were determined not to take any chances. Following a rumour that Oastler intended to lead 5,000 men from Huddersfield to Bradford on 4 December 1837, the day of the next Board of Guardians meeting, reinforcements were rushed to Bradford. Three hundred infantrymen arrived in Bradford on Saturday night, two hundred special constables were sworn in on Sunday, and the magistrates issued a notice advising the people to stay in their homes on Monday. It was also reported that pickets and parties of cavalry had been posted on the Huddersfield Road to intercept Oastler and his band. When he heard about the rumour, Oastler called it 'a Whig trick'. 'The "Oppressors of the Poor" ', he said, 'were very naturally fearful of the vengeance of the Poor, so they had with the help of *Power*, conjured up all this hobgoblin about myself and 5,000 armed men in order to meet under the protection of Bayonets and Bullets "to remove the landmark of the Poor".'[62]

In an effort to cool the situation in Bradford the opponents of the New Poor Law called a meeting at the Odd Fellows Hall on Wednesday, 13 December 1837. A woolcomber, William Sharman, was called to the chair. Addressing the capacity crowd of over 1,000, he said they should all come forward on this issue because 'their rights were invaded ... the rights of the poor'. 'That the poor had, and always had, an inherent right in the soil prior to all rights, he believed everyone would acknowledge.' Sharman said they should pursue every 'constitutional means' to defend these rights and obtain a repeal of the New Poor Law. He condemned the late disturbances and said it could not advance their cause. Other speakers, who included Peter Bussey and Richard Oastler, expressed similar views. Bussey even went so far as to say he was 'no fighting man'. In its report of the meeting the *Bradford Observer* was fulsome in its praise, congratulating the opponents of the New Poor Law on the 'rational way' in which they had expressed their opposition. 'How much better it is', they commented, 'to meet like free citizens, and condemn by speeches, resolutions, and petitions, than to assemble in a tumultuous manner, and by force resist the administration of the law.'[63] The problem was that the government in London only appeared to take any notice of their protests when they were accompanied by a forceful resistance of the law.

Notes

1. *Manchester and Salford Advertiser*, 28 January 1837.
2. *Halifax Express*, 1 February 1837; *Leeds Intelligencer*, 4 February 1837; *Halifax Guardian*, 30 January 1837.
3. *Manchester and Salford Advertiser*, 4 February 1837, and *The Times*, 11 February 1837.
4. *Leeds Times*, 11 February 1837.
5. Ibid., 14 January 1837; see also D. Fraser, 'Poor Law Politics in Leeds, 1833-1855', *Thoresby Society Publications*, vol.LIII, part 1, no.116 (1970), pp.23-9, 36. Although voting in Board of Guardians' elections was by ballot (the first time such a system had been used in Britain for elections to public office) it caused surprisingly few problems. It was corrupt or illegal practices on the part of the overseers, who acted as returning officers, which created most difficulties. Surprisingly the advocates of electoral reform in Britain never appear to have used the success of the ballot in poor-law elections to support their case for its introduction in parliamentary elections. The ballot was not used for the election of members of parliament until 1872.
6. For the reaction of some respectable ratepayers in the Huddersfield Union see: France to PLC, 10 March 1837; PLC to France, 14 March 1837; Bamforth to PLC, 10 March 1837, PRO, MH 12/15063.
7. *The Times*, 28 March 1837; *Manchester and Salford Advertiser*, 25 March 1837; *Blackburn Gazette*, 29 March 1837; *Manchester Chronicle*, 25 March 1837.
8. *The Times*, 30 March 1837, and *Manchester and Salford Advertiser*, 1 April 1837.
9. J. Foster, *Class Struggle and the Industrial Revolution* (Methuen, London, 1977), pp.47-72.
10. *Manchester Chronicle*, 11 March 1837; *The Times*, 3 April 1837.
11. *Blackburn Gazette*, 10 May 1837; Power to PLC, 21 September 1839, PRO, HO 73/55; Ormerod to PLC, 31 March 1837, PRO, MH 12/6272.
12. Unions where this appears to have been attempted include Ashton-under-Lyne, Bolton, Bury and Salford. *Manchester and Salford Advertiser*, 27 May 1837 and 12 May 1838; A. Sault, 'R.J. Richardson, A Working Class Radical', unpublished B.Ed. thesis, Elizabeth Gaskell College of Education, Manchester, 1976, pp.68-72.
13. Swain to PLC, 18 February 1837, PRO, MH 12/15063.
14. *Leeds Intelligencer*, 8 April 1837; *The Times*, 11 April 1837; Huddersfield Board of Guardian Minutes, 3 April 1837, KMBA.
15. Huddersfield Board of Guardians Minutes, 5 June 1837, KMBA, puts the population of the Union at 87,421; *Leeds Times*, 8 July 1837.
16. PLC to Huddersfield Guardians, 3 June 1837, PRO, MH 12/15063.
17. *The Times*, 9 June 1837, and *Halifax Express*, 10 June 1837.
18. E.P. Thompson, *The Making of the English Working Class* (Penguin, Harmondsworth, 1975), pp.612-17, and M.I. Thomis, *The Luddites* (Schocken, New York, 1972), pp.105-6.

19. *Halifax Express*, 10 June 1837.
20. Tinker to PLC, 8 June 1837, PRO, MH 12/15063; *Leeds Times*, 10 June 1837.
21. *Leeds Times*, 10 June 1837.
22. *Halifax Express*, 10 June 1837.
23. Tinker to PLC, 8 June 1837, PRO, MH 12/15063; *Leeds Times*, 10 June 1837.
24. M. Hovell, *The Chartist Movement* (first published 1918; Manchester University Press, Manchester, 1970), p.86, and M. Rose, 'Anti-Poor Law Movement in the North of England', *Northern History*, vol.I (1966), p.81.
25. *Halifax Express*, 10 June 1837; *Leeds Times*, 10 June 1837. 'Sen' is a regional slang term meaning self or own.
26. *Halifax Express*, 10 June 1837.
27. Tinker to PLC, 8 June 1837, Morehouse to PLC, 14 June 1837, PRO, MH 12/15063; Phillips to Battye, 13 June 1837, PRO, HO 41/13.
28. *Halifax Express*, 10 June 1837. Different spellings of Pitkethly's name exist, but this is how he spelt his own name.
29. *Leeds Intelligencer*, 10 June 1837, and *Leeds Mercury*, 10 June 1837.
30. PLC to Huddersfield Guardians, 10 June 1837, PRO, MH 12/15063.
31. Lockwood to PLC, 8 June 1837, and Shaw to PLC, 28 June 1837, PRO, MH 12/15063; *Leeds Intelligencer*, 17 June 1837.
32. *Leeds Intelligencer*, 17 June 1837.
33. 'Caution against Burning Effigies', 27 June 1837 (handbill), Brougham Papers, UCL 17802; *Leeds Times*, 1 July 1837.
34. Power to PLC, 19 August 1837, PRO, MH 12/14674; *Leeds Times*, 1 July 1837.
35. Russell to PLC, 26 June 1837, PRO, HO 73/52; Power to PLC, 15 July 1837, PRO, MH 12/15063.
36. *The Times*, 28 July 1837; *Halifax Guardian*, 18 July 1837.
37. Power to PLC, 18 July 1837, PRO, MH 12/15063; *Halifax Express*, 22 July 1837; Huddersfield Board of Guardians Minutes, 17 July 1837, KMBA.
38. *Halifax Express*, 5 August 1837; *Leeds Intelligencer*, 29 July 1837; *The Times*, 31 July 1837.
39. *Halifax Express*, 1 August 1837; *the Times*, 2,4,10,11 August 1837; R. Oasatler, *A Letter to Viscount Morpeth* (n.p., London, 1837), pp.7-8. See also C. Driver, *Tory Radical* (Oxford University Press, New York, 1946), pp.362-4.
40. Swain to PLC, 12 September 1837, PRO, MH 12/15063.
41. 'Fourth Annual Report of the PLC', *PP*, 1838, vol.XXVIII, pp.29-30.
42. *Manchester Times*, 26 August 1837; *Manchester Chronicle*, 26 August 1837.
43. *Bradford Observer*, 2 November 1837; Power to PLC, 5 December 1837, PRO, MH 12/5673.
44. Power to PLC, 30 October 1837, PRO, MH 12/14720.
45. *Bradford Observer*, 2 November 1837.
46. Power to PLC, 30 October 1837, PRO, MH 12/14720.
47. Power to PLC, 5 November 1837, PRO, MH 12/14720.
48. Ibid.
49. Thompson to Power, 4 November 1837, PRO, MH 12/14720; *Leeds Times*, 11 November 1837; Wagstaff to Power, 10 November 1837, PRO, MH 12/14720.
50. Report of Sergeant Wray, quoted in Thompson to Power, 8 November 1837, PRO, HO 73/52; *Halifax Guardian*, 21 November 1837.
51. *Halifax Guardian*, 21 November 1837.
52. Phillips to Lewis, 16 November 1837, PRO, MH 12/14720.
53. *The Times*, 23 November 1837.

54. Paley and Thompson to Harewood, 20 November 1837, Harewood Papers, Box 1, LCA; *The Times*, 24 November 1837; *Bradford Observer*, 23 November 1837; *Halifax Express*, 25 November 1837.

55. *The Times*, 24 November 1837; *Halifax Express*, 25 November 1837.

56. *Bradford Observer*, 23 November 1837; *Halifax Express*, 25 November 1837.

57. *Bradford Observer*, 23 November 1837.

58. *The Times*, 1 December 1837; *Cleave's London Satirist*, 2 December 1837; *Northern Star*, 2 December 1837.

59. Wagstaff to Power, 25 November 1837, and Power to PLC, 28 November 1837, PRO, MH 12/14720.

60. *Leeds Times*, 2 December 1837.

61. Power to PLC, 2 December 1837, H. Power to PLC, 30 November 1837, and PLC to H. Power, 2 December 1837, PRO, MH 12/14720.

62. *Bradford Observer*, 7 December 1837; *The Times*, 8 December 1837; Oastler to Editor, quoted in *Leeds Intelligencer*, 9 December 1837.

63. *Bradford Observer*, 14 December 1837. See also: *The Times*, 16 & 17 December 1837; *Northern Star*, 16 December 1837; *Halifax Express*, 16 December 1837.

8 THE HUDDERSFIELD UNION

After the disturbances at Bradford the government adopted a much tougher policy towards opponents of the 1834 Poor Law. Ordinarily military intervention was followed by a gradual withdrawal of troops from the disturbed area, but late in 1837 the military presence in the north of England was actually increased, with troops being dispatched to key centres in South Lancashire and the West Riding of Yorkshire. This was followed in early 1838 by attempts to bring the dissident Poor Law Unions into line. There was little that popular opponents of the New Poor Law could do when faced with a determined government which had a strong military force at its disposal. The co-ordinated campaign of demonstrations and petitions had failed to bring about any change in government policy, and all attempts at intimidation and violence had been met by gradually worsening confrontation. The Boards of Guardians were seen as the key to the struggle, and increasingly they were attracting the attention of both the authorities and the opposition forces. The opposition's campaign of boycotting had achieved some remarkable successes in the South Lancashire region, but it was the Huddersfield Poor Law Union, controlled by the anti-poor law Guardians, which was seen by both sides as crucial. Early in 1838 the proponents of the New Poor Law began planning their moves to defeat the opposition forces in Huddersfield.

I

The Huddersfield Board of Guardians had repeatedly refused to appoint a Union clerk. Late in September 1837 Assistant Commissioner Power and William Rookes Crompton Stansfield, the recently elected Whig MP for Huddersfield, met to discuss the problem. They decided that the only way to ensure that there were three Guardians on the Board willing to appoint a clerk was to create new magistrates, who in their capacity as *ex-officio* Guardians could force the appointment of a clerk. Power immediately wrote to the Poor Law Commission to suggest the creation of four new magistrates: Thomas and Joseph Starkey, John Sutcliffe and William Brook. All were large manufacturers and all prominent Whigs. Stansfield also wrote to the Poor Law Commission supporting the appointment of the four. He emphasised that new magistrates were needed to balance the anti-poor law Tory magistrates on the bench and on the Board of Guardians. The Poor Law Commission immediately forwarded the request to the Home Office.[1] The government decided that the sudden appointment of four new magistrates would be seen as an obvious attempt to stack the Board. Instead it was agreed only to appoint two new magistrates for the time being, the others to be appointed later.

The next meeting of the Huddersfield Board of Guardians was due to be held on 29 January 1838. The government and Poor Law Commission stepped up their pressure on the Guardians. As early as November 1837 Power was writing to Joseph Armitage, the chairman of the Bench at Huddersfield, to tell him that Swain and some other Guardians were willing to proceed with the appointment of a clerk if they could get the 'support, presence, and backing' of an *ex-officio* Guardian.[2] The Poor Law Commission also refined the legal sleight of hand they had attempted to use the previous June. Then, a minority of three had been empowered to appoint a clerk against the will of a majority. Now, the Commission advised, a minority of three could choose to ignore completely the existence of an opposition majority. Swain, the chairman, was instructed that

it is competent to you and ... it is your duty ... to refuse to put to the meeting any motion or amendment the obvious effect of which would be to defeat or postpone the election of a clerk; and secondly that, whatever course may be adopted by the majority of the guardians in contravention of the law, ... the candidate having the majority of votes will be duly elected although less than three may have voted for him, provided that three guardians at least have taken part in the election.[3]

The government's preparations did not go unanswered by the Huddersfield opposition. Pressure was put on the landlord of the Albion Inn, Mr Balderson, in which the Guardians normally held their meeting, to withdraw the use of his premises. Balderson succumbed to the threatened loss of business and informed the Guardians' Chairman that the Albion Inn was no longer available to them for meetings. The Guardians then applied to the landlord at the Rose and Crown and the directors of the Philosophical Hall, but both refused to make their premises available. Eventually, the Guardians were forced to hold their meetings in the Courthouse.[4]

To reinforce their opposition the popular opponents of the New Poor Law again decided to hold a demonstration on the same day as the Guardians' meeting. The government's response was immediate: two troops of the 15th Hussars were drafted into the town. The opposition replied with a blistering handbill. They asked why there should be so much 'Terror' over a demonstration, if the 'majority' of the people in Huddersfield was so 'decidedly in favour' of the New Poor Law as they had repeatedly been told they were by the *Leeds Mercury* and other Whig newspapers. The answer was clear: 'The Scoundrels know that they have told a base lie, and so does BAINES, else he would not have published it.' The opposition emphasised that they had no intention of causing violence and promised the 'villains' that they 'need not be alarmed'. After all they had 'their own Magistrates, the Police, and the soldiers to keep the Ghosts off'. In conclusion the handbill reminded the supporters of the New Poor Law that any 'CLERK, appointed by a MINORITY, will be NO CLERK AT ALL'.[5]

The day's events passed off peaceably. The two troops of cavalry arranged themselves in front of the Courthouse and despite the pouring sleet and snow a crowd of several thousand gathered to demonstrate in the Market Place. Oastler, Pitkethly and the Reverend Wood, of the Methodist New Connexion, addressed the crowd from the back of a wagon. Oastler told the crowd that they should 'preserve the strictest order'. The meeting then adjourned until the afternoon when the Guardians' decision on the appointment of a clerk would be known.

Inside the Guardians' meeting proceedings were less subdued. The anti-poor law stalwart, Samuel Midgley, immediately moved that the meeting be adjourned until 2 April. After a good deal of discussion and one joking suggestion that perhaps April Fools' Day might be a better date, Swain ruled the motion out of order because it set the law 'at nought'. Backed up by the two new magistrates and the instructions he had received from the Poor Law Commission, Swain indicated that he would let nothing stand in the way of the appointment of a clerk. The anti-poor law Guardians protested vehemently against the notion that a minority of the Board might appoint a clerk 'when the voice of the people (their constituents) were opposed to the introduction of the [New Poor] Law into that district'. Swain was unmoved and despite the opposition majority's loud and repeated objections, two candidates, Cookson Stephen Floyd and William Hesp, were proposed and seconded for the post. Swain then called for a vote to decide between them. Sixteen abstained, eight voted for Floyd and six for Hesp, whereupon Swain declared Floyd to have been elected.[6] After a year of delay, and against the opposition of a majority of elected Guardians, the Poor Law Commission had finally succeeded in getting a clerk appointed to the Huddersfield Union. It was a victory of sorts, but not one in which they could take any real comfort. To obtain their victory the supposed defenders of law and order had themselves set the law at nought.

News of the appointment angered the crowd in the market place. They were particularly outraged at the high-handed behaviour of the chairman and two new Whig magistrates. Pitkethly told the crowd that the Board meeting had been 'a mere farce' and that 'the appointment was altogether illegal'. Oastler agreed that 'not one act or deed of Mr Floyd would ever be worth a straw'. He said that if a 'minority was to rule, there was an end of society'. They, the protesters, had not broken the law; 'it [was] ... the commissioners and their tools'. Oastler said he was against the 'rebellion of the three traitor kings', and when they objected to the appointment of a clerk it was the opponents of the New Poor Law who upheld the law, not its supporters. He ended with a call for the crowd to remain calm in the face of Whig provocation, for nothing would suit the Whigs better than to have a 'row'. He was thankful to see the 'fine brave British soldiers' in Huddersfield and proposed three cheers for them. The crowd duly cheered. Later Oastler returned to the hustings to propose that the meeting raise a subscription to give the soldiers 'marching money'. A total of £3 was raised and presented to the troops. That night two of the public houses in the town put on a supper for the military at which they were able to drink the health of the 'Lads' of Huddersfield.[7]

The only violence of the day was a fist fight. The bellicose Huddersfield Postmaster, William Moore, an ardent Whig who had apparently over-indulged while celebrating the appointment of the clerk, challenged one of the opponents of the New Poor Law, a draper by the name of Fawcett, to fisticuffs. The two of them were seen later that evening, stripped to the waist, fighting in the snow outside one of the public houses.[8]

The appointment of a clerk failed to dissipate the opposition, who counterattacked at the next Guardians' meeting on 15 February 1838. The meeting had been called to divide the Union into districts and to appoint to each registrars for births, deaths and marriages. Lawrence Pitkethly led a large contingent of popular radicals into the Courthouse where the Guardians were due to meet. Although ordered out by George Tinker, one of the more outspoken of the pro-poor law Guardians, they insisted on their right to remain. At one stage Tinker was so abusive that one of the constables threatened to take him into custody if he did not moderate his tone. This caused consternation among the pro-poor law Guardians. Swain, the chairman, again repeated that all who were not Guardians should leave the room. He was asked on what authority he issued such an order. He replied that he did so on the authority of the Poor Law Commission. Pitkethly then told him they did not recognise that authority, but that if he put it to a vote and the majority of Guardians voted in favour of them leaving they would do so. In what was a confused and at times boisterous meeting, Swain was eventually forced to adjourn proceedings for a week rather than see the meeting completely taken over by the opposition Guardians.[9]

As a result of the rowdy meeting eleven of the pro-poor law Guardians immediately complained to the Poor Law Commission. They informed the Commissioners that

it will be impossible to carry the New Poor Law and Registration acts into effect without adequate protection being afforded to those Guardians who may in future attend the Meetings with an intention to forward the objects of the legislature and the Poor Law Commissioners . . . Without protection we beg to observe that we shall not feel justified in endangering our lives.

George Tinker, writing privately to the Poor Law Commission, attacked the 'ignorance' of the anti-poor law Guardians. He said that James Parkin, the Linthwaite Guardian, had assisted opponents of the New Poor Law in 'forcing their way into the room', and had 'encouraged the Blackguards ... to open violence, saying that if no one else did *he* would drag both chairman and Clerk into the street'. Tinker went on to suggest that, as 'the most active measures' were being taken 'to swamp the next Board with characters of this description', the Poor Law Commission might consider 'the propriety of raising the qualification of Guardians' to exclude such men from future Boards.[10]

Tinker was not the only Guardian disgusted by the behaviour of the Board. A number of anti-poor law Guardians were also losing their taste for the Board meetings. At the resumed meeting of the Huddersfield Board, on 22 February 1838, only twenty-two Guardians showed up. This time a force of special constables was on hand to keep out members of the public. For the first time the the the pro-poor law faction actually had a majority of Guardians in attendance, and against the vociferous opposition of a hard core of nine opposition Guardians they set about dividing the Union into districts and appointing assistant registrars. It was a clear reminder to the popular opponents of the New Poor Law that effective opposition was only as strong as the resolve of their elected Guardians. The only consolation for the crowd gathered outside the Courthouse was that they were able to give the Postmaster, William Moore, 'a rolling in the mud' when he foolishly appeared outside the building.[11]

II

New elections for Guardians were due to be held in the last week of March 1838. Once again popular opponents of the New Poor Law faced a difficult choice with regard to tactics. Oldham's total boycott had proved the only sure way of blocking the Poor Law Commission. As the experience in the Huddersfield Union had shown, even when a majority of anti-poor law Guardians were on the Board, London could evade them. But the difficulty of staging an effective boycott remained, and it had probably become harder to achieve in those Unions where Boards of Guardians had already been elected. At a meeting of delegates from the South Lancashire Anti-Poor Law Association held in Manchester on 5 February 1838, election tactics were discussed. Oastler and Pitkethly, who attended as observers from the West Riding Committee, proposed the selection of only the most strenuous opponents of the New Poor Law as Guardians. The Reverend J.R. Stephens and others opposed the idea. The majority of the South Lancashire delegates made it clear that they favoured a total boycott and the West Riding proposal was eventually withdrawn.[12]

Oldham again showed the way. In a surprisingly quiet campaign, the popular radicals in the Oldham Union easily maintained a total boycott of the elections. Similarly the opponents in the Todmorden Union were able to maintain the boycott in the cotton townships of Todmorden and Langfield. But in other South Lancashire Unions the task was much more difficult. In the Bury Union, a group of Tory candidates, who declared themselves not only opposed to the New Poor Law but also to illegal resistance, were nominated and refused to withdraw, breaking the back of the attempted boycott there. Only in the Ashton-under-Lyne Union did the opponents of the New Poor Law manage to throw out the existing Board of Guardians. Spurred on by Stephens, the local popular radicals staged a vigorous campaign of intimidation and succeeded in forcing all the candidates to withdraw their nominations before the election.[13] Elsewhere there were only sporadic boycotts and, like the year before, unless the boycott was total its impact was slight.

But outside the Lancashire and Cheshire border region, it was Huddersfield rather than Oldham which provided the model for resistance. Results were mixed. The opposition forces strengthened their hold in the Rochdale Union and had a spectacular victory in the Dewsbury Union, just north-east of Huddersfield. Elsewhere they were not so successful. In the Keighley Union the opposition forces suffered a severe setback, losing control of the Board of Guardians to a pro-poor law faction. In several Unions the anti-poor law forces fell to underhand tactics. In the Preston Union, Joseph Livesey, the cheese merchant and temperance reformer, led an apparently successful campaign of opposition only to see the votes of the anti-poor law Guardians disallowed by the presiding Tory magistrates in the election for the Union chairman.[14]

The most spectacular case of duplicity and underhand dealing, however, was in the Huddersfield Union. The Huddersfield Anti-Poor Law Committee had planned their election campaign with meticulous care. They met with delegates from local township committees, staged demonstrations, mobilised support, issued detailed instructions and acted as a clearing house throughout the campaign. When the results were first announced at the close of polling it appeared that they had won a clear victory. The *Northern Star* reported that again there would be a majority of anti-poor law Guardians on the Huddersfield Board.[15] What the opponents of the New Poor Law did not know was that the government had just appointed another two Whig magistrates and that the pro-poor law forces were already manoeuvring to get the election of some of the anti-poor law Guardians set aside.

Details of the chicanery and vote rigging are obscure. It appears, however, that in a number of townships the election result altered between the final count of poll and the declaration of results. In the Huddersfield township, for instance, four anti-poor law candidates and one pro-poor law candidate appeared to have been ahead at the close of counting, but the figures announced by the overseers the next morning showed only three anti-poor law candidates to have been elected. The opponents of the New Poor Law later charged the Huddersfield overseer with irregularities. They claimed that he added extra property votes to the pro-poor law candidates 'without having any voting papers'; that he had had 'a roll of votes, as thick as his arm ... that ... had not been summed up'; and 'that many votes were added from a book, containing entries of last year's claims', again without voting papers.[16] For their part, the pro-poor law candidates were adamant that the anti-poor law faction had acted illegally. They claimed that informal votes had been counted and that 'a great number of voting papers were improperly obtained at the Workhouse, filled up, and delivered to the overseers, by whom they were received and allowed as proper votes'. Stansfield, the town's Whig MP, was warned by a Mr Willan that the 'Oastlerites' were writing to the Poor Law Commission 'by this post' to get the election of one of the pro-poor law candidates 'set aside' and one of their own candidates put in his place. Willan said that a '[r]epresentation from *our* friends will be sent up tomorrow' and 'in the meantime' it was 'of the greatest consequence' to get the Commissioners to delay their answer until it arrived. He added that if 'they will direct a scrutiny I have no doubt we could turn out every anti-poor law Guardian to put the *friends* of the Law in'. Assistant Commissioner Power thought otherwise. He advised the Commission that the appointment of the two additional magistrates meant the pro-poor law faction now had a majority of two on the Huddersfield Board. He felt a scrutiny of votes would only upset matters, and therefore suggested that the Commission let the matter rest 'lest any proceedings of an extra-ordinary nature should have the effect of impeding in anyway the apparently favourable progress of affairs'.[17] Power's reticence about a scrutiny of votes was to be borne out by future events. It was the pro-poor law candidates who would suffer from an examination of the election result, not the opposition candidates.

The opposition, needless to say, was not prepared to let the matter rest. A few days before the new Board of Guardians was due to meet, James Brooke, one of the candidates in the election, complained to the Commission about irregularities in the election of the Guardians for Honley. He told how on the day of voting 'the Churchwardens, [and] Overseers of the poor together with three ratepayers for each candidate met at the Poor house to cast up the votes'. This count resulted in the two anti-poor law candidates, Henry Littlewood and himself, being elected as Guardians. In Brooke's words, however, 'the party of the loseing [sic] candidate not being satisfied demand[ed] a scrutiny'. The overseers acquiesced and the next day the ratebooks for 'near 20 years Back were sought up and every vote was struck off who in times of sickness poverty, and distress had been forgiven their rates'. Although

Brooke complained bitterly about this action, the overseers ignored him. The result of the scrutiny and recount was the election of the Tory candidate, Thomas Brooke (they were not related), in his place. James Brooke said that the 'proceedings have caused great unpleasantness in the township'. The fact that the Poor Law Commission's own legal advisors agreed that the overseers had indeed acted illegally, must have put the Commission in a dilemma. They solved it by simply ignoring James Brooke's letter. Brooke again wrote to the Poor Law Commission a few weeks later, vainly seeking a reply to his earlier correspondence.[18]

One letter which the Poor Law Commission did not ignore was from the former Guardian, George Tinker. He informed the Commission that the recently elected Guardian for Hepworth, 'who had done all he could to prevent the new [Poor] Law being brought into operation', was having 'wages for his attendance at the Board' paid by the ratepayers, 'in addition to his salary as overseer'. Tinker asked whether a person 'being ... a *salaried overseer ... can act as Guardian?'* In a tantalising postscript, Tinker added that he was 'credibly informed that several of the opposition Guardians .. have had *wages paid out of the poor rates'*. The Commission could hardly contain their excitement at the news. They immediately moved to discover whether this could provide grounds for dismissing the opposition Guardians. Unfortunately for the Commission, Tinker's information was wrong. The Guardian in question was an overseer, not a paid assistant overseer. The Commission's legal advice was that overseers could be Guardians, but that assistant overseers, who received payment, could not.[19]

The first meeting of the new Board of Guardians was held at the Huddersfield Courthouse on 9 April 1838. Despite the protests of the anti-poor law Guardians, one of the newly appointed magistrates, John Sutcliffe, assumed the chair and, together with the other three Whig magistrates, began examining the Guardians' credentials. In a blatantly partisan fashion all objections to the election of anti-poor law Guardians were upheld and those to pro-poor law Guardians dismissed. The result was to leave the Board equally divided between the pro and anti factions. However, by claiming and using a casting vote (although he had already voted once) the *pro tempore* chairman was able to secure the election of two pro-poor law Guardians, William Brook and Sidney Morehouse, to the positions of chairman and vice-chairman respectively.[20] The *Leeds Times* was scathing in its comments about the behaviour of the new Whig magistrates. 'If this be liberty', they said, 'save us from it.' The opposition Guardians immediately sent off a memorial to the Poor Law Commission protesting about the 'illegal' behaviour of the new *ex-officio* Guardians. Their protests were to no avail. Denied a hearing by the Poor Law Commission, the opposition Guardians resolved to pursue the matter in the courts.[21]

III

The first case involving election irregularities was heard before the Huddersfield magistrates on Tuesday, 17 April 1838. James Brooke brought a summons against the Honley overseers for non-performance of their duties. Although a minor charge, both sides were in no doubt as to the importance of the case. Feargus O'Connor came from Leeds to act for the claimant and the Union clerk, Floyd, appeared for the defence. In a long and powerful opening speech, O'Connor reminded the court that in Huddersfield, 'above all other places, it was absolutely necessary that the law should be administered with impartiality; especially with respect to the appointment of officers'. He said that one of the reasons why the law had been brought into contempt in Huddersfield 'was the imperious and anomalous manner in which partisan *ex-officio* Guardians were appointed'. It was therefore the 'duty of the Bench' to reassert their impartiality and give judgement against the defendants, whom he would prove 'had violated both the Act of Parliament and the Commissioners instructions'. O'Connor said he would show that one of the overseers, Thomas Brooke, was himself a candidate for the office of Guardian and had 'on his own behalf, violated the instructions'. After hearing the evidence of how the two anti-poor law candidates, Henry Littlewood and James Brooke, were at the top of the poll at the end of counting and how an illegal scrutiny had then taken place which put Thomas Brooke ahead of James Brooke, the court retired to consider its verdict.

An hour and a half later the magistrates returned to say that the Bench was divided and could not give judgement. Four of the magistrates had heard the whole case; the other two, the newly appointed Joseph Starkey and William Brook, had arrived late and heard very little of it. O'Connor immediately applied for fresh Bench summonses. He said that 'the people should be taught to respect the source of justice'; and from what he had seen, with two of the magistrates deciding as judges cases they had not even heard, he felt himself 'bound to direct his client to appeal to the Queen's Bench' if fresh summonses were not issued. The court agreed to O'Connor's request for fresh summonses and the hearing was set for the following week.[22]

O'Connor again presented the case for the claimant. This time, however, he adopted a more disarming approach. He admitted to the court that at the previous trial he had been unfamiliar with both the character of the defendants and the legal questions at issue. Since then he had familiarised himself with both. He said he was particularly struck by what he had learnt about the character of the defendant, Thomas Brooke. Here was a man of 'almost unbounded wealth', whose 'acts of beneficence, charity, and kindness, hold pace with his treasure'. O'Connor called him 'kind to the poor, affable to the rich, courteous to all, and beloved by all'. He said he regretted 'that so much worth should have been sacrificed and made a tool of by an artful and designing faction'.

O'Connor's was a polished and skilful performance. He played up to the feelings of the Tory magistrates on the Bench and made the Whigs appear to be at fault for leading poor Thomas Brooke astray. With his commanding courtroom presence and lively repartee, O'Connor again and again made Floyd, the defending counsel, look clumsy. While cross-examining the churchwarden, Mr Wilkinson, O'Connor asked if at the close of poll he had declared James Brooke to be duly elected. Floyd objected, saying a 'declaration' might not have been heard and that he should ask if he had announced it instead. Turning to Floyd, O'Connor asked, 'is there any difference'? Certainly, answered Floyd. 'Then you will have the kindness to state the difference', said O'Connor. 'I am sure that ... the Court, the public and myself will feel duly obliged.' But before Floyd could answer, O'Connor spoke: 'Perhaps he whistled the declaration ... [D]id you Mr Wilkinson'? Even the magistrates found it hard to suppress a laugh.

In his summing up, O'Connor said that if the New Poor Law was 'to be carried and executed, and administered contrary to law, popular power and popular discontent ... [would] strangle the monster'. Addressing the Bench he concluded: 'Gentlemen, your lives, your liberties, and your properties depend upon the due execution of the law, and if you cease to respect the rights of the poor, they will cease to respect your privileges and your estates.' It was a powerful and clear statement of why the defendants had to be found guilty. After deliberating for an hour, the Bench returned to find the defendants, Thomas Brooke, John Mellor and James Lancaster, overseers of Honley, guilty of having 'violated the law and the instructions'. They were fined five shillings each plus costs.[23]

Buoyed up by the success of the court case, the opposition Guardians determined to have a showdown with the pro-poor law forces at the next Board of Guardians' meeting. They would show that the election was not only 'a farce, but a real Whig juggle, from the beginning to the end'. Accompanied by Feargus O'Connor, the Reverend J.R. Stephens, Lawrence Pitkethly and their supporters, the opposition Guardians descended on the Board of Guardians' meeting in force. With the chairman away, it fell on the vice-chairman, Sidney Morehouse, to try to maintain order. As he started reading out the names of the Guardians, the opposition Guardians and their supporters 'began calling out in loud voices, "we have no Chairman [,] we have no Clerk" '. James Brooke, fresh from his victory in the courts, although still not officially a Guardian, then proposed that William Cooke, an anti-poor law Guardian for Huddersfield, should take the chair. The motion was overwhelmingly carried. Morehouse was quickly tipped out of his chair and the seat given to Cooke. In the noise and confusion which followed, Morehouse tried to clear the room of all persons whom he claimed were not Guardians. When this failed he moved for an adjournment. No sooner had Morehouse called for a vote on the motion than the cry went up to 'seize that book' – the Board of Guardians' minute book. Stephen Dickenson, James Brooke and James Parkin led the attempt to 'wrestle it away from Morehouse' and 'the respectable guardians'. Morehouse later informed the Poor Law Commission that he 'resisted as well as I was able, but they would have succeeded had not Mr F. O'Connor interfered and prevented them taking it from me'. The *Northern Star* reported that O'Connor fought his way into 'the thickest part of the fight' to rescue the minute book 'from the hands of the belligerents'. How much of this was a case of the reporter feeding his employer's ego is unclear. What is clear is that the fighting was restricted to the Guardians themselves. Floyd said that O'Connor appeared to exercise 'some influence' over the working-class onlookers and that it was his intervention which stopped them from taking part in the struggle.[24] One senses that perhaps the working men and women in the room were astounded at this display of ruffianism by their 'betters'; and it was this, more than anything else, which held them back.

As Morehouse was returning to his desk with the minute book, Joseph Hirst jumped up and snatched it away from him. Amidst great confusion Morehouse 'declared the meeting adjourned'. O'Connor then 'came forward and obtained order saying "he was astonished at their [the anti-poor law Guardians] conduct, it was disgraceful [and] they ought to permit Mr Morehouse to take the Chair again and go into [the] business" '. He said 'he attended there professionally on their behalf but he was ashamed of them'. Morehouse and the other pro-poor law Guardians then withdrew, leaving the opposition Guardians with the room to themselves. Although Floyd, the Union clerk, also tried to leave, he was not allowed to go. The anti-poor law Guardians ordered him to stay and 'do our work'. Floyd said the reason they wanted him to remain was 'to clothe their proceedings ... with something like legality'. The ploy did not succeed. The Poor Law Commission was later to recommend to the Home Office that a number of the anti-poor law Guardians be charged with assault. At the York Assizes in April 1839 two Huddersfield Guardians were tried and found guilty of assault and bound over on their own recognisances.[25]

With the anti-poor law Guardian William Cooke in the chair, the rump of the Huddersfield Board of Guardians now set about conducting its own business. A subcommittee was set up to examine the disputed election returns. An earlier order making the *Leeds Mercury* and *Halifax Express* the official advertising media for the Board was rescinded, and the *Leeds Intelligencer, Leeds Times* and *Northern Star* were substituted for them. And finally the Guardians adopted Joseph Hirst's proposed petition to the House of Lords. The petition, which called for a halt to the imposition of the New Poor Law in the Huddersfield Union, offered no 'popular' critique of the New Poor Law; it reflected the views and concerns of the lower-middle-class Guardians, the shopkeepers, tradesmen and small farmers, who adopted it. They claimed that the able-bodied unemployed did not impose on the poor rate, and only desired 'to have task work at such wages as may afford food in return for a full day's work'. But there was no mention of 'rights' and again and again the petition returned to the theme that the old system of relief was much cheaper and much more convenient than the new.[26]

Meanwhile legal proceedings over alleged irregularities in the Board of Guardians' elections continued before the Huddersfield Bench. In May 1838 a Mr Bower, a former overseer from Melthan, appeared in court charged with acting contrary to the instructions of the Poor Law Commission. The court was told that on the day of the poll Bower had delivered fifty to sixty votes to the scrutineers, all filled out for the pro-poor law candidate James Redfearn. Bower admitted he had been given the voting papers by Redfearn. The court was then told how

Redfearn had earlier called on the printer who produced the voting papers and placed an order for sixty additional voting papers to be given to him. The implication was clear: Redfearn had forged the votes on his own behalf. As Redfearn had only been elected with a majority of fifteen votes over the anti-poor law candidate, John Taylor, it threw the whole election into doubt. However, the validity of the election result was outside the court's jurisdiction and it was not Redfearn but the luckless Bower who was standing trial. The court found him guilty and fined him 40s plus costs. It was an embarassed Union clerk who informed the Poor Law Commission that one of the pro-poor law Guardians had been 'involved in some questionable actions in the election'.[27] Eventually the Commission was forced to declare Redfearn's election invalid.

The succession of court cases, the convicted overseers and the clear evidence that a number of pro-poor law Guardians had engaged in questionable practices continued to preoccupy the Huddersfield Board of Guardians. As early as 22 April 1838, Morehouse had complained to the Poor Law Commission that the disputed election results had made it 'impossible to proceed with ... business'. When the Board of Guardians met again on 21 May 1838 it was the disputed elections which once more dominated proceedings. With 'a posse of constables' guarding the doors and the public excluded, the pro- and anti-poor law factions screamed accusations at one another. The only positive result of the meeting was to adjourn the Board for another two months. When the Board next met in July the issue of the disputed elections had still not been resolved. The Board's subcommittee testified to 'great irregularities', but could offer no decisions about which candidates were entitled to serve as Guardians because the overseers had repeatedly denied them access to the voting papers. The continual bickering meant that the Huddersfield Board of Guardians was virtually moribund. On a number of occasions not a single Guardian bothered to turn up for the Board meeting. The Board's minute book contains only a forlorn note by the clerk: 'no Guardian attended at the time fixed ... and that one hour elapsed without any such attendance'.[28]

As the year drew to a close, there was yet another reminder of the depth of anti-poor law feeling in Huddersfield, when a visit by the pro-poor law lecturer, James Acland, sparked violence. Acland, a former editor of the Whiggish *North Cheshire Reformer*, had decided early in 1838 that a comfortable living could be made by giving public lectures on the 1834 Poor Law. He would hire a theatre or hall in a town, advertise the lecture extensively and charge one shilling admission. The lecture itself usually consisted of little more than a resumé of the history of the poor laws, with special emphasis on the evils of the Old and the merits of the New Poor Law. Henry Ashworth, a leading Bolton cotton manufacturer, told his friend Edwin Chadwick that the lectures 'answer very well for spreading a more correct feeling on this abused subject'. Throughout early 1838 Acland gave lectures in a number of South Lancashire towns. One of the ways in which he helped ensure a full attendance was to invite a leading opponent of the New Poor Law to debate the subject with him. In Oldham he debated with Fielden, at Bolton with Myerscough and in Preston with Livesey. The meetings were often very lively with loud booing and hooting, but apart from one incident at Bolton, where a stone was thrown at Acland, there was no real violence.[29] There was no violence, that is, until Acland decided to give a lecture in Huddersfield.

Acland arrived in Huddersfield early in November 1838. He immediately issued his usual challenge to the leading opponents of the New Poor Law to debate the subject. They agreed to the debate, but only if the profits of the meeting were donated to charity. This Acland refused to do. On the night of the lecture a large crowd, many carrying torch-lights, gathered outside the Philosophical Hall to boo and jeer at those who went inside. As soon as Acland began his lecture the mood of the crowd became more belligerent. One fellow tried to set alight the door of the hall with his torch. Pitkethly and the other leaders who were present attempted to calm the crowd, but failed. The gas lamp outside the hall was put out and stones were thrown at the door and windows. At some stage the crowd got hold of a builder's trestle and using it as a battering ram, forced in the panels of the door. Then they rushed into the hall, yelling revenge on those inside. Most of the audience fled through the back door, while Acland and the leading Whigs sought shelter in the coal cellar. It was perhaps lucky for Acland that the crowd believed he had already escaped because 'it was the declared intention of the women to have converted him to a very different *animal* by the application of tar and feathers'. After throwing a few stools through windows to celebrate the rout, the crowd quietly made their way home. Only one person, Benjamin Cragg, the fellow who had tried to set light to the door, was charged over the incident. He was fined one shilling, plus costs.[30]

IV

In March 1839 a majority of pro-poor law candidates were returned at the Huddersfield Board of Guardians' election. Floyd, the Union clerk, was ecstatic: 'we have achieved ... a glorious victory [,] instead of a Board composed of ignorance [,] impudence and vulgarity as before, we have now a well constituted Board of respectable [,] intelligent and honest men'.[31] How the opposition forces could have allowed this to happen after two years of bitter struggle is not clear. Certainly 1838-9 was the period of greatest Chartist activity in Huddersfield and it could have been that the allure of achieving power nationally deflected the attention of popular radicals from resisting the New Poor Law at home. Whatever the reason, the labouring population of Huddersfield township momentarily stood aside from the struggle. It was the inhabitants of the outlying rural villages who now took up the fight.

On Monday, 1 April 1838 the newly appointed relieving officer from the Kirkheaton district was mobbed. He had gone to the local poorhouse to make arrangements to take over the administration of poor relief from the parish authorities. As soon as it became known he had arrived a large crowd gathered, forced him out of the building and chased him across the open countryside. The relieving officer's bag, containing books and papers, was seized by the crowd and thrown in the river. At Dalton, where he attempted to take refuge in a cottage, the officer was again turned out and chased. And at Bowling Green Inn he had the misfortune to run into a gathering of 'shepherdesses ... holding their anniversary'. The women told the publican that either the officer was turned out, or they would take their custom elsewhere. Looking bruised and bloody, and with his clothes torn off his back, the luckless relieving officer finally made it back to the relative safety of Huddersfield, shocking the Board of Guardians as he burst in on their meeting. Over the following days threats were made that a similar fate awaited the Lepton relieving officer should he be foolish enough to venture into that district.[32]

Disturbing as the crowd violence was, it was the opposition of the old parish officials which caused the pro-poor law Huddersfield Guardians the most difficulty. At Lepton the overseers refused to hand over what monies they held, or 'give up their books'. When summonses were taken out against the overseers they were able to tell the magistrates that the town's secretary now had the books. After a further delay and the issuing of yet more summonses the town's secretary duly appeared before the bench. Again, the ratebooks were not in evidence. The secretary told the magistrates that 'he had orders from the ratepayers . . . not to give them up'. Their patience at an end, the magistrates informed the Lepton officials that if the books were not brought to the Courthouse within three hours they would 'inflict the full penalty and also enter a distress warrant upon their premises'. The overseers and town's secretary immediately set off to fetch the books. No sooner had they collected them, however, than a large crowd gathered and forcibly removed them from the officials. Eventually cooler heads prevailed and the churchwarden was able to convince those who had seized the books to tell him where they had hidden them. He found them buried in a wood and handed them over to the magistrates.[33]

In August 1839 the Huddersfield Board of Guardians attempted to take over the operation of all existing workhouses in the Union. The five larger workhouses at Huddersfield, Almondbury, Kirkheaton, Golar and Honley would continue operating (albeit under the Board's control) and the other smaller workhouses would be closed down. The Guardians had no sooner made their intentions known than they encountered opposition from the old parish authorities. At Huddersfield a special subcommittee of the Vestry was established to investigate what rights the town's ratepayers had over the workhouse and the land (ownership of which was vested in the Vicar and church wardens), and whether they could resist the Union's takover. The Vestry eventually resolved that the terms of their tenure precluded the workhouse and land being used for 'any other purpose than that to which they had hitherto been applied, namely the accommodation of the paupers belonging to the Township of Huddersfield'. Unsure of their legal position the Huddersfield Board of Guardians asked the Poor Law Commission to take the matter in hand. What advice the Commission had for the Guardians is not clear, but three months later the Huddersfield Vestry issued a directive that no valuation was to be allowed of the furniture and fittings in the workhouse. The *Halifax Guardian* explained that had a valuer been appointed 'it would have been a tacit allowance of the Guardians' authority over the house, furniture, paupers, and all'. The Vestry also took steps to ensure the loyalty of Burton, the workhouse master, increasing his salary to £70 per annum and giving clear instructions not to admit any agent of the Guardians or Commissioners.[34]

Frustrated in their efforts to assume authority over the Huddersfield workhouse, the Board of Guardians decided on a policy of confrontation. In November 1839 they issued dismissal notices to the

workhouse master and his wife. When the Guardians advertised the
positions, however, Burton responded with his own advertisement
warning potential applicants that the ratepayers were the sole
proprietors of the workhouse and that the Guardians had no authority
to dismiss him. In an effort to resolve the impasse Assistant
Commissioner Power wrote to the Commission to ask them to dismiss
the workhouse master. He explained that Burton was a 'strenuous
opponent' of the New Poor Law and had even taken in the *Northern
Star* for the benefit of workhouse inmates. Despite his obvious
unsuitability the Commission found itself unable to dismiss summarily
the workhouse master. The Commission's law officer explained to
Power that the only grounds for dismissal were a failure to obey
workhouse regulations and orders, and as none had been issued Burton
could not yet have disobeyed any. His advice to Power was to issue the
orders and then dismiss the workhouse master when he failed to
comply. In late December 1839 the Guardians turned up at the
workhouse gates to demand possession of the building from Burton. He
refused, and was summoned before the magistrates, convicted and
fined £5. The magistrates told Burton that the fine would be suspended
if he immediately resigned his position. This Burton did, but instead of
delivering possession of the workhouse to the Guardians he handed it
over to Mr W. Poppleton, one of the overseers. The Huddersfield
Guardians had been frustrated yet again.[35]

With an overseer in possession of the workhouse, the Guardians'
legal claim to occupancy was not nearly as clear cut as it had been with
the workhouse master. Poppleton was summoned before the
magistrates, but this time the case was dismissed. The Vestry passed a
vote of thanks to Poppleton for his 'manly' actions. He was told to
'keep possession of the workhouse' for as long as he could do so legally.
A subscription was raised to indemnify him against any pecuniary loss.
Finally in June 1840 some of the overseers rebelled against the
intolerable position they had been placed in by the Vestry and allowed
the Guardians to gain possession of the workhouse. The guilty parties
were soundly condemned by the Vestry:

> Mr John Dent deserves the unqualified censure of the inhabitants of
> this Township for his treacherous conduct towards Mr Poppleton
> his fellow Overseer, towards the ratepayers, and towards the poor of
> Huddersfield.

Two other overseers who had assisted Dent were reminded that next year they had to deliver to the new overseers 'all property placed in their hands or ... belonging to the ratepayers and the Poor of this township'.[36]

Despite their apparent victory, the Huddersfield Board of Guardians' troubles were not at an end. They even managed to make difficulties for themselves in their appointment of a new master and mistress for the Huddersfield workhouse. In March 1837 Elizabeth Ainsworth, the then matron of the Huddersfield workhouse, had been accused of misconduct and forced to resign her position. Despite this, the Huddersfield Guardians now announced their intention to appoint Mrs Ainsworth and her nephew Robert Holbert Taylor as workhouse matron and master respectively. Opponents of the New Poor Law in Huddersfield responded by formally charging Mrs Ainsworth over her previous misconduct. She was accused of having misappropriated township property for the benefit of herself and fiends, and with having behaved with cruelty towards the inmates. Assistant Commissioner Power, who investigated the charges for the Poor Law Commission, found little evidence to support the charge of misappropriation but a good deal of evidence to support the charge of cruelty. He admitted that 'there is some truth in the imputations regarding the treatment of the paupers', but concluded that 'Mrs Ainsworth has been a most valuable servant to the township, and . . . would prove equally so to the Guardians if her appointment should be confirmed.' Although clearly unhappy about the Board of Guardians' choice, the Commission informed them that they would sanction the appointment of Mrs Ainsworth if the Guardians still wanted her. Ainsworth and Taylor were confirmed in their appointments at the Huddersfield Board of Guardians' meeting on 31 January 1840.[37] Mrs Ainsworth's presence as matron of the workhouse would serve as a public reminder of the harshness of the New Poor Law in Huddersfield for years to come.

Notes

1. Power to Lefevre, 15 October 1837; Stansfield to Lefevre, 24 October 1837; Lefevre to Maule, 16 October 1837, PRO, HO 73/52.

2. Power to Armitage, 22 November 1837, PRO, MH 12/15063.

3. Power to Swain, 23 November 1837, PRO, MH 12/15064.

4. Swain to PLC, 10 January 1838; Wrigley to PLC, 20 January 1838, PRO, MH 12/15064; *Leeds Times*, 13 January 1838; *Northern Star*, 3 February 1838.

5. 'Appointment of Clerk to the Huddersfield Poor Law Union' (handbill), 19 January 1838, PRO, HO 40/40, f.137.

6. *The Times*, 1 February 1838.

7. *Northern Star*, 3 February 1838.
8. Ibid.
9. *Leeds Times*, 17 February 1838; *Northern Star*, 17 February 1838.
10. Huddersfield Board of Guardians Minutes, 15 February 1838, KMBA; Tinker to PLC, 17 February 1838, PRO, MH 12/15064.
11. Huddersfield Board of Guardians Minutes, 24 February 1838, KMBA; *Northern Star*, 24 February 1838.
12. *Northern Star*, 10 February 1838; *The Times*, 7 February 1838; *Leeds Times*, 10 February 1838. N.C. Edsall, *The anti-Poor Law Movement* (Manchester University Press, Manchester, 1971), p.140, wrongly claims that a total boycott was the semi-official policy of opponents of the New Poor Law for the Guardian elections in 1838, and that it was supported by the *Northern Star*, the South Lancashire Anti-Poor Law Association and 'almost all the popular anti-Poor Law Leaders'. Before the elections the *Northern Star* was inconsistent in its advice, see 24 February and 31 March 1838, and most of the anti-Poor Law leaders in the West Riding viewed a boycott as impractical and favoured the elections of anti-poor law Guardians.
13. *Northern Star*, 31 March and 14 April 1838; *Manchester and Salford Advertiser*, 7 April 1838.
14. *Northern Star*, 14 April 1838; *Preston Chronicle*, 14 April 1838.
15. *Northern Star*, 24 February and 3 March 1838, *Leeds Times*, 10 & 17 March 1838; *Northern Star*, 31 March 1838.
16. Whitworth to Shepherd, 31 March 1838, Whitworth to PLC, 2 April 1838, PRO, MH 12/15064; *Northern Star*, 14 April 1838.
17. Memorial to PLC, 2 April 1838; Willan to Stansfield, 2 April 1838; Power to PLC, 6 April 1838, PRO, MH 12/15064.
18. Brooke to PLC, 7 & 18 April 1838, PRO, MH 12/15064.
19. Tinker to PLC, 31 March 1838; Memo on Eligibility of Assistant Overseers to the Office of Guardians, 4 April 1838, PRO, MH 12/15064.
20. *Northern Star*, 14 April 1838, and Huddersfield Board of Guardians Minutes, 9 April 1838, KMBA.
21. *Leeds Times*, 14 April 1838; *Northern Star*, 12 May 1838.
22. *Northern Star*, 21 April 1838.
23. Ibid., 28 April 1838.
24. Ibid., Morehouse to PLC, 9 May 1838; Floyd to PLC, 9 May 1838, PRO, MH 12/15064; *Northern Star*, 12 May 1838.
25. Morehouse to PLC, 9 May 1838; Floyd to PLC, 9 May 1838, PLC to Russell, 22 May 1838, PRO, MH 12/15064; Floyd to PLC, 4 April 1839, PRO, MH 12/15065.
26. *Northern Star*, 12 May 1838; Petition of Huddersfield Guardians, 17 May 1838; PRO, MH 12/15064.
27. *Northern Star*, 19 May 1838; Laycock to PLC, 25 May 1838, PRO, MH 12/15064.
28. Morehouse to PLC, 27 April 1838, PRO, MH 12/15064; *Leeds Times*, 26 May 1838; *Northern Star*, 28 July 1838; Huddersfield Board of Guardians Minutes, 7, 21 & 28 September 1838, KMBA.
29. Ashworth to Chadwick, 21 April 1838, Chadwick Papers, UCL 203; *Manchester and Salford Advertiser*, 28 April 1838; *Bolton Chronicle*, 14 May 1838; *Northern Star*, 26 May 1838.
30. *Halifax Express*, 17 November 1838; *Halifax Guardian*, 17 November 1838; Moore to Maberly, 12 November 1838, PRO, HO 40/40, f.239; *Bradford Observer*, 11 July 1839.
31. Mott to PLC, 1 April, 1839, PRO, MH 12/15065.
32. *Halifax Guardian*, 6 April 1839; Mott to PLC, 3 April, 1839, PRO, MH 12/15065.

33. Mott to PLC, 3 April 1839; Walker to PLC, 1 May 1839; Mott to Lefevre, 3 May 1839, PRO, MH 12/15065.

34. Huddersfield Vestry Meeting Minutes, 1 August, 19 August and 14 November 1839, KMBA; Floyd to PLC, 19 August 1839, PRO, MH 12/15065; *Halifax Guardian*, 16 November 1839.

35. Power to PLC, 22 November 1839; Lumby to Power, 29 November 1839; Power to PLC, 11 January 1840, PRO, MH 12/15065.

36. Ibid.; Huddersfield Vestry Meeting Minutes, 16 January, 20 February and 18 June 1840, KMBA.

37. Ibid., 30 March 1837; Power to PLC, 20 January 1840; PLC to Floyd, 23 January 1840; Power to PLC, 4 February 1840, PRO, MH 12/15065.

9 DRAWING THE MONSTER'S FANGS

The opposition movement never succeeded in forcing the government to repeal the 1834 Poor Law. They did, however, succeed in lessening its impact. As early as 1838 some of the leaders of the anti-poor law movement in the north of England were claiming partial victory. The Poor Law Commission's introduction of watered-down regulations in a number of northern Unions provided the proof to support such a claim. The radical surgeon and leader of the opposition campaign in Bury, Matthew Fletcher, told a meeting in July 1838 that the campaign of popular agitation

> was not only efficient in keeping out this accursed law, but had also had the effect of obliging them [the Poor Law Commissioners] to treat their poor victims of the South with much more kindness, and with much less of devilish cruelty, than they would otherwise have been. This was a gratifying fact; for even if they should fail in their efforts to repeal this accursed measure, (which they certainly would until they obtained Universal Suffrage,) it was something to know that [they] ... had the power of drawing some of the fangs of this monster.[1]

Fletcher overstated the opposition's success, but he was correct to see the Poor Law Commission's revised regulations as a significant backdown. The process of lessening the impact of the New Poor Law was a gradual one; it depended not on an overwhelming opposition victory in a single Union, but on the accumulation of many small victories in many different Unions.

I

Throughout 1838 the Poor Law Commission continued with its policy of piecemeal implementation of the New Poor Law. In the first half of the year the watered-down regulations were put into force in Stockport, Haslingden, Wigan, Burnley, Preston and Keighley. The Poor Law Commission's apparent success in introducing the revised regulations into these Unions encouraged it to believe that the regulations would be equally effective in some of the more doubtful Unions like Dewsbury and Todmorden.

During the 1838 Board of Guardians' elections the opposition forces had staged a spectacular victory in Dewsbury. At the first meeting of the new Board, it was resolved that as the previous Guardians had put the Registration Act into force, it was 'neither expedient nor necessary to proceed any further with the New Poor Law'. The Guardians also decided that all Board meetings would in future be open to the public. Late in March 1838 one of the Dewsbury Guardians, Joseph Ellison, gave evidence before the House of Commons Select Committee investigating the New Poor Law. He declared the New Poor Law unsuited to the manufacturing districts of the north of England. Assistant Commissioner Power, eager to counter this argument, asked the magistrate and pro-poor law chairman of the Dewsbury Board of Guardians, Joshua Ingham, to give evidence in favour of the New Poor Law. Ingham told the Select Committee that the New Poor Law would 'work beneficially' in Dewsbury and that there was 'nothing in the character of the population of Dewsbury, or the circumstances of that Union, which should make it inexpedient to introduce'. A week later Power recommended that the Poor Law Commission direct the Dewsbury Guardians to assume responsibility for administering poor relief. This the Commission did, giving as one of their reasons the recent statement made before the Select Committee 'by a member of the Board of Guardians, showing ... the advantages which would arise from introducing ... the Poor Law Amendment Act into the Union'.[2]

The first Board of Guardians' meeting held under the authority of this order took place in the Church School Room, Dewsbury, on 23 July 1838. Apart from the Guardians, a large number of spectators also attended. Power had earlier conferred with Ingham, outlining what needed to be done at this meeting. He also instructed the clerk in the manner in which the Board was to proceed. No sooner had the order from the Poor Law Commission been read to the Guardians than an angry discussion began over Ingham's evidence to the Select Committee. A Mr Penny moved that as the Board was ignorant of the evidence they should postpone the business of the meeting until they had had a chance to consider it in detail. Ingham refused to put the motion. Penny then observed that if the chairman refused to put the motion he would move another 'more obnoxious', and moved 'that the meeting do adjourn for one whole week'. Again Ingham refused to put the motion, saying he would refuse to put any motion which he considered contrary to either the law or the instructions. In a repetition of what had happened earlier in the year at Huddersfield, Ingham declared 'that if two Guardians voted with him he would carry out the law in spite of all they could do'. Assistant Commissioner Power in his report commented: 'Mr Ingham who is nowise disposed to shrink from his duty through dread of the unpopularity to which he has been exposed, firmly insisted upon the Guardians proceeding in execution of the Order, and finally the resolutions were passed'.[3]

On the following Wednesday the opposition Guardians in Dewsbury held a public meeting in the market place to get advice from the ratepayers on how they should respond to this new development whereby a minority could overrule the majority at the Board of Guardians' meetings. The large crowd asked the opposition Guardians to continue to attend the Board meetings and to use whatever means were available to prevent the adoption of the New Poor Law. The crowd then stayed to hear Feargus O'Connor and Richard Oastler address them on the subject of the New Poor Law. O'Connor told the crowd that 'until the people were enabled to protect themselves by means of Universal Suffrage, all attempts to repeal isolated Acts of Parliament would be worse than useless'. The liveliest speech of the evening, however, came from Oastler. In a sarcastic and biting speech Oastler attacked Ingham's character. He had the audience howling with laughter when he alluded to how Ingham had 'acquired' his 'property', or rather his wife's property; and how he now wanted 'to deprive his neighbours of *all* the rights they possess', a clear reference to rumours of Ingham's lecherous behaviour. It was a savage speech from a bitter man. Two months earlier Oastler had learnt he was to be dismissed from his post as Steward of Fixby Hall. He was in no doubt that the cause of his dismissal was his active opposition to the New Poor Law. Oastler's employer, Squire Thornhill, was a friend of the chairman of the Poor Law Commission, Thomas Frankland Lewis, and they 'had correspondence together' about him. Small wonder Oastler was angry: at forty-nine years of age and after eighteen contented years at Fixby Hall, his world was collapsing around him. '[T]hey had as much right', Oastler told the crowd, 'to go to Mr Ingham's house and burn it down and destroy his property as he had to put the new law in to force'. The crowd cheered enthusiastically.[4]

In the days immediately following the public meeting the Chief Constable of Dewsbury, William Pearson, reported 'much violent language and general threats . . . among the lower orders'. The threats were 'directed particularly against the putting in force of the New Poor Law and against Mr Ingham'. As if to give substance to Pearson's claim, Ingham received a threatening letter later in the week. Although the letter was obviously written by someone who was barely literate (significantly they had no trouble spelling the word bastile), there is a certain wit about the notion of a 'Pill' (a ball, or a bullet) being the remedy for Ingham's malaise:

> Mr Ingham your sines is gone Be fore you your damnethan is just you have rolead [ruled?] the conteree the fatherless and the widdow pray your det [dead] and your the first Man for the Bastile ... you have a broter [brother] A Layere [Lawyer] and you whant to get your self and im rased up in the sight of government by puting your self for wred [forward] But there is a Pill ... for you that will hele [heal?] you all your mallad of self Congate [congratulation?] the medesen [medicine] is sereten [certain?] for thee.[5]

A foretaste of this medicine came at the next Board of Guardians' meeting on Monday 6 August 1838. A large crowd of onlookers were in attendance. The audience was well behaved, however, until 'Mr Ingham ... declined to put several propositions to the meeting.' The audience now 'became very violent & ... made a rush towards that part of the Room where the Guardians were assembled and several stones were thrown'. With the crowd jostling the magistrates, and crying 'pull them out, pull them out', Ingham read the Riot Act and adjourned the meeting. Thomas Rylah, an attorney who was present at the Board meeting, reported some people near him crying, 'Mr Ingham ought to be murdered, he ought to have his soul pulled out.' No sooner had Ingham got outside the meeting room than a woman in the crowd 'made a personal attack on [him] ... and endeavoured to drag him to the ground'. Ingham lost a shoe in the scuffle and was pelted with mud and stones. Eventually Ingham was able to find shelter in the Derwents Hotel. The Chief Constable approached several of the 'respectable inhabitants' to see if they would 'come forward and protect the authorities', but 'they declined to interfere'. Apparently most of them were shopkeepers and they feared the loss of custom that might result should they be seen to be supporting the New Poor Law.[6]

Troops arrived from Leeds during the afternoon. Crowds still filled the streets but there were no clashes with the military. The crowd appeared more intent on celebrating their victory in the public houses than on engaging in any further disturbances. As Greenwood and

Ingham lived some distance out of town a military escort was provided to accompany them home. A crowd followed them for about a mile, occasionally pelting them with stones and mud. Over the next few nights a military guard was placed on the homes of both Greenwood and Ingham.[7]

II

Both sides sought to blame the other for the violence. The opposition Guardians sent a memorial to the Poor Law Commission complaining about the chairman's dictatorial conduct and suggesting it had provoked the outburst. Ingham was equally sure that 'agitators' were to blame. 'I am only astonished', he said, 'that I am alive — How I escaped is only known to a merciful providence.' He believed the disturbance had been caused by the anti-poor law meeting on 1 August 1838 and asked that the government instruct the Attorney General to prosecute those who had spoken at the meeting. He warned that unless the government protected him and 'proceed[ed] against these agitators with Vigour and without delay', he would resign his magistracy and return to private life.[8]

The Home Secretary, Lord John Russell, gave the *ex-officio* Guardians at Dewsbury no comfort in his reply. Russell pledged that 'should' the Board continue to meet 'they shall have all the support the Government can give them'. The *ex-officio* Guardians interpreted this as meaning that it was up to themselves whether the New Poor Law was put into force or not. The Union Clerk, William Carr, informed the Poor Law Commission that the Guardians did not want to be placed in such a position: 'unless the Government determined to enforce the law and support that determination with all its power the Magistrates have no wish to attempt to enforce the law in defiance of an infuriated mob'. Carr went on to say that it was clear that the New Poor Law could not be enforced without the presence of strong military and civil forces and it would be madness for the magistrates to proceed without the protection of such forces. He added that 'if the Law is not enforced at the present time it never can be at any future time; and the Government must therefore determine whether the Law shall be now enforced or abandoned altogether'. He warned that if the 'mob ... consider that they have obtained a Victory' it would 'not be long before they follow the [same] example when any Law which is not quite palatable to them is attempted to be enforced; and thus there will be an end to obedience to the Laws altogether'. The Poor Law Commission immediately replied that they were sending down twenty Metropolitan Policemen for the next Guardians' meeting.[9]

That same week Power was removed from his responsibilities as the Assistant Commissioner for Dewsbury. It is unclear what prompted the Poor Law Commission to take this action. Possibly it was simply a belated recognition of the fact that Power was unable to cope with his large and troublesome area. Charles Mott, a former workhouse contractor, who had been one of the first Assistant Commissioners appointed under the New Poor Law, was drafted north to assist Power. The Poor Law Commission also seems to have finally realised that Power had actually provoked trouble in a number of Unions. Details are obscure, but it appears that Power had struck up a close personal friendship with hardliners like Ingham and not only supported them, but actively encouraged their belligerent and arrogant behaviour.[10] Charles Mott was not nearly as haughty as Power and on occasion was even prepared to allow opponents of the New Poor Law to state their case, something Power would never have allowed.

The difference in approach between the two Assistant Commissioners can be seen in Mott's assessment of the difficulties the Poor Law Commission faced in Dewsbury. Mott said he was 'induced to believe that not a small part of the dissatisfaction was created by the Chairman Mr Ingham'. He continued:

> I am not insensible to the value of the support which a Gentleman of Mr Ingham's firm character can give to an Union ... but it must not be forgotten that an unbending and overstrained zeal ... is calculated to increase the excitement and dissatisfaction which prevails...
>
> I have reason to believe also that much of the dissatisfaction which has existed at the Huddersfield Board of Guardians has arisen from a dislike of too prominent an interference on the part of the Ex-Officio Guardians... I was ... told by Mr Hirst the leader of the opponents that much of the bad feeling amongst their Guardians had been created by the Chairman and other Ex-Officio Guardians from their unbending manner of treating their suggestions.

One cannot imagine Power talking to Hirst, much less passing his views on to the Poor Law Commission. But on one issue both Power and Mott agreed: the unimportance of popular opposition when compared with respectable opposition. As far as the prospects of the Dewsbury Union were concerned, Mott said that he regretted that a majority of the Guardians are opposed to the introduction of the New Poor Law. The rabble are easily quieted but where a majority of a Board of Guardians is opposed to the Commissioners, the whole proceedings are attended with extreme difficulty.[11]

The government and local authorities were determined to make sure the 'rabble' stayed quiet in Dewsbury. One hundred 'Lancers', 76 riflemen, 600 special constables and 20 Metropolitan Policemen were on hand for the next meeting of the Dewsbury Board of Guardians. The majority of Guardians chose to stay away, rather than participate in a meeting where their views were ignored. This time the public was excluded from the meeting.[12] Despite the display of force the populace was not cowed.

The meeting itself passed off peacefully, but outside in the street the crowd became more and more restive. Once again it was the women who took a leading part in the disturbance. One of them, an old woman named Mary Hey, was spotted by a Metropolitan Policeman, Edward Tarleton. He saw her 'standing in a ring with a large mob of people round her [,] she cried out [,] "no Bastile" [and] if you stand by me we'll give it them this Evening'. Tarleton cautioned Hey and told her the law would be put in force. '[U]pon this she went away followed by a great mob of people.' Later Tarleton 'saw her in the market place with a mob around her'. As the Guardians emerged from the meeting room, flanked on each side by London police, the crowd of 5,000 to 7,000 broke into loud jeering. The women were particularly vocal. There were cries of, 'Go it lads!', 'Down with em!', 'Damn that Ingham!', 'Murder them London ‒‒‒‒‒‒‒‒'. The Guardians and their escort were heading for the Royal Hotel, and as they arrived on the bank of the river they were hit by a hail of stones thrown from the other side. For the moment the police were powerless to stop them. It was only after the Guardians had reached the safety of the hotel and the Riot Act had been read that the police were able to set off after the culprits. The Inspector of Police, George Martin, spotted Mary Hey again, this time outside the Royal Hotel:

I saw this woman with a great crowd about her using very violent language towards the Constables and ... the Magistrates. Several of the people around her were getting very violent[.] I begged her to go away. She refused to do so. She continued using very violent language against Bastiles.

Martin therefore arrested Hey. He said he had 'no doubt if she had not been taken into custody she would have stirred up a serious riot'.[13]

Eventually the troops were called in to disperse the crowd. Eight people were arrested that day. One of them, a young man named William Brook, was found in possession of a loaded pistol. Evidence was later given that Brook had earlier shown the pistol to an ironmonger's apprentice and told him he was going to shoot Mr Ingham if he got a chance. The threat was probably bravado on Brook's part, but Ingham saw it as clear proof that without the presence of the military the day would not have passed off without serious violence.[14]

For the time being the Dewsbury crowd appeared to be quelled. The next Board of Guardians' meeting passed off peaceably enough. Peaceably enough outside the meeting, that is; inside, things were not nearly as quiet. The opposition majority on the Board of Guardians expressed deep and bitter dissatisfaction with the conduct of Ingham. Assistant Commissioner Mott, who was in attendance, said it was only with 'the greatest possible difficulty' that he prevented the Guardians from passing a resolution overturning all the Board's earlier decisions. He said the 'impetuosity of the *Ex-officios*, Mr Hague and Mr Ingham, and the rancour of the ... elected Guardians frequently exceeded the bounds of propriety'. Eventually Mott's restraining influence prevailed and the meeting broke up amicably enough.[15]

Popular ill-feeling and bitterness towards Ingham and the police continued in Dewsbury for some time. On the night of Saturday, 8 September 1838, four of the London policemen were set upon by a band of about thirty men armed with bludgeons. The police were given a serious beating and it was only after reinforcements arrived that they were able to drive off their attackers. Two men arrested for their part in the attack turned out to be respectable tradesmen with no criminal records.[16]

III

The other scene of major resistance to the New Poor Law in 1838 was Todmorden. Situated in the Pennines on the Lancashire-Yorkshire border, the Todmorden Union had been a problem for the Poor Law Commission ever since it was first formed in February 1837. Through the judicious use of intimidation and threats of 'exclusive dealing', popular opponents of the New Poor Law had ensured that no

Guardians were returned for two of the largest townships in the Union, Todmorden-Walsden and Langfield. During the March 1838 election of Guardians the two townships again failed to return any Guardians. Assistant Commissioner Power was in no doubt that John Fielden, the Todmorden cotton manufacturer and radical MP for Oldham, was behind the campaign of intimidation.[17] Clearly Fielden actively encouraged the opposition forces in Todmorden, but he was certainly not the initiator of the opposition, nor its only leader. In a letter written to his son Samuel, in March 1838, John Fielden indicated his support for *the men's* decision over exclusive dealing:

> The men are right, and I like them will not buy of any shopkeeper who is for having Guardians appointed to work out the oppressive new poor law. The men feel on this subject as they should do. The poor law would not only deny them parish relief but it would at once operate to reduce their wages. If the shopkeepers could only see this they would be convinced that they are committing a suicidal act.[18]

Although an effective opposition movement had existed in Todmorden for some time, it was not given an institutional form until late in March 1838. William Clegg, the treasurer of the South Lancashire Anti-Poor Law Association, advised John Fielden's son Samuel on what they needed to do. Clegg told them they need not bother with rules and regulations at this stage because the 'object of the society [is] ... so simple'. All they needed to do was 'just ... name a committee ... fix "its meetings" once a week; and suggest that it sho[ul]d correspond occasionally' with the committee in Manchester. The Working Men's Association of Todmorden was formed at a meeting held at the Unitarian Chapel, Todmorden, on 28 March 1838. In a placard issued not long afterwards the Association said that it aimed 'to obtain the repeal of the Poor Law Amendment Act' and that a committee of six had been established for that purpose. Members were asked to contribute 'one penny per month' to help finance the Association. It was a small price to pay to help rid the country of the 'monster' New Poor Law, a cross between 'a SERPENT and a VAMPIRE'.[19]

At first the Poor Law Commission seemed prepared to ignore Todmorden for yet another year, but in the Spring of 1838 on the advice of Assistant Commissioner Power it was decided to introduce the revised regulations into the Union. There were a number of reasons for making such a move at this stage. Firstly, Todmorden was the home of John Fielden, the parliamentary spokesman for the anti-poor law movement, and any success the Commission had in the Union undermined his position. Secondly, the new Guardians returned by the four Yorkshire worsted townships were reported by Power to be 'friendly' to the New Poor Law. And thirdly, the fact that Fielden, the largest employer in the area, was opposed to the New Poor Law made the pro-poor law Guardians more determined than ever to press ahead with its introduction. Any delay, reported Power, 'has the appearance of [giving in] ... to Mr Fielden's ... influence' and that was something the Todmorden Board of Guardians wished to avoid at all costs.[20]

In June 1838 the Poor Law Commission instructed the Todmorden Board of Guardians to take over the administration of poor relief in the Union, and scheduled their first meeting for 6 July. The opposition's response was immediate. A public demonstration was called for the same day and Fielden wrote an open letter to the Guardians calling on them to resign and threatening to close all his mills if they did not immediately do so. The growing agitation had some effect, but not the one the opposition desired. Troops at Burnley were placed on alert and the Guardians secretly brought their meeting forward one day to avoid confrontation with the demonstrators.[21]

On Thursday, 5 July 1838, Fielden made good his threat to close his mills. And the following day the planned anti-poor law demonstration was held at Eastwood. A procession of some 3,000 people marched to the gathering in the pouring rain from Todmorden. The meeting passed resolutions condemning the New Poor Law and called on the Guardians to resign. Over the next week ratepayers in a number of townships were asked to sign a memorial calling on the Guardians to resign immediately. The ratepayers overwhelmingly supported the call. Armed with the memorial a deputation of respectable tradesmen called on the Guardians asking them to resign their office. On Monday, 9 July 1838 the deputation reported the result of their efforts to a large public meeting in Todmorden. The meeting was told that despite the fact that the overwhelming majority of ratepayers were in favour of the Guardians resigning, the Guardians themselves still refused to do so. Fielden gave a speech in which he attacked the New Poor Law and called on the crowd to remain peaceful.[22]

John Fielden's attempt to force the Guardians to resign by closing his mills was a curious one. The implied threat was one of violence: the distressed workers would take out their anger on the offending Guardians. And yet it was only ever a threat, not a real possibility. Fielden secretly continued to pay all his workmen for the time they lost because of his decision to stop the mills. Thus, the only people to suffer from the action were the shareholders in the firm of Fielden Brothers. After visiting Todmorden, the officer commanding the troops at Manchester, Colonel Wemyps, reported that Fielden's brothers were annoyed about his decision to stop the mills. He said it was only because John Fielden was 'Head of the Firm' that his brothers were 'obliged to submit to his dictation'. Wemyps predicted, correctly as it turned out, that 'self interest, the declaration of the Guardians that they will Act, and the determination of the Government to support them ... will force him [Fielden] to give up 'ere long'.[23]

On 16 July 1838, eleven days after he had first closed the mills, John Fielden reopened them. He informed the Guardians that he took the decision 'out of the interests of peace' and of those he employed. The Guardians and the government had called Fielden's bluff and won. But in his announcement Fielden intimated that he was neither defeated nor would the campaign of opposition cease. 'To oppose force to force', he wrote,

we are not yet prepared [,] but if the people of this and the surrounding districts are to be driven to the alternative of either doing so or surrendering their local government into the hands of an unconstitutional Board of Law Makers the time may not be far distant when the experiment may be tried and I would warn those who provoke the people to such a combat of the danger they are incurring.

Fielden went on to outline the future tactics which would be used by opponents of the New Poor Law:

your *real* difficulties may only commence when the period arrives for the relief of the poor being administered by your Board and the officers acting under it. Supplies will be required [,] the Rates will have to be collected and after having disregarded the entreaties of your brother Ratepayers this may be much more difficult to accomplish than you expect even with the threatened force at your back. You have heard that tithes could not be collected in Ireland and if you persevere you may have the *satisfaction* of knowing that rates cannot be collected in England.

Fielden's comments only earned a reprimand from Assistant Commissioner Power. Power wrote to the Home Office suggesting that Fielden be immediately struck off the list of magistrates for the county of Lancashire. The Home Office advised that although qualified as a magistrate Fielden had never actually been sworn in and therefore could not be struck off.[24]

IV

Following the reopening of Fielden's mills the Todmorden Board of Guardians pressed ahead with the implementation of the revised regulations. The aim was to bring all the townships in the Union under the control of the Board of Guardians by 12 August 1838. They immediately ran into difficulties. Overseers in the townships of Todmorden-Walsden, Erringden and Langfield refused to hand over their funds to the Board of Guardians. Warrants were issued demanding that monies be paid to the Union Treasurer. On 4 August the overseers of Todmorden-Walsden called a meeting of ratepayers to receive advice on whether they should comply with the warrants. The ratepayers, '99 in 100 of whom were opposed to the Guardians' and indemnify them should the Board of Guardians take any further action against them. The Guardians decided to take the intransigent overseers to court and summonsed them to appear at the Rochdale Petty Sessions on Monday, 13 August 1838. In their defence the two overseers, William Robinson and J. Crossley, said that in refusing to pay money to the Union they were acting under the orders of the ratepayers, '99 in 100 of whom were opposed to the Guardians' and that the Union was illegally constituted because one of the townships refused to return Guardians. The Rochdale magistrates found them guilty but did not impose the full penalty of £5 for a first offence and, much to Power's and the Todmorden Guardians' chagrin, fined the overseers only 40s plus costs.[25]

Still the overseers refused to pay the money over to the Union. At the next Board of Guardians' meeting it was decided to issue further orders against the overseers. After a series of court cases distress warrants were eventually issued against the overseers. When some of these seized goods were first offered for sale at Todmorden in late October 1838 there was a disturbance. The crowd refused to allow anyone to bid for the goods and chased the auctioneer out of town before returning the goods to their rightful owner.[26]

Matters came to a head in early November 1838 when William Ingham, the Langfield overseer, received a distress warrant for nonpayment of fines imposed by the Halifax Petty Sessions. The two Halifax constables who served the order marked his goods and told him that if the money was not paid they would return the following week and take his goods. Ingham was reported to have told the constables that he 'most assuredly should not pay the fine'. Later Ingham was to claim that pressure had been brought to bear on him not to pay any money to the Guardians. In a letter to the *Manchester Guardian* he said that no sooner had he received the Guardians' first demand for £20 than his life was threatened.

> I was threatened ... by three or four men upon Todmorden bridge ... 'that, if I paid any money to the Bastile guardians, they would tear me to picces'... [S]ince then I have been frequently threatened, and on one occasion was savagely told, 'that if I paid either money or fine, I should be trod into the earth, and my body cut up to make garter bands with'.

It was also decided that any attempt to seize Ingham's goods would be resisted by force. William Robinson, the overseer for Todmorden and a steward of Joshua Fielden's, is reported to have arranged for the factory bell at Lambutts Mill, near where Ingham lived, to be rung and a message sent to the Waterside Mill as soon as the constables appeared.[27]

Two days later, on Friday, 16 November, James Feather, the deputy constable of Halifax, and William King, the sergeant of the watch, arrived at Ingham's to take possession of the marked goods. Leaving their horse and cart at the bottom of the yard they made their way up to the house. They had hardly been in the house for ten minutes when an angry crowd began gathering outside. James Feather later explained what happened.

> I ... went to look for the cart followed by King – the cart was gone. I followed it ... near a mile – part of the mob followed me and a great many other persons came from the mills below and attacked me and took away the Horse and Cart. I then attempted to escape. I was knocked down by the mob and they said they would give me two chances, whether I went back with the horse and cart or was made unable to walk. There were repeated cries from other parts of the crowd saying 'Kill him'[.] I then ... returned with the horse and cart to Mr Inghams house. [T]he Stande [horse?] and cart were then seized by the mob and thrown down and I was thrown upon the

horse. I then got up and was immediately struck on the side of my head with a large stone which again knocked me down. Stones were at this time flying in all directions and I was severely kicked ... I then ran up to Mr Inghams window and ... was seized by the crowd who said 'Hold him by the ears until he sees the cart burn' [,] they were breaking the Cart with Malls and Mattocks. Mr Ingham opened the door and let me into his house, where I found King. We were concealed in Mr Ingham's House for near an hour – whilst we were so concealed I heard cries outside the house ... that if he did not turn us out they would pull the house down stone by stone. In consequence ... we came down stairs – I went to the window and spoke to the crowd and asked them if they would spare our lives and cries came from all parts of the crowd 'if you will take an oath before Mr Ingham that you would not be concerned in anything of the kind in future'... Mr Ingham then took a book which he shewed the crowd through the window as if he was about to administer an oath. Mr Ingham then opened the door and I then begged of the mob to spare our lives ... and they said 'we will spare your lives [,] Mr Fielden said we must spare your lives'.[28]

The crowd of mill workers, and railway labourers from the nearby construction works, then marched the constables off to Wood Mill, where the Board of Guardians were meeting. Although a number of people tried to protect the two men from further violence, they were forced to desist after their own mouths had been stuffed with dirt by some of the crowd. Women took the lead in abusing the hapless constables; they were knocked, kicked, yelled at and dragged through the mud. As a result, Feather lost most of his clothes and arrived in Wood Mill clad only in the remnants of his drawers and stockings. Eventually the two men were able to make their escape and the crowd rounded off the day by smashing the windows at the inn where the Guardians were holding their meeting.[29]

Tension remained high in the area over the next few days and on Wednesday, 21 November 1838 an even more serious disturbance took place. It is unclear what sparked the disturbance. During Wednesday morning an order was issued by the magistrates calling on the respectable inhabitants to be sworn in as special constables to protect the Guardians at their meeting on Friday. A rumour quickly spread that the constables and the military were to proceed to Langfield to enforce the seizure of the overseer's goods. Early that afternoon a crowd of over 1,000 persons, many armed with clubs, assembled at Langfield to prevent any attempted seizure. Although the crowd soon realised the rumour was unfounded they were slow to disband. Months of pent-up frustration and anger at the Guardians burst out in a savage display of destruction. Crossley, the Todmorden magistrate, was the first to raise the alarm. In a hasty note to the Commanding Officer at the Burnley Barracks, he wrote:

> Sir, I do hereby request you to send here forthwith a Squadron of Dragoons and some infantry, as I have this moment received Information on oath of a *large mob* which are now engaged in breaking windows and threatening the lives of persons engaged in putting into force the New Poor Law here.[30]

For something like four hours in the late afternoon and early evening the crowd toured the district attacking and ransacking the homes of Guardians and known supporters of the New Poor Law. At Wood Mill the homes of two Guardians, Samuel and Royston Oliver, were broken into and sacked. The windows at the inn where the Guardians normally met were smashed for the second time in a week. At Stones Wood the crowd attacked the home of Abraham Ormerod, another Guardian, destroying the windows, doors and furniture. The crowd then turned west and proceeded rapidly through Todmorden and up the Devil's Gate Pass to Frith's Mill, where they attacked the home of William Helliwell, another Guardian. Helliwell was entertaining a party of friends at the time, and all had to flee when the crowd began smashing their way into the house, destroying the furniture. The home of William Greenwood, another Guardian, was attacked next. The crowd were fast running out of Guardians' houses to attack and they now began broadening their aim. The home of Jeremiah Oliver, the surgeon and registrar for births, deaths and marriages, was attacked. His windows, doors, furniture and the contents of his surgery were smashed. He later estimated his loss at £300. Ann Holt, a draper, had the window of her shop smashed. Although a sister-in-law of Joshua Fielden, she had drawn the crowd's vengeance for her 'many speeches over the shop counter in favour of the New Poor Law'. Henry Atkinson, shoemaker, and James Stansfield, solicitor and clerk to the Guardians, were next on the list. At Todmorden Hall, the home of James Taylor, the magistrate and *ex-officio* Guardian, the crowd smashed all the windows, destroyed a carriage in the yard and attacked the doors with shovels. Entering the house, they destroyed the furniture and paintings and made off with wine and spirits from the cellar. Before they left they set the lot ablaze. Luckily for Taylor, his servants were able to put out the fire before it damaged the house itself. James Suthers, a beer-shop keeper and collector of rates for the Guardians, was the next victim. The crowd smashed his windows, doors and furniture; they would have set it all ablaze had not a neighbouring woman pleaded with them that if the fire got hold, the whole row of buildings would be endangered. The crowd finished their tour of destruction at Hare Hill, the home of Mr Greenwood, another Guardian. They smashed the windows, threw the silver plate in the stream and set the house on fire. Only the speedy arrival of the engine from the Fielden Brother's Mill at Waterside saved the house from serious damage. William Robinson, the Todmorden overseer, was eventually able to calm the crowd and persuade them to go home. By the time the troops arrived at 8.00 pm the area was once again quiet.[31]

Obviously frightened and shocked by the outbreak, the local authorities began rounding up suspects. The operation had all the appearance of a military exercise deep in enemy territory. Travelling across country and avoiding the roads, the troops surrounded each Mill in turn. The magistrates and special constables would then enter the Mill to arrest those suspected of having participated in the disturbance. Forty-seven persons were taken in this way and conveyed back to Todmorden for examination. Fourteen were committed for trial at York Assizes and two to Liverpool. All were charged over the assaulting of the constables on 16 November. The magistrates admitted that they were having great difficulty in procuring any evidence against those involved in the wild destruction on the evening of 21 November. Despite the offer of a £100 reward no evidence was forthcoming. Assistant Commissioner Power was convinced that intimidation was the cause of the silence: 'The system of intimidation practised under Messrs Fielden's infuence and the more active agency of the Working Men's Association is so effective that even the respectable persons whose property has suffered are some of them supposed to know more than they dare mention.' Meanwhile he reported that the magistrates had employed 'Secret Agents' to procure information.[32]

The effect of the disturbance on the already shaken Guardians was dramatic. Five of the Guardians immediately sought leave to resign from the Poor Law Commission. They gave as their reason 'fear of *personal* violence'. The Poor Law Commission was also told that other Guardians were contemplating resigning and that the relieving officer and rate collector had tendered their resignations. Power informed the Commission in the gravest terms that he had engaged to attend a meeting with 'such Guardians as may deem it prudent to assemble' on 29 November and that 'it is probable that on that date the fate of the Poor Law Amendment Act in Todmorden will be decided'. He concluded: 'The consequence[s] to the whole district are incalculable should the Guardians then resign.'[33]

The Guardians did not resign, but the New Poor Law remained unenforceable. Starved of funds by the overseers' persistent refusals to hand over money, the Guardians could do little. By appealing against every court decision which went against them, the overseers of Todmorden-Walsden and Langfield were able to delay the introduction of the New Poor Law for years. To add to the Poor Law Commission's difficulties it was soon realised that the intransigent townships were managing their own affairs more cheaply than the Union was able to do. Todmorden and Langfield had poor-rates of one shilling in the pound while the other townships in the Union were rated at two to three shillings in the pound. This was despite the fact that Todmorden and Langfield were 'notorious for behaving well towards the poor'. Finally in March 1840 the Todmorden Board of Guardians revolted. They sent off a memorial to the Poor Law Commission, signed by every Guardian in the Union, asking that the Poor Law Union be dissolved.[34]

V

As the cost of poor relief began to rise in the late 1830s and early 1840s, quite a few Boards of Guardians turned against the New Poor Law. In February 1839 the Maldon Union Board in Essex resigned *en masse* after the Poor Law Commission ordered them to stop providing relief for the children of families earning inadequate wages. The Guardians claimed that the relief offered 'was more economical to the Union, and less subversive of the good feeling that should subsist between the master and those employed by him, than sending the whole family ... to a workhouse'. When the Commission replied that there could be no grounds for relieving able-bodied families out of the workhouse, the Guardians all resigned. In March 1840 the Dewsbury Board of Guardians requested the Poor Law Commission to dissolve the Union. And in December 1840 the Macclesfield ratepayers complained of the 'injurious and unsatisfactory working of the Poor

Law union'. They said that the poor-rates had risen £1,600 per annum since the introduction of the New Poor Law, and 'without any special causes arising from want of employment or depression of trade'.[35]

The Poor Law Commission tried to ignore such criticisms. But one thing the Commission could neither ignore nor deny was that the full rigour of the New Poor Law had still not been applied in the manufacturing districts of the north of England. Assistant Commissioner Power, in a report he wrote in September 1838, admitted that he was still unable to classify a single Poor Law Union in his area which was operating the New Poor Law. This position remained unchanged for at least a decade. Despite the Poor Law Commission's concessions and the revised poor relief regulations, northern Poor Law Unions began to backslide in the early 1840s. In April 1841 a rather embarrassed Assistant Commissioner Mott admitted that many of the old 'abuses' in the administration of poor relief, including the villainous 'relief in aid of wages', had reappeared in the northern counties. He added that, luckily, the industrious habits of the manufacturing population 'are of exemplary tenacity or we should have ... to regret more striking instances of their corruption by these illegal modes of relief'.[36]

Northern Boards of Guardians continued to give 'illegal relief' because it was not as expensive to administer and because it was better suited to the needs of the recipients than the relief authorised by the Poor Law Commission. When an outdoor work test order was issued to the Bradford Union in early 1843 the Guardians condemned it as impractical. They told the Poor Law Commission that the work test would cost more to administer than simply giving outdoor relief to the able-bodied. Three years later the Bradford Guardians were of the opinion that the able-bodied woolcombers who applied for relief should not have to perform labour which exposed them 'to the inclemency of the weather'. One thing was certain, there was no workhouse test applied to poor-relief recipients in the north of England. When Assistant Commissioner Alfred Austin submitted his report for the December Quarter 1848 it revealed that over 90 per cent of male able-bodied paupers were still receiving outdoor relief.[37]

Scandal also helped weaken the impact of the 1834 Poor Law. In August 1845 the reforming editor of the *Lancet* and Radical MP for Finsbury, Thomas Wakely, asked the then Home Secretary, Sir James Graham, whether he had received any information concerning the conditions experienced by inmates of the Andover Union workhouse in Hampshire. Wakely 'understood that one of the guardians ... had complained to the Poor Law Commissioners that the paupers of the

Union were employed in crushing bones, and that, while so employed, they were in the habit of quarrelling with each other about the bones, of extracting the marrow from them, and of gnawing the meat which they sometimes found at their extremities'. Graham replied that 'he could not believe such an abuse existed, otherwise he should have heard of it'. He promised however to institute an immediate inquiry. *The Times* quickly took up the story and when Assistant Commissioner Henry Walter Parker arrived in Andover a few days later to begin his investigation a special correspondent was on hand to report his findings.[38]

Not only did the allegations prove to be true, but Parker's report suggested grave mismanagement in the running of the Union stretching back over a number of years. The Poor Law Commission quickly sought to distance itself from the affair. Proceedings were begun against the workhouse master and the responsible Assistant Commissioner, the luckless Parker, was dismissed. The attempt to set up the two scapegoats went badly astray, however, and the government was eventually forced to establish a Select Committee of the House of Commons to investigate. The Committee revealed a long list of cruelties, abuses and mismanagement going back to the formation of the Union in 1835. But it refused to heap all the blame on the workhouse master and the Assistant Commissioner. The Board of Guardians, the Poor Law Commission and even the Treasury shared in the guilt. The dietary table which the Poor Law Commission had recommended to the Andover Guardians was inadequate, and although this had subsequently been discovered by the Poor Law Commission no one had seen fit to inform the Union Board. The Guardians had failed to carry out adequate inspections of the management of the workhouse which might have revealed the master's abuses. They had also sold to themselves, at a discount price, the blood and bone which the paupers produced. The Committee also found that the threat of starvation in the workhouse had been used to force farm labourers to accept reduced wages. While the Guardians had undoubtedly acted harshly in enforcing the workhouse test, the Committee found that they had only been acting 'in accordance with the frequently published views of the Poor Law Commissioners'. The Committee even found that the Commission discouraged its Assistants from taking any notice of rumours of cruelties and abuses. Chadwick and Nicholls were blamed for their rigour and the other two Commissioners for their neglect. And finally the Treasury was blamed for reducing the number of Assistant Commissioners from twenty-one in 1839 to a wholly inadequate nine in 1842.[39]

The Committee's report was devastating: it did everything but demand a repeal of the New Poor Law. Clearly the existing Poor Law Commission could not survive such an onslaught and in 1847 it was replaced by a Poor Law Board, directly accountable to Parliament. The New Poor Law survived, albeit in watered-down form. It survived because neither the Whigs nor the Tories had an alternative policy. A few parliamentarians still advocated a return to the Old Poor Law, but generally the criticisms contained in the *Report* of the 1832 Royal Commission held sway. The harsher aspects of the New Poor Law were removed and a work test rather than a workhouse test became the primary means of determining a person's eligibility for poor relief. In December 1852 the Outdoor Relief Regulation Order legitimised what had always been the practice with poor relief in the manufacturing districts of the north of England: the able-bodied were to receive outdoor relief on certain conditions and the aged and infirm without restriction.[40]

VI

Popular opposition to the 1834 Poor Law continued well into the twentieth century. There was not the fervour there had been earlier, but just occasionally some incident would occur to illustrate the depth of popular feeling. In 1855 a plan by Guardians to build a new workhouse in Sheffield sparked a vigorous campaign of opposition. At the next Board of Guardians' elections the pro-workhouse Guardians were swept from office. And during the 1860s Lancashire Cotton Famine there were serious disturbances after local officials attempted to tamper with the scale and type of relief paid to the unemployed. When the Local Government Act of 1894 removed both the property qualifications for Guardians and the plural voting system for ratepayers, working men and women began to appear on Boards of Guardians. The result was the gradual adoption of a more generous policy of relief than was sanctioned by the central authorites. Such a watering-down of regulations reached its zenith, of course, with the activities of the Socialist-dominated Popular Borough Council and Poor Law Union in the 1920s. Ironically the very problem that the 1834 Poor Law had been specifically drawn up to deal with — the problem of the able-bodied unemployed — led to its final demise. By the 1920s the principles of less eligibility had finally shown themselves to be totally inadequate (if not irrelevant) to the needs of a modern industrial society. In 1930 the administrative machinery of the New Poor Law was finally dissolved and power transferred back into the hands of local government. The monster had not been slain, it had died of natural causes.

Notes

1. *Northern Star*, 4 August 1838.
2. Resolutions of Dewsbury Guardians, 23 April 1838, PRO, MH 12/14830; *Northern Star*, 28 April 1838; 'Reports from the Select Committee on the Poor Law Amendment Act', *PP*, 1837-8, vol.XVIII, part II, pp.1-17, and part III, pp.25-31; Power to PLC, 2 April and 2 July 1838; Chadwick to Dewsbury Board of Guardians, 7 July 1838, PRO, MH 12/14830.
3. *Northern Star*, 28 July 1838; Power to PLC, 24 July 1838, PRO, MH 12/14830.
4. *Northern Star*, 4 August 1838; Examination and Deposition of Thomas Rylah, 6 August 1838, Harewood Papers, Box 1, LCA. There is no doubt that Lewis pressed Thornhill to dismiss his wayward steward. Thornhill to Lewis, 11 April 1837, PRO, MH 12/14974, indicates that the final straw for Thornhill was the decision by his tenants not to elect a Guardian for Fixby parish for the second year running. See also C. Driver, *Tory Radical* (Oxford University Press, New York, 1946), p.382.
5. Examination and Deposition of William Pearson, 6 August 1838, Harewood Papers, Box 1, LCA; [Anon.] to Ingham, [August 1838], PRO, MH 12/14830.
6. Examination and Deposition of John Greenwood, Thomas Rylah, & William Pearson, 6 August 1838, Harewood Papers, Box 1, LCA; *Halifax Express*, 11 August 1838.
7. Carr to PLC, 7 August 1838, and Greenwood to Ingham, Tuesday morning [7 August 1838], PRO, MH 12/14830.
8. Memorial Dewsbury Guardians, [August 1838]; Ingham to PLC, 7 August 1838, PRO, MH 12/14830.
9. Carr to PLC, 11 August 1838; PLC to Carr, 13 August 1838, PRO, MH 12/14830.
10. To save itself embarrassment the Commission appears to have kept information concerning Power's role out of the official records. Rhodes to PLC, 4 September 1838, PRO, MH 12/14830, has pencilled comments on it referring to Lefevre's private letter to Mott, 8 September 1838. The letter is not to be found amongst PLC correspondence. Ingham to PLC, 7 August 1838, PRO, MH 12/14830, indicates that Power was a regular house guest of Ingham.
11. Mott to PLC, 16 & 20 August 1838, PRO, MH 12/14830.
12. Ingham to Harewood, 21 August 1838, Harewood Papers, Box 1, LCA; Carr to PLC, 20 August 1838, PRO, MH 12/14830.
13. Depositions against Mary Hey, n.d., Harewood Papers, Box 1, LCA; *Halifax Express*, 25 August 1838.
14. Depositions against William Brook, n.d.; Ingham to Harewood, 21 August 1838, Harewood Papers, Box 1, LCA.
15. Mott to Lefevre, 4 September 1838, PRO, HO 73/54.
16. Mott to PLC, 14 September 1838, PRO, MH 12/14830.
17. Ormerod to PLC, 31 March 1838; Power to PLC, 23 April 1838, PRO, MH 12/6272.

18. J. Fielden to S. Fielden, 26 March 1838, Fielden Papers, JRULM.
19. Clegg to S. Fielden, 27 March 1838, Fielden Papers, JRULM; 'Address to the inhabitants of Todmorden ... from the Working Men's Association of Todmorden', 2 April 1838 (placard), PRO, MH 12/6272. The original committee members were all working men and employees of the Fieldens. One of them, the Secretary John Lord, later helped supplement his income by acting as the Todmorden correspondent to the *Northern Star* and other radical journals. In 1849 Lord was appointed manager of Fielden's Robin Wood Mill.
20. Power to PLC, 15 April 1838, PRO, MH 32/63; Power to PLC, 24 April 1838, PRO, MH 32/64.
21. 'Public Meeting New Poor Law', 2 July 1838 (poster); Riley to PLC, 3 July 1838; Todmorden Guardians' Resolution, 5 July 1838, PRO, HO 40/38; Maule to Wemyps, 4 July 1838, PRO, HO 40/13.
22. *Manchester and Salford Advertiser*, 7 July 1838, and *Northern Star*, 14 July 1838. In Todmorden and Walsden only 9 out of 804 ratepayers refused to sign the memorial; in Longfield 6 out of 315 refused; and in Stansfield 16 out of 683 refused. *Manchester and Salford Advertiser*, 14 July 1838.
23. *Halifax Express*, 21 July 1838, and *Manchester and Salford Advertiser*, 28 July 1838; Wemyps to Phillips, 14 July 1838, PRO, HO 40/38.
24. *Northern Star*, 21 July 1838; Fielden's placard, quoted in Power's Report, 12 April 1839, PRO, MH 32/64; Power to HO, 17 July 1838, PRO, HO 40/38.
25. Power to PLC, 11 August 1838; Stansfield to Power, 13 August 1838; Power to PLC, 14 August 1838, PRO, HO 73/54; *Manchester and Salford Advertiser*, 18 August 1838.
26. Power to PLC, 20 August 1838, PRO, HO 73/54; J.M. Cobbett to Fielden, 31 October 1838, Fielden Papers, JRULM.
27. *Halifax Guardian*, 24 November 1838; *Manchester Guardian* letter quoted in Power to PLC, 22 November 1838, PRO, MH 12/6272; Wemyps to Phillips, 24 November 1838, PRO, HO 40/38.
28. Examination of James Feather, 24 November 1838, PRO, HO 40/38.
29. *Halifax Guardian*, 24 November 1838; Shuttleworth, Holgate and Roberts to Power, 17 November 1838, PRO, HO 40/38.
30. Crossley to CO Burnley Barracks, 5.00 pm, 21 November 1838, PRO, HO 40/38.
31. *Halifax Guardian,* 24 November 1838; *Manchester and Salford Advertiser,* 24 November 1838; Todmorden Magistrates to Russell, 23 November 1838, PRO, HO 40/38.
32. Wemyps to Phillips, 24 November 1838; Crossley and Taylor to Russell, 25 November 1838; '£100 Reward' (poster), November 1838; Power to PLC, 27 November 1838, PRO, HO 40/38.
33. Foster, Riley, Lister, Sutcliffe and Ashworth to PLC, 24 November 1838; Power to PLC, 27 November 1838, PRO, HO 40/38.
34. *Halifax Guardian,* 28 March 1840.
35. *Chartist*, 23 February 1839; *Halifax Guardian*, 7 March and 26 December 1840.
36. Power Report, 13 September 1838, PRO, MH 52/64; Mott to PLC, 30 April 1841, PRO, MH 12/5594.
37. Wagstaff to PLC, 25 April 1843, PRO, MH 12/14723; Wagstaff to PLC, 13 November 1846, PRO, MH 12/14725; Statement of the number of persons receiving relief in Mr Austin's district, December Quarter 1848, PRO, MH 32/7. The exact percentage was 92.88. Able-bodied males accounted for only 9.53% of those receiving relief. 91.58% of all paupers received outdoor relief.
38. *Hansard*, 3rd series, vol.LXXXII, cols 1320-1; *The Times*, 13 August 1845.

39. 'Report from the Select Committee on Andover Union', *PP*, 1846, vol.V, part 1, pp.iii-x.

40. S. and B. Webb, *English Poor Law History, Part II* (Frank Cass, London, 1963), vol.I, pp.183-8 and 202-5; G. Nicholls, *A History of the English Poor Law* (Putnam's Sons, New York, 1898), vol.II, pp.456-7.

41. D. Fraser, 'The Poor Law as a Political Institution' in D. Fraser (ed.), *The New Poor Law in the Nineteenth Century* (Macmillan, London, 1976), pp.119-22; M.E. Rose, 'Rochdale Men and the Stalybridge Riot', in A.P. Donajgrodzki (ed.), *Social Control in Nineteenth Century Britain* (Croom Helm, London, 1977), pp.185-206; N. Branson, *Poplarism, 1919-1925* (Lawrence & Wishart, London, 1979).

PART THREE

BELIEFS

10

RUMOUR AND FEAR

Popular opposition to the 1834 Poor Law was characterised by rumour and fear. Unfortunately, this has led many historians to assume that the opposition movement merely resulted from 'ignorance'. We are told, for instance, that 'every arsenal of superstition and ignorance was ransacked to provide reasons against [Poor Law] reform', that northern opposition to the New Poor Law was '[s]purred on by fear and anger', and that 'pathetic misconceptions ... played a large role in bringing about the riots'.[1] One can search the histories of the New Poor Law for an illustration of the popular beliefs and assumptions which gave rise to these 'pathetic misconceptions', but in vain. All we are told is that '[w]ild rumours spread as to the intentions of the ... Act'.[2]

Rumour and fear helped determine the texture and tone of the campaign of popular opposition to the 1834 Poor Law. They served as powerful reminders of the legislation's alleged intentions and provided the inspiration for the black humour which characterised so much anti-poor law propaganda. Furthermore, we would be wrong to assume that all the rumours and fears concerning the New Poor Law were necessarily the result of either ignorance or irrationality. While some rumours sprang from the 'primitive fears' of the labouring population as a whole, others were derived from a popular understanding as to what could be expected of those who championed a radical reform of poor relief. By examining these rumours and fears we can gain some insight into the beliefs and assumptions which guided popular opposition to the 1834 Poor Law; we are also enabled better to understand the emotional impact of that campaign.

I

As soon as the New Poor Law began to be introduced into southern England in the spring of 1835 extravagant rumours started circulating as to the Act's intentions. Assistant Commissioner William John Gilbert reported some of the rumours he had heard in Devon:

Among other ridiculous statements circulated, the peasantry fully believe that all the bread [being given as poor relief] was poisoned, and that the only cause for giving it instead of money was the facility it afforded of destroying the paupers; that all the children beyond three in a family were to be killed; that all young children and women under 18 were to be spayed; that if they touched the bread they would instantly drop down dead; and I saw one poor person at North Molton look at a loaf with a strong expression of hunger, and when it was offered to her, put her hands behind her and shrink back in fear lest it should touch her. She acknowledged she had heard of a man who had dropped down dead the moment he touched the bread.

Gilbert said that still others 'believed that to touch the bread was like "taking bounty" and the Guardians would immediately seize them, kill their children, and imprison the parents'. Nor was it only the poor and destitute who were subject to such rumours. Gilbert went on to report that the small ratepayers had their own tale of horror:

The chairman [of the Board] was to have 1,200 *l.* a year, and all the guardians in proportion, and ... 20,000 *l.* were to be immediately levied on the rate-payers for a workhouse.[3]

Popular fears very like those in Devon were reported throughout southern England. The Reverend Thomas Spencer, the first chairman of the Bath Union, was told by a pauper at Bradford-upon-Avon that the people feared the black bread that they now received as relief; apparently it was believed that 'the poor [who ate the bread] would die off like sheep with the rot'. When the Archdeacon of Lewes, who had recently joined the local Board of Guardians, generously invited pauper school-children to a boat outing, it was whispered that they were to be taken out into the English Channel and drowned. During the 1835 General Election, people in Worcester were told that the sitting members 'had voted in Parliament that all the old people in England should be killed'. And in the Royston Union in Cambridgeshire the 'wildest and most extravagant notions' circulated about the New Poor Law. Assistant Commissioner Power reported that the labouring population 'believe ... every form of cruelty not excepting that of death by hanging is to be inflicted on them as part of the Workhouse System'.[4]

Nor were such fears alleviated by the utterances of many of those charged with implementing the New Poor Law. 'Our intention', admitted one Assistant Commissioner at a public meeting, 'is to make the workhouses as like prisons as possible.' Assistant Commissioner Mott openly told Richard Oastler that 'the object of building these union [work]houses is to make them a terror to the poor and prevent them from entering'. In the Wayland Union in Norfolk the paupers went around in mortal terror that they would be branded with the letter P and that their meagre possessions would be confiscated, after the Union's new relieving officer made a series of threatening remarks.[5]

What is surprising about these rumours and fears is not that they should have existed, but that the authorities (and for that matter later historians) found them so inexplicable. Certainly there was nothing new about them. Whenever there were attempts to introduce a stricter system of workhouse relief, there were rumours of cruelties. And, of course, the Reverend Thomas Malthus had been part of the demonology of popular radical discourse since the Napoleonic Wars. There were few labouring men and women who had not heard of Cobbett's 'check-population parson' and his scheme to reduce the 'surplus population'. Of course, few of them had read Malthus for themselves and their understanding of both his doctrine and his proposed solution was necessarily distorted. Nevertheless, in the atmosphere of excited debate which raged over Malthusianism in the post-war years, there were times when it appeared that Malthus and his followers were advocating nothing short of mass murder.

In a little-known play written in 1831, William Cobbett had satirised Malthusianism. 'Surplus Population: A Comedy in Three Acts', was the rollicking tale of two young lovers, the dairymaid Betsy Birch and the farm labourer Dick Hazle, and the obstacles placed in the way of their marriage by the leering Sir Gripe Grindum. Although professing to be a disciple of Malthus, Sir Grindum's real reason for wanting to stop the marriage was so he could have Betsy for himself. Eventually Grindum got his 'cumuppance' when his evil scheme was discovered and the farm labourers threw him in the pond. Cobbett used the simple story-line to good effect, presenting a very funny and at times, witty critique of Malthusianism. Apart from the leading protagonists there were the visiting Malthusian philosopher, Peter Thimble (a thinly veiled tilt at Francis Place), the stout-hearted Farmer Stiles, the village's radical shoemaker, Last, and a whole collection of country men and women.

Cobbett used the character of Peter Thimble, and his constant harping about the dangers of surplus population, to ridicule Malthusianism. When told by young Betsy that she came from a family with seventeen children, Thimble was horrified:

> Hold your tongue! Hold your tongue! *(aside)* It is quite monstrous!
> Nothing can save the country but plague, pestilence, famine, and
> sudden death. Government ought to import a ship-load of
> arsenic...

But Thimble's Malthusianism met its match in the common-sense
logic of the radical village shoemaker, Last.

Squ. Thim. ... Mr Last, do you not know that there is in nature, a
              tendency, in every country, for the people to increase
              faster than the food that they usually live on?
Last.   I do not only not know that fact, but I know that, besides
              being contrary to reason and experience, it is next to
              blasphemy to assert it... [I]f there be *in nature* this
              tendency, how comes it that it never was discovered
              before; and that ... until ... that Scotch fellow, Malthus,
              wrote his book, no man in England even dreamed of our
              having too many people?
Squ Thim.   The evil has not existed until of late years.
Last.   But if it be *in nature*, why did it not exist before?[6]

It was a question many working people also asked the supporters of
Malthusianism.

In 1835 Cobbett revised the play and added new material relating
directly to the New Poor Law. In what must be one of the most original
protests staged against the New Poor Law, Cobbett actually presented
performances of the play in the area around his farm near Farnham,
Surrey. When he announced plans to take the play on a tour of
Hampshire, Sussex and Kent, the authorities stepped in and banned it.
Whether the play actually influenced popular opinion is hard to gauge.
Assistant Commissioner a'Court did not think it had much effect.[7] In
all events it was Cobbett's last swipe at the authorities; the grand old
man of popular radicalism died on 18 June 1835.

II

Lurid stories of the torture and cruelties allegedly taking place in the
new Union bastiles were the staple of the anti-poor law press.[8] They

not only sated the appetite of a sensation-hungry readership but helped fuel popular fears about the New Poor Law. The *Halifax Guardian* reported how a 'brute of an overseer' had forced a mother and her young infant to be removed from Tuplon to Cambridge in the middle of winter. The child had subsequently died. A coroner's jury was supposed to have returned a verdict of manslaughter against the overseer. The *Manchester and Salford Advertiser* told how two sick paupers in the Crediton Union workhouse in Devonshire had been shut in a dark outhouse with only straw to lie on in the middle of winter. One of the workhouse officials is even alleged to have expressed impatience at the length of time it took for the two paupers to die. At one stage they are supposed to have been taken out naked in the freezing weather and washed with a mop at the courtyard pump. *The Times* alleged that a man preparing to leave a workhouse had asked after his wife, that she might join him outside, only to be told that she had been buried three weeks previously. No one had seen fit to inform the man. The *Northern Star* told how an unemployed weaver named Coleman had been sent before the Nottingham magistrates by the Guardians on a charge of sleeping out of the workhouse. When the bench heard evidence that he was actually trying to obtain work at the time, they dismissed the case. Apparently the Guardians were so angry at this that they stripped his wife of her shoes and socks and her newborn infant of all its clothes and expelled them from the workhouse.[9]

Of course, many of these reports were at best half truths, but the newspapers' readers were not to know that. By the time the Poor Law Commission had checked the allegations and issued a denial there were another dozen or so reports to investigate. The Poor Law Commission could not keep pace with the rumours. In the case of Oastler's claim that a workhouse inmate had not been informed of his wife's death, it was almost three months before the Poor Law Commission could inform the Home Secretary that they could find 'no evidence which would substantiate the rumour'. The Commission said that Oastler had heard the rumour from a Mr Kettlewell, who heard it from some friends, who heard it from a man in Lepton, who heard it from his brother, 'to whom it had been related by a pauper, who said he had been in the same [work]house, but whose name and abode he confessed he did not know'.[10] When the Reverend Mr Bull told a horrified Bradford meeting that a young woman in a workhouse had been stripped and flogged 'like a soldier', Chadwick immediately wrote asking him if he could prove these charges. Bull replied somewhat lamely that he would only give his evidence to a duly constituted court of law. Eventually he was forced to admit that the woman had only been slapped by the workhouse matron.[11]

But there were always stories with enough truth in them to cause the Poor Law Commission and the government acute embarrassment. Certainly the Poor Law Commission could not argue with the *Sheffield Iris* when it reported that conditions in the new Pershore workhouse, near Worcester, were so bad – with damp walls and damp bedding – that the inmates were dying off. The verdict of a local Coroner's Jury into the death of a former child inmate was that she had 'Died from inflammation of the lungs, brought on by cold caught in the newly-erected workhouse at Pershore'. In fact the verdicts of several Coroner's Juries caused the Poor Law Commission unease. When Mary Wilden, an epileptic, died in the Worksop Union workhouse, an inquest found that her death was caused by the ill-treatment she had received there. And when Mary Whiting died after being forcibly removed from Heston to St Pancras, a Coroner's Jury attributed it to the New Poor Law. John M. Cobbett informed his patron John Fielden that 'the Coroner's Juries are not bad fellows, though they are shopkeepers' and he went on to say that as far as the case of Mary Whiting was concerned 'the Poor-law Commissioners have very nearly placed themselves within the claws of a Coroner's writ!'.[12]

If the New Poor Law was not directly killing off the paupers, it was treating them like felons. George Troth, an 81-year-old inmate of the Hereford workhouse, was sentenced to seven days' imprisonment with 'hard labour' after he had refused the workhouse master's orders to break stones. And when two young boys ran away from the Tingoe Union workhouse in Suffolk, they were taken into custody and charged with stealing the clothes they were wearing. The Bury St Edmunds magistrates found them guilty and sentenced them to fourteen days' hard labour. The *Halifax Guardian* sarcastically commented: 'And yet we are told that workhouses are *not* prisons'.[13]

In December 1840 a number of newpapers shocked (and no doubt titillated) their readers by reporting the flogging of girls and young women by James Miles, the master of the Hoo Union workhouse at Rochester in Kent. 'Upwards of half-a-dozen girls', reported *The Times,*

> have ... had their persons exposed in the most brutal and indecent manner, by the Master, for the purpose of inflicting on them cruel floggings; [they have] ... been compelled ... to strip the upper parts of

their persons naked, to allow him to scourge them with birch rods on their bare shoulders and waists . . .

Apparently, the workhouse master might even have been able to continue his nefarious activities undetected, had he not 'flogged little Jemmy (a pauper's illegitimate child, then two years of age) with a birch rod ... because it cried for its mother'.[14] This finally proved too much for the long-suffering women inmates and they got up enough courage to complain. The workhouse master was eventually prosecuted and convicted of assault.

III

Because of the rumours, the fears and the sensational revelations, there grew up in the popular mind an almost mythical view of the New Poor Law. It centred on the bastile – the hated union workhouse. In October 1836 the *Champion and Weekly Herald* presented its readers with an engraving of the new Union workhouse at Bridge, near Canterbury. The building was in the shape of a quadrangle with separate quarters for men, women and children on three of the sides, and the fourth side towering over the rest, housing the Guardians' Board room, waiting rooms and lodging rooms for the master. There was only one entrance to the building, through an archway under the Guardians' Board room. The only windows to face out were also on the Guardians' side; all the other windows looked in towards the central courtyard. In a written commentary which accompanied the engraving, readers were placed in no doubt as to what the building looked like – 'a prison!'[15]

Life inside these 'hell-holes' was portrayed as one of unremitting terror. Inmates were separated from their spouses and children; they had their heads shaved; and they were forced to work at degrading and menial tasks. A cartoon, probably dating from 1836, purported to show the interior of an English workhouse under the New Poor Law. Four paupers (three men and a woman) are shown beating hemp – which is 'worse than breaking stones' – while the children, with tears running down their cheeks, are picking oakum. An old man who asks for ten minutes' rest is forced back to work by an official, whip in hand. The official abuses him:

Rest, indeed! you lazy old thief, d'ye think ye came in here to be a gentleman. Old and young must labour here – what was the poor made for but to work?

In the background, some paupers are chained to the wall, while others hang hog-tied from a beam. Notices on the walls give the workhouse regulations. One of them states that 'all able-bodied paupers who conduct themselves in a mutinous or disorderly manner will be knocked on the head without a trial and their bodies sold to the surgeons'. Just to reinforce the point, a cart is shown being dragged away. One of the officials asks what is in it. The answer:

The infant poor wot's *died*, I'm going to take one to the hospital to sell for the surgeons have generally have such a load as this here once a week.[16]

A belief that the aim of a workhouse was actually to kill off the paupers and make a profit by selling their bodies to the surgeons for dissection was a persistent fear of popular opponents of the New Poor Law. Again there was nothing particularly new about such fears. During the 1832 cholera epidemic there had been rumours that the 'disease' was merely an excuse to get people into the special cholera hospitals where their bodies could be used for anatomical study. The use of paupers' bodies for such a purpose would, of course, be the final indignity, a symbol of the way the rich and powerful treated the poor and helpless. This is what one anonymous Welsh working man thought:

We know that the Framers of the laws of our land will not make any law to amend or ameliorate our condition. Loading heavier, that is the religion of wealth. *Lower, lower* with the condition of workmen and more labour add 'that's the rub'. And after the workman fails to work, to the Bastile with him to be plagued, to be separated from his wife and children, and to be slowly starved with water-porridge; and after he dies, thro' the visitation of God, *of course!* his corpse will be given up to the skilful butchers to be hacked and sawed asunder with their tools for *'dissecting for the benefit of science and the faculty'*...

As Peter Bussey told an audience at Bradford in June 1838: 'If they were poor they imprisoned them, then starved them to death, and after they were dead they butchered them.' As we shall see in the next chapter, such fears were not entirely without substance.[17]

But by far the most evocative symbol of life in the 'bastiles' was the atrocious food. The Reverend J.R. Stephens repeated to a meeting at Hyde in February 1839 what he had been told by a former inmate:

> their meat was the nastiest that could possibly be conceived, and ... in the skilly he detected lumps of resin which had been boiled in it... [Apparently] the skilly ran through them like water through a pipe, and they put the resin into it to make it stick in their belly.

Stories about the 'skilly', or workhouse soup, abounded and it quickly became the subject of some bitter satire. The *Champion and Weekly Herald* printed a recipe allegedly taken from the memorandum book of a Poor Law Commissioner:

> Take ten quarts of ditch-water, and stir it well with the body of a farthing rushlight, till it boils. Season it to your liking with old tealeaves, and it will be ready for use. The wick, which will not dissolve, is a delicious relish, and may be bottled whole, and, if you *should* want a desert, suck your fingers.

But probably the most imaginative description of the making of workhouse soup was this send-up of the Witches scene from *Macbeth*:

(Workhouse Laboratory – a Cauldron boiling – Groans.
Enter three Guardians.)

1st Guardian.	Thrice hath the dying pauper groan'd.
2nd Guardian.	And once his starving child hath moan'd.
3rd Guardian.	Rot-gut cries, 'Tis time',
1st Guardian.	Round about the cauldron go;
	In the loathsome victuals throw;
	Bone that in the shambles' drain
	Thirty days and nights hath lain,
	Taken from sheep that had the rot,
	Boiled here in the charmed pot.
All.	Double, double, toil and trouble, Fire burn and cauldron bubble ...

1st Guardian.	Cool it with a pauper's blood
	Then the charm is firm and good ...
	Now for water; make it thin,
2nd Guardian.	Put of that a plenty in
3rd Guardian.	That will make the paupers grin.
All.	Around, around, around, about, about, all bad come running in — all good keep out.

Supporters found it impossible to defend the New Poor Law from humorous attacks like this.[18]

Satire was one of the most potent weapons available to opponents of the New Poor Law and they used it to savage effect. The Tory *Wigan Gazette*, for instance, informed its readers that because a 'saving' was always put forward as the main justification of the New Poor Law it was strange that 'a much more economical and infinitely more humane method of avoiding the wasteful extravagance of maintaining unproductive old paupers should have been overlooked'. This was a system 'practised by the ancient Germans' and apparently cost virtually nothing. The newspaper continued with biting irony:

These [ancient] political economists enclosed the aged, the infirm, and even the deformed, in crates, and suffocated them at once in muddy pools, by which means they rid themselves of the trouble and cost of supporting them, and at the same time provided them with a coffin and grave. Strengthened in our opinion by physiological inquirers, who declare strangulation to be an easy kind of death, we deem the method now recommended to the notice of our political economists preferable, in point of humanity, to starving the poor by such a slow process as that to which the ... paupers are now condemned.[19]

Handbills were used for the dissemination of many anti-poor law satires. One of the most elaborate of these was 'The Mirror of the Age; or, the State Galanti Show', printed at Sheffield in November 1834. Signed 'The Showman', it was probably written by that inveterate pamphleteer, Samuel Roberts. The handbill purports to be a description of a fairground sideshow and the reader is invited to see what is taking place in this 'show of shows'. Looking through a special eye-glass the reader is first shown a 'large grand room' with three fine Lords – Brougham, the Bishop of London, and Althorp – seated at a table with 'heaps of golden money ... upon the scarlet table cloth'. Brougham addresses his companions:

'My Lords, we must either rob or be robbed. If we do not get more this will not be ours another year. We cannot fleece Lords, we cannot fleece the rich, who must we fleece?' 'Fleece the poor! fleece the poor! ... Yes, fleece the poor!' they all exclaim.

The reader then observes the three Lords making 'hodge, podge, or Althorpiano', for the poor to eat. Lord Althorp says 'we must accustom the poor to coarser food'. The next scene is of a grand dinner where the three Lords are eating. The Poor Law Commissioners enter bringing in 'a plate full of money'. Althorp asks:

'And you got all this already, from the overfed poor?' 'Yes, my Lord [answer the Commissioners], but it required very close scraping'.

The reader is next invited to look in on one of the new workhouses. First 'a large mean-looking room . . . long bare tables . . . a crowd of *men* all dressed alike . . . all looking sorrowful, many ill humoured'. Then a similar scene in the women's quarters, the children are

all dressed alike... Look what pale faces they have, and how many of them are crying. Little dears, many of them will perhaps never see their daddies and mammies again.

Finally the reader is invited to look in on a 'dismal little room' full of 'rough coffins'. The showman addresses the reader:

Look the men are bringing the body of a poor woman, – they put it into a coffin ... and the doctors take it away. No, not to bury it, but to cut it into pieces as butchers do calves. I could show you them at work, but you would not like it...[20]

Cartoons were also used to mount satirical attacks on the New Poor Law. The radical engraver, Charles Jameson Grant, produced a succession of anti-poor law cartoons in his *Political Drama* series in the mid-1830s. 'Effects of the New Bastardy Law' purport to show Brougham and the Bishop of London wheeling barrow-loads of infants into a workhouse. Althorp, in the uniform of a parish beadle, stands guard at the door. In the background four 'gentlemen' stand talking:

I say, Sir John, there are a few specimens of *good breeding* at all events exercised under the new [Poor] law.

Ha! ha! I suppose you would call this the fruits of the new Bastardy law.

Delightful idea. The sensualist can now enjoy himself without the fear of *corroborative testimony*.[21]

One of the best cartoon satires on the New Poor Law was 'Sunday Amusements in a Union Workhouse'. It lacks the savagery of Grant's work or the simplicity of 'England's Infernal Machine', but as a means of pointing up the duplicity of the Whig government, the cartoon is unequalled. The background to the cartoon was a request to the government by a 'respectable deputation' that workhouse inmates be allowed out on Sunday to attend their respective places of worship. The Home Secretary, Russell, refused 'on the ground that the poor old creatures, if let out ... might spend their time improperly'. The government's concern for the souls of the poor suggested the idea that the same care was needed for the rich. Hence the cartoon. In a commentary which accompanied the cartoon the scene in the workhouse was explained.

Here is represented one of the small rooms in a new Union Bastile, appropriated to able bodied men. In this room six of the zealous Noble Advocates of the pauper imprisonment system are seen confined, on the Sabbath day, to prevent their spending it improperly, they being there dieted as they have ordered the poor to be. On the right-hand side, Lord Brougham has got Lord John Russell upon his shoulders in order to enable him to get a peep into the prison yard out of one of those high placed small windows common in the new Bastiles. The time is after dinner, when the bells are ringing for afternoon service. Lord John [Russell] is supposed to be saying, 'why, Brougham! I think this must be as bad as being at Church!' to which the late Chancellor replies, 'I really think it is, but I cannot tell' ... Next to them is Lord Melbourne, attempting with the poker, to make an opening through the wall into the adjoining apartment in which the younger women are confined. He has a packet in his pocket addressed to *'Mrs. Norton, on State Affairs.'* Farther on is seen Lord Howick amusing himself by drawing shadowy outlines of *'Liberty and Plenty.'* In the foreground, on the left hand, Lord Althorp and the Bishop of London are seated on stools with a small table between them; the former has a placard on his knee headed *'Improved method of fattening Cattle,'* while the latter has a roll under his arm, inscribed, *Bastardy Clause.'* There are cards upon the table with which the two have been playing at *'Beggar my Neighbour'.* There is likewise an Old Weather House, which the Bishop has been altering so as to bring the woman out during storms – while the man is snug within. He is now, with doleful countenance, exhibiting to his noble companion the empty plate and wooden spoon; over his head is inscribed on the wall *'Wanted for Dissection'* – under his stool a famished mouse lies dead. On the wall, over Lord Althorp, the Chancellor has written *'Our Estates will not be our own another year.'* Over Lord Melbourne are two placards, one headed *'The Last Scale of Reduced Pauper Diet,* and the other, *'Commissioners Last Orders'*. On the floor are several empty gruel basons.[22]

Apart from being an amusing attack on Whig hypocrisy, the cartoon was a summary of the fears of popular opponents of the New Poor Law.

IV

Of all the rumours and fears concerning the New Poor Law, the most infamous were the Marcus pamphlets. This series of pamphlets, which appeared in the winter of 1838-9, purported to advocate a state-controlled system of infanticide in order to restrict the size of working-class families. They caused a furore. The pamphlets and the response they caused are worth examining in detail, not only because they help point out the way rumours and fears were mobilised by the anti-poor law movement, but also because they help illustrate the difficulties historians can face when trying to distinguish between the satirist and the crank whose intentions were deadly serious. On 8 December 1838 the *Northern Liberator* carried a small item on 'a pamphlet, privately printed at first, but now openly published' which appeared to recommend 'the MURDER *by wholesale of new-born infants*, by a scheme called *"Painless Extinction!"* ' The paper said it had the pamphlet in its possession and would publish extracts in future editions of the paper. Two weeks later, under the heading 'Practical Philosophy of the Men now in Power', the newspaper gave further details of the pamphlet. The pamphlet began with the old Malthusian argument that 'populousness *must* be limited by some means, or misery ... [will] go on increasing'. Where it differed from Malthus, however, was in the belief 'that no moral checks, such as prolongued or entire celibacy will ever be found to be effectual to the end proposed'. Other means had to be found to check the growth in population, and the means suggested was the 'EXTINCTION of certain number of infants as soon as born!' The pamphlet suggested every third infant and argued at great length 'that we have a *moral right* to commit this sort of murder, and that all we have to be careful about is, that it be a *painless extinction!*'[23]

The first anti-poor law leader to make mention of the pamphlet was the Reverend J.R. Stephens. In a speech he made immediately after being released on bail in late December 1838, Stephens not only condemned the pamphlet but also suggested that one of the Poor Law Commissioners was the real author. Stephens continued:

> There is, then, to be a sort of *Parish Registry* of all *married persons* (poor, of course) who may happen to have three children; and when the mother of any such family happens to be *enceinte* of the 4th, a parish officer, a spy, is to report to an official professional man-midwife; and such man-midwives alone are to attend all such accouchements. When the travail is over ... when the baby ... is born, the *remorseless midwife is to tear it away from its mother, without the permission of a single embrace... The child ... is then, with all convenient speed, to have an end put to its existence, by the introduction into its slender frame of a small portion of noxious gas.*[24]

Stephen's revelations caused a sensation and not only amongst the labouring population. Assistant Commissioner Power quickly contacted the Poor Law Commission, informing them that Stephens had committed a 'gross libel'. Edwin Chadwick immediately denied Stephens's charge that one of the Poor Law Commissioners was the author of the pamplet: 'Mr Nicholls, Mr Lewis and Mr Lefevre were not, collectively or individually, the authors or author of it.' According to Chadwick the Commissioners were not even aware of the pamphlet's existence prior to Stephens's announcement. Unfortunately for the Commission, the public denial only earned the rejoinder from Stephens that 'there are other [Assistant] Commissioners, a score or two, besides these three, and then there was Mr Chadwick himself, his patron Lord Brougham, and his bosom friend Mr Francis Place, and their female assistant Miss Martineau'.[25]

There is little doubt that Chadwick was truthful in his claim that the Poor Law Commission had not even heard of the pamphlet before Stephens had brought it to their attention. When Power wrote complaining of Stephens's slanderous statements, he had to admit that he was 'wholly unacquainted' with the pamphlet, 'not having been able as yet to procure any copy'. A few days later, when Chadwick wrote asking Power to try to discover the identity of the author of the work 'advocating infanticide', Power had to admit that he had 'not yet been enabled to ascertain that any such work [actually] exists'. All he had to go on was 'the report of Mr Stephens's sermon' and the fact that the pamphlet was 'spoken of by other parties, besides Mr Stephens'. Power promised he would 'continue to inquire into the fact of its existence'.[26]

There were in fact two pamphlets. An anonymous pamphlet, *An Essay on Populousness*, had been printed in London in 1838. It carried the note 'printed for private circulation' on its title page. This pamphlet presented the neo-Malthusian argument that over-population was the cause of distress and coyly suggested that something should be done about it. There was no mention of infanticide, or painless extinction. The second pamphlet, *On the Possibility of Limiting Populousness* was written under the pseudonym Marcus and was printed in London by John Hill in 1838. It was this second work that was the one to suggest the scheme of 'painless extinction'. The two pamphlets are written in such a similar style and express such similar views that one can only assume they were both the work of 'Marcus'. Despite attempts by Power and the Poor Law Commission to discover the identity of Marcus, it has remained a mystery. The *Manchester Guardian* suggested that the pamphlets might well be English translations of French originals. The suggestion is not as odd as it might first appear: quite a few words have French spelling and some of the phraseology is reminiscent of direct translation from French into English. The Poor Law Commission took up the suggestion and tried 'tracing the work to its origin', but without success. No evidence has come to light which would either support or disprove the speculation that Marcus might have been French. It remains merely an interesting *possibilité*.[27]

Equally puzzling is whether the Marcus pamphlets were meant as a clever satire against the New Poor Law or whether they were the work of a neo-Malthusian crank and were therefore supposed to be taken seriously. If they were meant as satire they certainly were not very well written satire. The most obvious comparison is with Swift's *A Modest Proposal*, a satire suggesting the breeding of children for food in famine-torn Ireland. And yet there is none of the biting irony that one finds in Swift. The Marcus pamphlets are long and turgid with none of the witty remarks one would expect to find in a work of satire. Certainly when cheaper versions of the Marcus pamphlets came to be published, it was thought necessary to add a racy introduction to give them more pep.[28]

The Marcus pamphlets were not only verbose, they were also expensively produced. The first edition of *On the Possibility of Limiting Populousness* ran to nearly a hundred pages, used a large and expensive typeface, and was printed in octavo form on high-quality paper. It sold for 2 shillings. The price and quality were much higher than one would expect for a satire or squib aimed at the popular market. Furthermore, the first edition of the pamphlet was sold, not by the network of radical and working-class booksellers, but by a perfectly respectable London bookshop. James Whittle, the Liverpool Chartist leader, bought his copy of the pamphlet at the shop of Sherwood and Company early in January 1839. James Paul Cobbett informed his brother John that he was 'quite at a loss to conceive how such a thing c[oul]d come from such a source'. Sherwood and Company were reputable London booksellers and he could not understand what had 'induced them to touch anything so perilous'. Possibly the booksellers did have second thoughts once they had discovered what was contained in the pamphlet, because when Whittle returned to buy further copies he was told that it was 'out of print'.[29]

The question of whether the pamphlet was intended as a satire or to be taken seriously remains unanswered. It is hard to conceive of the scheme of 'painless extinction' being put forward as a serious proposal, and yet why would a satire be produced in such an expensive form? Despite Stephens's claim that it was written by one of the Poor Law Commissioners, the weight of opinion amongst leading Chartists and popular opponents of the New Poor Law was that the pamphlet was the work of some enemy of the New Poor Law. James Paul Cobbett was probably closest to the truth when he claimed that it came 'from some Tory quarter, to injure the Whigs'.[30]

If the intentions of Marcus in writing the pamphlets remain obscure, the purposes to which they were put by popular opponents of the New Poor Law are not. Throughout the first half of 1839, Marcus and his evil scheme were used to attack the New Poor Law and its proponents unmercifully. The authorities even managed to give the Marcus pamphlets greater publicity by making a rather ham-fisted job of trying to suppress them. No sooner had the pamphlets disappeared from bookshops than some enterprising radical printers began publishing their own cheap editions. The *Northern Star* advertised a 'Peoples Edition', which combined the two Marcus pamphlets and was published under the title *The Book of Murder*. The author was described as 'Marcus, one of the Three'. In order to make it more palatable to the general reader, the 'Peoples Edition' contained an introduction which not only gave it added bite but also made sure that the reader drew the correct conclusions from Marcus's turgid prose. The reader was informed that

> the most atrocious conspirators ... have actually plotted, and schemed, and prepared the means of perpetrating the MURDER OF MORE THAN ONE-HALF THE CHILDREN TO BE BORN INTO THE WORLD! – THE ASSASSINATION OF MORE THAN HALF OF THE FUTURE RACES OF ALL MANKIND.

Who were these atrocious conspirators? '[A]n active and powerful philosophical and political PARTY IN THE STATE, comprising both public writers and public men' – in other words the Philosophical Radicals.[31]

That the Philosophical Radicals lay behind Marcus's proposal was a theme taken up by the *Northern Liberator* in an open letter it published to the Home Secretary, Lord John Russell, in January 1839. Marcus would have been of little account, it said, had it not been for the fact that the principles of Malthus

> which have given rise to this murderous proposal, *are known to be the principles of many of the men now having political power*, and especially of those who framed and helped to pass a measure the most abhorrent to the people of England of any that had been passed for centuries — THE POOR LAW AMENDMENT BILL. Of that bill the people complain that it actually *does* (though by worse means) that which Marcus *recommends*... Hence all this agitation ... MARCUS, MALTHUS, MURDER, THE [NEW] POOR LAW, AND THE GOVERNMENT, are now all MIXED TOGETHER in the minds of the people... The people now deem it ... to be '*one concern*'...

The *Northern Liberator* took the theme up again in a satirical story it ran on Marcus in March 1839. The author of the piece claimed he had been invited to witness 'the brilliant dawn of a new era in science' – Marcus's experiment on a new-born infant. Marcus allegedly said that he was there 'to do what that great man [Malthus] had left undone'. An engraving which accompanied the story showed Marcus conducting his experiment before representatives of the Church, the law, government and Philosophical Societies. Marcus finished his lecture by performing 'the experiment of the "painless extinction" of an infant'. As the infant slid off into extinction the audience applauded. With savage irony the author alleged that a select few of the assembled audience, including Aristocrats, Philosophical Radicals, and 'two or three of Her Majesty's Ministers' had the honour to sup with Marcus afterwards. He concluded: 'we fondly hope that from this auspicious moment, we may date the diffusion of a more liberal science in England than she has yet witnessed'.[32]

It is unclear how many people actually believed that Marcus and his proposal were supported by the Poor Law Commission or the government. The evidence is conflicting. Assistant Commissioner Mott spoke to several operatives soon after Stephens had claimed that Marcus was a Poor Law Commissioner and said that they were of the opinion that Stephens was insane. John Moxon, one of the anti-poor law Guardians at Huddersfield, is alleged to have declared 'that no person *could believe* such a work to have emanated from the Poor Law Commissioners'. On the other hand, when Assistant Commissioner Power asked the Preston agent of the *Northern Star*, from whom he had just bought a 'cheap edition' of Marcus, what was meant by the words on the title page, 'one of the Three', the man replied without hesitation 'one of the "Three Poor Law Commissioners to be sure" '. The *Bradford Observer* expressed surprise that 'so many working men' could have given credence to the notion that Marcus was a Commissioner. And in Loughborough, Leicestershire, the 'lower orders' were reported to have 'swallowed' Marcus's lies whole.[33]

What was significant about Marcus and his proposal, of course, was not that people believed it to be true but that they were able to conceive of such a possibility. In a sense, Marcus's proposal was just the logic of Malthus and the Philosophical Radicals carried to an absurd conclusion. When the Poor Law Commission issued their denial that they had anything to do with the Marcus pamphlet, George Condy, the editor of the radical *Manchester and Salford Advertiser*, reminded them that they shared a common parentage with Marcus. The Poor

Law Commissioners 'know', he said,

> and *'Marcus'* and Lord Brougham boast, that their calculations are
> founded on that terrifying revelation made as to population, and
> what was to be done with its overplus, by that priest of Satan,
> MALTHUS. Here there must — there shall be no mistake.
> Whoever works in, or abets, or approves of the New Poor Law, is,
> whether he knows it or not, a child slaying, anti-procreation
> Malthusian.

As the *Northern Liberator* pointed out, the New Poor Law 'actually
does' what Marcus only recommended, and by worse means.[34]

V

Rumour and fear helped shape the campaign of popular opposition to
the New Poor Law. Much of the language and most of the symbols
which were used to attack the New Poor Law had their roots in the
'primitive fears' of the labouring population at large. Because we live in
a modern, rationalist age it is often extremely difficult for us to
appreciate the 'primitive' beliefs and assumptions of a different time
and place. And yet we must if we are to understand the motivations of
the mass of people who opposed the New Poor Law. There was
something sinister and frighteningly different about the New Poor
Law: it turned social relationships, human values and Christian
worship on their head; it was part of a general attack on the rights and
customs of the labouring population of England and Wales. The
language of 'fear' and 'horror' provided popular opponents of the New
Poor Law with a means of explaining the measure to themselves and
ultimately of mounting a challenge to it.

> Thus was the three-fold chain of tyrants forged;
> Thus was the blood-stained Moloch trebly gorged,
> As soon it gave a hideous monster birth,
> Fierce as Hell's furies, terrible as death,
> Hear the Ex-Chancellor in bloated pride,
> Eliza's long-tried act with scorn deride,
> And in its stead produce a famous scheme,
> To check our populations onward stream;
> To feed the peasantry on 'coarser fare',

And drive our ruined daughters to despair;
To build huge prisons, paupers to confine,
And punish honest poverty as crime;
To tear asunder each domestic tie,
To snatch the infant from the parents eye; ...

Such was the cursed device, the child of hell,
And public plunderers loved the monster well.
Tories and Whigs, Lords, Commons with good will
Grasped at the plan, and passed the Poor Law Bill.[35]

This is more than a mere catalogue of horror and injustice; it is the basis of a sustained critique of the New Poor Law.

Notes

1. J. Redlich and F.W. Hirst, *History of Local Government in England* (Macmillan, London, 1971), p.115; D. Frazer, *The Evolution of the British Welfare State* (Macmillan, London, 1973), p.47; N.C. Edsall, *The anti-Poor Law Movement* (Manchester University Press, Manchester, 1971), p.38.

2. M. Bruce, *The Coming of the Welfare State* (Batsford, London, 1967), p.89.

3. 'Second Annual Report of the PLC', *PP*, 1836, vol.XXIX, part 1, Appendix B, no.9, p.328.

4. T. Spencer,*The Successful Application of the New Poor Law...* (Ridgway, London, 1836), p.24; N. Longmate, *The Workhouse* (Temple Smith, London, 1974), p.73; Power to PLC, 19 August 1835, PRO, HO 73/51.

5. C. Driver, *Tory Radical* (Oxford University Press, New York, 1946), p.332; A. Digby, *Pauper Palaces* (Routledge & Kegan Paul, London, 1978), p.224.

6. W. Cobbett, 'Surplus Population: A Comedy in three Acts', published in *Cobbett's Political Register*, 28 May 1831, and *Cobbett's Two-Penny Trash*, vol.1, no.12 (June 1831). M.L. Pearl, *William Cobbett: A Bibliographical Account* (Oxford University Press, London, 1953), p.171, suggests that the character Peter Thimble lampoons Francis Place, and that the wicked seducer, Sir Grindum, was meant as an attack on Sir Francis Burdett.

7. *Cobbett's Political Register*, 6 June 1835; a'Court to Chadwick, 5 April 1835, Chadwick Papers, UCL, 152.

8. A surprisingly large number of northern provincial newspapers were opposed to the New Poor Law. They included Tory-controlled newspapers like the *Blackburn Standard, Bolton Chronicle, Halifax Guardian, Leeds Intelligencer, Manchester Chronicle,* and *Wigan Gazette.* Radical newspapers which opposed the New Poor Law included the *Champion and Weekly Herald, Leeds Times* (at least until Samuel Smiles took over as editor in 1839) and *Northern Liberator.* Another important anti-poor law paper was the *Sheffield Iris,* although its politics were slightly whiggish. Nationally the most important anti-poor law papers were *The Times* and *Northern Star.*

9. *Halifax Guardian*, 26 January 1839; *Manchester and Salford Advertiser*, 5 September 1840; *The Times,* 11 July 1837; *Northern Star,* 31 March 1838. Many of these horror stories were later collected together and published in G.R.W. Baxter, *The Book of the Bastilles, History of the New Poor Law* (Stephens, London, 1841).

10. PLC to Russell, 16 September 1837, PRO, MH 12/15063.

11. *Bradford Observer*, 2 February 1838; G.S. Bull, *Horrors of the Whig Poor Laws!* (W. Strange, London, [1837]), p.6; M. Rose, 'The Anti-Poor Law Movement in the North of England', *Northern History*, vol.1. (1966), p.78.

12. *Sheffield Iris,* 28 February 1837; S. Roberts, *Mary Wilden, A Victim of the New Poor Law* (Whittaker, London, 1839); J.M. Cobbett to Fielden, 23 August 1836, Fielden Papers, JRULM.

13. *The Times*, 3 July 1837; *Halifax Guardian*, 20 October 1838.

14. *The Times*, 26 December 1840.

15. *Champion and Weekly Herald*, 2 October 1836.

16. [Charles Jameson Grant], *The Political Drama*, no.57, bound collection in Working Class Movement Library, Manchester.

17. *Udgorn Cymru [Trumpet of Wales]*, no.1, translation supplied to HO by Marquis of Bute, PRO, HO 40/57; *The Times*, 8 June 1838. See also my forthcoming article, 'Popular Attitudes to Death and Dissection in Early Nineteenth Century Britain: The Anatomy Act and the Poor', *Labour History*, no.49, November 1985.

18. *Northern Star*, 23 February 1839; *Champion and Weekly Herald*, 8 January 1837; *Northern Liberator*, 24 March 1838.

19. *Wigan Gazette*, 23 December 1836.

20. 'The Mirror of the Age; or, the State Galanti Show' (handbill), PRO, MH 12/15465.

21. [Charles Jameson Grant], *Political Drama*, no.60, bound collection in the Working Class Movement Library, Manchester.

22. S. Roberts, *England's Glory; or, the Good Old Poor Laws...* (n.p., London, 1836), pp.31-2.

23. *Northern Liberator*, 8 & 22 December 1838.

24. *Leeds Mercury*, 5 Janaury 1839.

25. Power to PLC, 6 January 1839, PRO. MH32/64; *The Times,* 10 & 15 January 1839.

26. Power to PLC, 6 & 10 January 1839, PRO, MH 32/64.

27. *Manchester Guardian*, 20 February 1839; Power to PLC, 20 February 1839, PRO, MH 32/64. I have also attempted to locate a French original for the Marcus pamphlets. But none of the more obvious French bibliographies for the 1820s and 1830s, especially those concerning the debate over Saint-Simonism, reveal a pamphlet with a title like those of the Marcus pamphlets.

28. Marcus [pseud.], *The Book of Murder!* (Dugdale, London, 1839).

29. J.P. Cobbett to J.M. Cobbett, 16 January 1839, Fielden Papers, JRULM.

30. Ibid.

31. *Manchester and Salford Advertiser,* 19 January 1839; *Northern Star,* 9 February 1839; 'Introduction', Marcus [pseud.], *The Book of Murder!*, pp.3-4. S. and B. Webb, *English Poor Law History, Part II*, vol.1 (Frank Cass, London, 1963), p.163, wrote that Francis Place believed George Mudie, the Owenite printer and journalist, to be the author of the introduction.

32. *Northern Liberator*, 26 January and 2 March 1839.

33. Mott to Lewis, 11 January 1839; Mott and Muggeridge to Chadwick, 15 January 1839, PRO, MH 12/15065; Power to PLC, 2 March 1839, PRO, MH 32/64; *Bradford Observer*, 17 January 1839; Brock to PLC, 27 February 1839, PRO, HO 73/55.

34. *Manchester and Salford Advertiser*, 19 January 1839; *Northern Liberator*, 26 January 1839.

35. T.B. Smith, 'Gradual Oppression of the Labourer', *Northern Star*, 28 April 1838.

11

'THIS MODERN MOLOCH'

The 1834 Poor Law was a focus for popular discontent, rather than its sole cause. When the popular radicals of Bradford drew up *A Petition to Parliament Against the New Poor Law Act* in early 1835, they did not confine themselves to criticising the Act's poor relief policy; they also mentioned the hardship and suffering caused by the use of steam power and machinery in factories, and of the failure of the 1832 Reform Act to extend the franchise to the labouring population.[1] Immense changes were taking place in British society at the time. Technological development had created new industries and just as quickly forced long-established trades into decline. Whole towns had appeared where not long before there had been green fields and swift-running streams. And throughout it all, men and women had worked, played and struggled to survive. They also struggled to understand events in order that they might control what was happening to them. Boom and depression punctuated their lives; they were frightened by the 1832 Anatomy Act and the introduction of the New Police; the 1832 Reform Act and the 1833 Factory Act fell well short of their demands; and now the 1834 Poor Law held out the spectre of lower wages and possible starvation. It was hard to escape the conclusion that all these things were part of an orchestrated attempt to grind the labouring population down even further.

I

Mark Hovell has claimed that the leaders of the anti-poor law movement 'drew their inspiration from the Bible, from a belief that the Act was a violation of Christian principles'.[2] Although one could quibble about the exclusive nature of the claim, there is no denying that Christianity provided a powerful weapon with which to attack the 1834 Poor Law. And, what is perhaps even more important, it also provided a set of beliefs and assumptions with which people could begin to grasp and comprehend the New Poor Law's significance.

'The Old Poor Law was of God,' claimed Samuel Roberts, 'the New one is of the Devil.' In a long series of pamphlets written by the former

Sheffield cutler between 1834 and 1848, this theme occurs again and again. 'If the Devil himself', Roberts wrote in 1841,

> had ... been permitted for the sins of this nation to concoct a measure *which the legislature would enact*, the most calculated to cause the people to draw down upon it the vengeance of the Almighty, and lead to the speedy and entire destruction of the State; I cannot conceive one which would have been so likely as the *Poor Law Amendment Act.*

In another pamphlet, written in the same year, he reminded people that Christ had said they would be judged on how they treated the poor. Christ, he said,

> even considers *that* which we do to the *poor* as if it had been done to HIMSELF... Well then (horrible as it is) our impious rulers have had the selfish, audacious effrontery to concoct and establish a decree (for the sole purpose of adding a little to their enormous heaps of wealth) to impoverish, afflict, and destroy JESUS CHRIST himself in the persons of the poor...[3]

Such notions undoubtedly appealed to members of universalist sects like the Primitive Methodists, but one did not need to be a believer in immanentism to accept that the New Poor Law was unchristian.

Richard Oastler, a long-time supporter of the established Church, gave one of his pamphlets the title *Damnation! Eternal Damnation to the Fiend-Begotten 'Coarser-Food' New Poor Law.* In a foreword to the work he asked readers not to be

> alarmed at the sound of the title. I can not *bless* that, which God and NATURE CURSE. The Bible being true, the Poor Law Amendment Act is false! The Bible containing the will of God – this accursed Act of Parliament embodies the will of Lucifer. It is the Sceptre of Belial, establishing its sway in the land of Bibles!! DAMNATION: ETERNAL DAMNATION to the accursed Fiend!!

Like many Ultra-Tories, Oastler's religion and politics were tightly bound together:

> I gather my politics from the Holy Scriptures; I read them in the books of the Church, and I learn from the Judges of the land, that

'Christianity is part and parcel of the Law', and that, 'Christianity is interwoven in our Constitution'.

This, of course, only made the New Poor Law an even greater affront: 'had the Church of England been faithful to her mission the New Poor Law could not have been passed'. For the Church, the 'rights of the poor' were 'a sacred trust'. Hence, one of the reasons why Oastler sought a repeal of the 'infidel legislation' was to enable the Church to be 'presented to the people in her true position, as the guardian of their rights and liberties'.[4]

But it was the erstwhile Methodist preacher, the Reverend Joseph Rayner Stephens, who presented the most forceful Christian critique of the New Poor Law. 'The battle we are now fighting' over the New Poor Law, he told his parishioners at Stalybridge in January 1839,

is not the battle which most men take it to be. It goes much further . . . It is not a battle of party against party... It is not a struggle for power or for place... It is the working of the mystery of iniquity mentioned in Holy Scripture ... the struggle of Christ in his spirit ... against Belial in his spirit... It is the battle between God and Mammon – between Christ the Prince of Peace, and Belzebub, the Prince of the Devil. The question is, whether God shall reign in England, or whether Satan shall domineer...

Thus the New Poor Law was not only a product of the Devil, it heralded his possible rule on earth. 'For many years', claimed Stephens,

England has been a mark at which the devil has shot his most insidious but most destructive bullets. Covert and unobserved for a while, but at length more openly, and now at last without disguise. England is claimed by Satan as his lawful inheritance and prey.

To defeat the Devil, Stephens recommended that the 'Children of God' fight 'boldly and fearlessly' against the New Poor Law. The struggle would be a hard one, he said, but they must fight 'at all risks and at all hazards, even unto the death' if the terrible consequences were to be avoided. For if they lost the battle, Stephens could foresee the day when

an Act of Parliament, called the Word of God Amendment Bill

[would be] brought into the House of Commons... The time is not far off when it will be forbidden to read – when it will be forbidden to have, and above all, when it will be forbidden to preach the Bible.[5]

There is no doubt that many people actually believed in the existence of the Devil and the reality of his intervention on earth. Joseph Lawson, recalling his adolescence in the West Riding weaving village of Pudsey in the 1830s, tells us that

Such was the superstition at the time ... that the whole atmosphere was supposed to be full of good and bad spirits on errands of mercy or mischief; the later mission always preponderating – the evil spirits mostly prevailing over the good.

Nor was Pudsey unusual in this regard. James Obelkevich notes how a belief in the Devil as a living presence was accepted in the rural communities of South Lindsey until at least the middle of the nineteenth century.[6]

Some people even claimed to have seen the Devil on one of his many errands of temptation and deception.

He appeared to one man who was very devout... [The man had been] fretting about his clothes being so ragged, and wondering how he would be able to get new ones, as he found it hard to get sufficient food; when all at once a person with the appearance of a gentleman presented himself and offered him lots of gold. The poor man suspected his benefactor, and looking down at the gentleman's feet, saw that he had a 'cloven foot' ... The poor man immediately said, 'Satan, I defy thee'; whereupon the gentleman instantly vanished, leaving a strong smell of sulphur behind, which was a certain proof of his identity.[7]

For members of sects like the Primitive Methodists, who had most effectively incorporated popular beliefs about witches, spirits and the physical presence of the Devil into their theology, such sightings served an important practical function: they warned against backsliding and drew the devout even closer together.

Popular religious beliefs, including a belief in the Devil, helped provide the labouring population with a conceptual framework with which they could seek to comprehend and explain the immense changes taking place in society. After all, if the New Poor Law was inhuman and contrary to God's law did it not follow that it must be a product of the Devil? Thus the terms used to attack the New Poor Law – 'the Devil-King law', 'the Whigs' Hell-born bantling', and 'the Beast' – were more than rhetoric; they were metaphors with which working men and women helped to explain the New Poor Law to themselves and to others. In 'England's Infernal Machine', probably the most striking of all the anti-poor law cartoons, the concept is captured with wit and humour. The Devil is shown poised over England. In his hands he holds a flag labelled 'The New Poor Law Bill' and he thrusts it deep into the heart of London. As the Devil, with his bat-like wings extended either side of him, peers out from behind the flag there is just the hint of a grin on his face. The message is clear: the Devil would use the New Poor Law to spread his influence throughout the country.

The heathen Whigs and the greedy factory owners were to be the instrument for spreading the Devil's influence. The Reverend F.H. Maberly, who led a vigorous campaign against the New Poor Law in Cambridgeshire, claimed that he was opposed to both

> the abominable Poor Law Amendment Act, and the present Whig administration, the authors of this act, because that under *neither*, is God regarded. The Poor Law Amendment Act is in direct violation of his command, and as to our Whig rulers, they puff at all reference to the Deity.[8]

Samuel Roberts expressed similar views. The New Poor Law, he wrote, has been a suggestion of

> the arch-enemy of Christ – (MAMMON) – to those who seem neither to fear God nor regard men – to men wallowing in luxury on the spoils of the nation – striving to increase their own abundance by depriving the poor of that needful sustenance, which God and their country has awarded them.[9]

The hellish images of greed and avarice keep recurring. George Condy, editor of the radical *Manchester and Salford Advertiser*, referred to what he called 'the vampire spirit of the New Poor Law', 'prowling commissioners' and 'the clutches of greedy landlordism'. But it was with the factory system that the New Poor Law appeared to work in most perfect harmony. 'The existing factory and pauper systems,' wrote the radical Bury doctor, Matthew Fletcher, those monstrous Whig engines for dealing destruction upon thousands of our indigent and infant population, appear to be working together with a harmony of effect not dissimilar to what we sometimes see in real machinery, where the teeth of a particular mill-wheel are nicely adjusted to facilitate the grinding operation of another.[10]

In other words the 1834 Poor Law was specifically designed to provide factory fodder for industry.

II

It was the Factory Réform movement and the network of local Short Time Committees which had initially provided the organisational basis for the campaign of popular opposition to the 1834 Poor Law in the north of England. The move from factory reform to anti-poor law agitation was no mere accident. From the beginning the New Poor Law was viewed as a direct attack on wages. According to William Cobbett, the New Poor Law would compel the labouring population of England and Wales to live on lower wages and poorer quality food. He argued that as

no one but the weakest would accept relief under the new system, labourers would be prepared to work for any wages they could get. Thus the English labourer would be screwed down to Irish wages and Irish diet.[11]

No sooner had Cobbett issued his warning than the first moves were being made to bring about a lowering of wages in the manufacturing districts of the north. Early in June 1834, while the Poor Law Amendment Bill was still before Parliament, two leading Bolton cotton manufacturers, Henry and Edmund Ashworth, wrote to Edwin Chadwick suggesting that the future Poor Law Commission establish a labour migration scheme. Henry Ashworth said that as the rural counties were 'burthened with a superabundant population' and the cotton and woollen industries were 'very inadequately supplied with labourers' it would be to their mutual advantage if the rural unemployed were forced to migrate to the manufacturing districts. 'I am ... of [the] opinion', continued Ashworth, that if an alteration in the Poor Laws and an overturning of Trades Unions were effected (the sooner the better [this was later crossed out]) our manufacturing employments would then be fairly opened for general unrestricted competition, – the rate of wages would assimilate more nearly with those paid for the general labour of the Country and little or nothing would be heard again of superabundant population.

The Poor Law Commission jumped at the suggestion. They sent a circular letter to the leading manufacturers in the north in March 1835 and were gratified to learn, that 'there existed the greatest demand for labourers'. Before long the Poor Law Commission had established migration offices at Manchester and Leeds, and suitable pauper families in the south were being approached by local Boards of Guardians to see if they would be willing to move north.[12]

The number of paupers who eventually migrated north was relatively small. Despite what Ashworth and the other manufacturers had said, there was no real shortage of labour in the northern textile mills. What the factory owners required were child factory workers, not unskilled farm labourers. The figures tell the story. Of the 988 persons who migrated from the agricultural south to Yorkshire in 1836, nearly 70 per cent were children. Nor did all the children necessarily find jobs in factories. Samuel Walker, a coal merchant from Mirfield near Dewsbury, wrote to the Poor Law Commission seeking twenty to thirty boys to be apprenticed to coal miners. He requested that they be no more than eight to ten years of age 'as they are generally too tall after that age to learn the employment'. The Commission replied that they had no suitable applicants at present, but they would make enquiries. What they did not bother to do was to make enquiries about the conditions of work faced by the children employed in the mines. When the *First Report of the Children's Employment Commission* was published in 1842, it revealed the widespread practice of sending children from Union workhouses to work in coal mines. A rather shamefaced clerk to the Dewsbury Union later revealed that pauper children as young as five years of age had been sent down the mines by the Board of Guardians.[13]

The northern workers viewed the Poor Law Commission's labour migration scheme with serious misgivings. To the operatives in the Lancashire cotton mills it appeared to be nothing more than an attempt to smash their Trade Unions and force down wages. And to be fair, such results were not very far from the minds of those who had first suggested the scheme. When four unemployed labourers from Buckinghamshire arrived in Manchester in May 1835 to take up work at one of the cotton mills, they were threatened by the other workers 'if they worked under the price'. Within days they had all returned to their home parish of Coddington, saying 'they wo[ul]d not work for 14s. as they found the men there got more'. Assistant Commissioner Gilbert took a dim view of the whole affair, claiming the men were simply lazy, and advised the relieving officer to give them 'no relief if possible or at the most only bread'.[14]

The northern factory operatives and popular radicals soon came to realise, however, that the able-bodied paupers from the south offered no real threat to skilled workers and were merely the victims of scheming southern Guardians and the Poor Law Commissioners. Matthew Fletcher claimed that in numerous southern Unions

> vast numbers of destitute labourers and their families are shamefully coerced and hurried off to manufacturing towns, under the most discreditable pretexts. Partly by flattering promises and partly by dint of threats ... and it appears that unless they acquiesced, relief under any circumstances was often denied.[15]

Such victims needed to be pitied, not threatened.

Certainly those southern paupers who were shipped north arrived in a miserable condition. Robert Baker, the Poor Law Commission's migration agent in Leeds, reported their arriving 'without furniture ... [or] beds, and very badly clad, and almost always without a farthing to supply their immediate necessities'. Families with children had little trouble finding work because of the shortage of child factory workers. But single men were much more difficult to place. One of these men, who had had no food since morning and was 'without a penny to provide a lodging for the night', returned to Baker's office after unsuccessfully searching for work. He told Baker that he came from Suffolk where the local Guardians had refused him 'both work and relief and [he] was therefore obliged to come hither'. Baker informed the Poor Law Commission that he had been 'obliged to relieve such cases with 1/- and a little bread and cheese'. The relief came from Baker's own pocket and he expressed some concern about 'from whence I am to be repaid'.[16]

The conditions experienced by the southern paupers on their arrival contrasted greatly with the rosy picture many of them had been given of life in the north. A Mr Markwell, who came from the Oxon Union in

Suffolk, had allegedly been told by Assistant Commissioner James Kay that in Yorkshire 'he would get as much coal for 6d. as would last him a month, buy beef for 2½d. lb and obtain clothing almost for nothing – as it was made there'. Markwell signed what he thought was a contract guaranteeing him three years' employment and set off north with his family to this land of cheap coal and beef. He found that not only was the coal and beef as expensive as it was in Suffolk but that his 'contract' only bound him to serve his employer for three years and did not guarantee him any employment. When Markwell attempted to leave to obtain better-paid work he was taken before the magistrates and threatened with imprisonment, but as soon as trade declined he was sacked.[17]

The main threat caused by the labour migration scheme to the northern factory operatives came from the employment of children. The 1833 Factory Act had set the maximum period of labour for children under thirteen years at eight hours a day. What it did not do was restrict hours for adults or ban night work for children. The factory operatives therefore feared that the factory owners would institute a double-shift, or relay system, for the children and work the adult operatives up to sixteen hours a day. A shortage of child labour had so far precluded the factory owners from instituting such a system, but the New Poor Law and its labour migration scheme now made it all too possible. Matthew Fletcher warned that 'the teeth of the New Poor Law are made available to give them the requisite impetus'.[18]

For a brief period in late 1836, before depression hit the textile industry in the north of England, the mill owners did institute a double-shift system. 'Both in Yorkshire and Lancashire' reported the Leeds Mercury in December 1836,

> great numbers of mills are working on the relay system. In some places there is a scarcity of hands, which has inconvenienced the mill owners; but this has been partly remedied by the removal of families from the overpopulated agricultural districts... It is obvious that the success of the relay system removes every pretence for demanding a Ten Hours Bill.

Popular radicals and factory reformers agreed that the New Poor Law and factory system were working in harmony, but came to a radically different conclusion about the need for a Ten-Hours Bill. The Reverend J.R. Stephens told a meeting at Stockport in February 1838, that in supporting the Ten-Hours Bill he had been advocating a repeal of the New Poor Law and 'vice versa'.

The manufacturers could not stand without a poor-law bill; and if the poor-law bill was fastened upon the working people, good bye to the ten-hours bill. If once the poor-law was come, they would be no better than a set of cattle. Wages would be down to the starvation point; just sufficient to keep body and soul together. But if the [New Poor] law was repealed the manufacturers must reform.[19]

III

The 1834 Poor Law had two main functions: to save the property-owning class money and to act as an instrument of social discipline. The well-regulated workhouse with its strictly enforced classification would not only discourage paupers from seeking relief, but also inculcate them with the habits of industry and independence. In fact some proponents of the New Poor Law wanted to reinforce its role as an instrument of social discipline by linking the administration of poor relief directly with the provision of a New Police. Charles Mott suggested to his friend Edwin Chadwick that 'the *Roads Trust* and *Surveyorship of Highways* for *Pauper Labour* might be combined with *a system of Police'*. He proposed the establishment of Police Houses at regular intervals along roads to render assistance to 'trampers, travellers, Accidents on the Roads &c.' According to Mott an efficient signalling system set up between the Houses would enable large numbers of policemen to be assembled 'at a very short notice, at any given point in disturbed districts – where Rioting or Burnings existed'. And when not busy suppressing disturbances, Mott thought the policemen 'might superintend the Pauper Labour &c.'[20]

Luckily for the poor and destitute of England and Wales nothing came of Mott's proposal, but nevertheless the New Poor Law remained inextricably bound up with the issue of social discipline and in particular with the establishment of a rural Police Force. When the Assistant Commissioners began moving in to the north of England in late 1836 the prospect of the introduction of a new Police Force was yet another issue on which the popular radicals could attack the 1834 Poor Law. George Condy told an anti-poor law meeting at Manchester in March 1837 that there was a 'secret clause' attached to the New Poor Law. 'The secret clause ... was the introduction of the Bourbon police, to enforce upon the people the observances of this [New Poor] law.'[21] Certainly the Poor Law Commission maintained a keen interest in the establishment of a rural Police Force. When the Assistant

Commissioners began establishing the New Poor Law in the southern counties early in 1835 a clear need was shown for a new civil force. Local officials were only too well aware of the problem. Two Norfolk magistrates informed Lord John Russell, the Home Secretary, that as

the Assistant Commissioners are now carrying into effect the provisions of the Poor Law Amendment Act ... we beg to press upon your Lordship the necessity of forthwith establishing some local civil force to meet any emergency which may arise. The common Constables are notoriously unequal to this duty and we are satisfied His Majesty's Ministers cannot wish it to devolve upon the Military.

And as for special constables: 'when riots and tumults are apprehended it has been found, not only that the persons so appointed have been indisposed to act, but also that it has been too late for them to do so effectively'. Local officials throughout the country expressed similar views. The foreman of the Norfolk Grand Jury said there was an urgent need for an efficient civil force to meet 'any emergency which may arise in carrying the provisions of the New Poor Law Act into operation'. The petty constables, he informed the Home Secretary, are 'notoriously unequal to such a duty'.[22]

The Home Office and Poor Law Commission solved the problem in the short term by using the Metropolitan Police. At the first sign of trouble in a Union, a force of London policemen would be sent down and sworn in as special constables. In most cases they proved more than adequate in dealing with the troublesome farm labourers. And of course if the crowd got out of hand there was still the military to fall back on.

The long-term solution was to establish a rural Police Force. In 1837 a Commission was set up to inquire into the best means of establishing such a force. The proposal for setting up the Commission came from the Secretary to the Poor Law Commission, Edwin Chadwick. He informed Home Secretary Russell that 'repeated communications received at the Poor Law Commission Office' showed the need for an efficient New Police force. Chadwick recognised that any 'efficient plan' would run into opposition from 'corrupt interests' and that these might endanger the government by throwing 'unpopularity' on it.

The cry of Gendarmerie and of attacks upon the liberties of Englishmen will be raised in the village by every jobbing constable or Magistrates clerk; by every Brewer for Beer shops; by the Cobbettite Politicians and the press which has not yet ceased to assail the Metropolitan Police as being French and an instrument of despotism.

Chadwick therefore believed that the subject could only be safely brought forward 'by means of a Commission'. He reminded Russell that this procedure had worked well with the 1834 Poor Law. Russell approved the proposal and asked Chadwick if he would like to be a member of the Commission.[23]

Chadwick's views on the role of the police are worth examining in detail. As A.P. Donajgrodzki has recently pointed out, Chadwick's experience as secretary to the Poor Law Commission had led him steadily to broaden his view of the constituents of social policy. Chadwick informed Russell:

The view generally taken of the functions of a Police force have always appeared to me extremely narrow. Popularly they are for the most part viewed as a mere agency for the apprehension of criminals...

Chadwick, on the other hand, believed their duties should extend into non-penal areas. He foresaw the police 'superintending the labour on the turnpike roads', 'being in charge of Fire Engines, ladders and escapes' and looking after 'lost or found goods or children'. The provisions of such services, Chadwick believed, would render the New Police 'less obnoxious' in the eyes of the public. In one area of social legislation Chadwick thought the police had a central role to play:

the complete operation of the principles of the poor law Amendment Act is largely dependent on the aid of a rural Police whose chief functions would necessarily be clearly connected with the poor law business of a Board of Guardians in respect of casual poor or mendicants and vagrants, the pursuit and apprehension of runaway parents, the punishment of refractory paupers, the suppression of tumults connected with the administration of relief.[24]

When Chadwick came to write the Constabulary Forces Commission Report in 1839 he obtained most of his evidence through the agency of the Poor Law Commission. He painted a frightening picture: 100,000 people annually convicted for some form of criminal activity, and an annual prison population of 20,000 and rising. Of course the Report found that none of the crime was due to poverty or destitution: it was merely the result of greed, caused by the temptation to obtain property without working for it. The Report's recommendations were straightforward enough: a paid Constabulary Force was to be set up in all the counties of England and Wales on the same principles as the Metropolitan Police.[25]

Although there had been no specific mention of poor relief or of the 1834 Poor Law in the *Constabulary Forces Commission Report*, popular opponents of the New Poor Law were in no doubt that the rural police were intended to work in harmony with the hated measure. As early as February 1837 James Walton had warned an anti-poor law meeting at Haworth that 'after this essay of tyranny [the New Poor Law], Lord John Russell had thrown out another feeler, and that the rural police and the silent system would follow up and enforce the Poor Law Bill'.[26] The appearance of London policemen on the streets of northern towns in 1837-8 protecting Assistant Commissioners and keeping the populace out of Boards of Guardians meetings only served to reinforce the warning.

Popular radicals feared that the proposed rural police would restrict both their democratic liberties and their opportunities for protest. Some of these fears were caught up with the traditional English apprehension over a standing army, with which the police were initially identified in many quarters. The Reverend J.R. Stephens even alleged that 'the New Poor Law Bastiles [were] ... intended to be a chain of barracks round the country, each capable of holding 500 to 1,000 men, and each intended to be garrisoned in part by regular military and in part by the Russellite military police'. Others remembered Oliver the Spy and the use to which government agents and informers had been put in the immediate post-war years; they feared the New Police would be used a spies or *agents provocateurs*. John Foster tells us that by mid-1842 the spy system in Oldham was in full operation, with plain-clothes country police acting as agents. But it was a fear of the police being used as an auxiliary to the New Poor Law which caused most concern. 'The New Poor Law and the rural Police', warned one anonymous pamphleteer,

are both intended for the same class of persons, or supposed to be so intended; they are merely parts of the same system. But, bad as the

New Poor Law is, I believe it is mercy itself to what it is intended to be; or what it will be, if a Police Force be generally established.[27]

IV

At first glance the 1832 Anatomy Act would appear to have had little to do with the 1834 Poor Law. For the labouring population of England and Wales, however, the Anatomy Act (like the factory system, New Police and New Poor Law) was perceived as yet another example of how little those in positions of power and authority cared for the lives or feelings of working men and women. It was also linked to the New Poor Law because under the terms of the Act the unclaimed bodies of paupers could be sold to anatomy schools for dissection.

The Anatomy Act, like the New Poor Law, had its origins in changes which had taken place in British society in the eighteenth century. The old trade of barber-surgeon had been slowly transformed into a science, a science based on the findings of empirical research carried out in the dissecting room. These new research methods brought with them a new emphasis on the practical training of doctors. It was no longer sufficient for a medical student simply to witness dissections; he was expected to gain practical, first-hand knowledge and experience in the dissecting room. The combination of the requirements of empirical research and the new practical teaching methods resulted in an increased demand for corpses.

Traditionally the scaffold had provided subjects for dissection, but increasingly the medical profession was forced to find other sources. The bodies of deceased hospital patients were acquired and increasingly even graves were robbed. As public awareness of dissection and the nefarious trade in bodies grew, so did bitterness against the surgeons and 'resurrection men'. In 1801, a London crowd wrecked a public house used by resurrection men. Any surgeon or anatomist who offended popular sensibilities could also expect to become the target of crowd anger. And in Glasgow troops had to be called out on no less than four occasions to protect members of the medical profession after it had been discovered that they were being supplied with bodies from local graveyards. With increased awareness came an increased vigilance at the graveyard. Paid watchmen had always been available to those who could afford them. By the beginning of the nineteenth century the poor were also organising to keep a watch over the graves of their relatives and friends.[28]

Crisis point for the medical profession was reached in February 1828 when William Gill, a 'respectable teacher of Anatomy', was tried and convicted by a Lancashire court for having in his possession a dead body, 'knowing it to be unlawfully disinterred'. He was fined £30. Until then those receiving corpses had been ignored by the law and only persons actually involved in the disinterment had been prosecuted. The new ruling meant that henceforth all teachers of anatomy who used illegally obtained corpses were liable to prosecution. The Royal College of Surgeons immediately brought pressure to bear on the government with the result that a House of Commons Select Committee was set up to inquire into the manner of obtaining subjects for dissection in schools of anatomy. The Committee took evidence from distinguished members of the medical profession, a number of magistrates and three unnamed resurrectionists. Its recommendations were that murderers should no longer be dissected, but that the bodies of paupers dying unclaimed in workhouses, hospitals and other public institutions should be used in their place. '[W]hat bodies ought to be selected', argued the Committee, 'but the bodies of those, who have either no known relations whose feelings would be outraged, or such only as, by not claiming the body, would evince indifference on the subject of dissection [?]' That a person might experience anguish or apprehension on his or her own account was ignored. Nor was it accepted that what appeared as 'indifference' to the Committee members, in not claiming the body of a relative, was in fact only an indication of poverty.[29]

The scandalous revelations concerning the Burke and Hare murders in Edinburgh assisted in getting the Committee's report accepted. Burke and Hare had murdered their victims so as to be able to sell their bodies to the surgeons. But although a Bill along the lines recommended was introduced, it was eventually withdrawn after the Bishops in the House of Lords objected to the want of provisions for the Christian burial of remains. This proved to be only a temporary setback. In November 1831 the country was scandalised by the arrest of Bishop and Williams for committing a series of murders similar to those of Burke and Hare. The brutality of Bishop and Williams, and the fact that the crimes were committed in London, was a spur to renewed parliamentary activity. A new Bill, based on the 1829 proposals, was introduced. This time it contained provisions for the christian burial of the remains. Although the Bill satisfied the Bishops and most of the medical profession it was not without its opponents.

In Parliament it was the popular radicals and old fashioned Tories who led the attack. Henry Hunt tabled amendments to almost every clause. He spoke of the fear of dissection being one of 'the natural feelings of mankind' and cited the case of Dr William Hunter, the most famous of the eighteenth-century anatomists, who although 'he had dissected so many himself, up to the very last moment of his life declared that he objected to the operation being performed on him[self]'. Hunt suggested that every surgeon who conducted dissections should give an undertaking to allow his body to be dissected after death. One of the arguments used by supporters of the Anatomy Act, both in the 1828 Select Committee Report and in the parliamentary speeches in favour of the Act, was that the poor and destitute who were maintained at public expense should repay society by allowing their bodies to be used for scientific research after death. Hunt skilfully showed the blatant hypocrisy of those who used such arguments, when he moved that the bodies of all sinecurists and government pensioners should also be given over for dissection.[30]

In the House of Lords the Tory opposition to the Bill was less biting, but no less forceful. The Earl of Harewood 'did not see why the bodies of the poor and friendless should be particularly selected for the dissecting knife'. Lord Wynford supported him and said it was preferable that criminals should be dissected, rather than 'honest members of the community'. He admitted that something needed to be done, but he contended that there were other places, besides workhouses, hospitals and debtors' prisons, from which an ample supply might be procured. However, the opposition was unavailing and the Anatomy Act was passed into law.[31]

Most of the radical press do not appear to have taken up the issue of the Anatomy Act, at least not while it was still before Parliament. Part of the explanation is that they were too preoccupied with the 1832 Reform Crisis. Furthermore, radical opinion was deeply divided on the issue. Such prominent radicals as Major Cartwright and Augustus Hardin Beaumont, founder of the radical Newcastle *Northern Liberator*, had bequeathed their own bodies for dissection. And Francis Place's National Political Union supported the Anatomy Act. They admitted 'that the bill was defective in some particulars', but thought that ultimately it was in the interest of the working people. But the closer one moves towards popular radicalism, the stronger the cries of dissent. William Cobbett, the supreme spokesman for the popular conscience, was in no doubt that the 'Dead Body Bill' was a blatant attack on the poor and labouring population. '[T]his is a thing in which you are all most deeply interested,' he told his readers; 'the House of

Lords will now soon decide whether you and your parents and wives and children, be, after death, to sleep quietly in your graves, or whether you be ... sold and cut up, like dogs and horses'. Cobbett pointed out that body-snatching only constituted a misdemeanour, 'that is to say, a crime punishable by fine and imprisonment ... and I pray you mark, that to steal the dead body of *a sheep*, or *pig*, or *calf*, or an *ox*, or *fowl* of any sort, is a *capital felony*, punished with DEATH'. For Cobbett the implication was clear: 'If the poor had votes as well as the rich, members of parliament would not pass laws *to sell the bodies of the poor.*'[32]

The Anatomy Act did not become a burning popular issue, however, until after the passage of the 1834 Poor Law. This is not to say that dissection and the activities of some surgeons and resurrection men did not continue to cause popular concern; they certainly did so during the cholera epidemic. But generally such incidents were perceived as being the fault of a particular surgeon or obnoxious anatomy school. What the New Poor Law appeared to do was provide the machinery for the introduction of a national scheme of dissection. The Anatomy Act and New Poor Law would work in harmony, serving up the bodies of the poor for the surgeon's knife. Such views were current across the whole popular political spectrum. Giles Marsh, a member of the Bolton Operative Conservative Association, told a local branch meeting that

Warburton's [Anatomy] Bill robs the grave of its victims, and the new Poor Law Bill provides the schools of anatomy with subjects, – the former whets the knife which is to be plunged into my body, and the latter prepares me for the dissecting table!

The Salford popular radical and Trade Unionist, R.J. Richardson, found himself in complete agreement. He told a meeting of Manchester Trades that the 'Dead Body Bill' had paved the way for the New Poor Law. And in Sheffield the inveterate pamphleteer, Samuel Roberts, claimed that the 'Dissection Bill, with the Workhouse Coarse-food Bill, will ... convert those places into little better than *Burking houses*'.[33]

Although popular radicals claimed the Anatomy Act to be part of a general conspiracy, the question arises as to whether this view can be supported by any hard evidence. To what extent, for instance, did the Home Office and Poor Law Commission actually accommodate themselves to the requirements of the Anatomy Act? The answer is that they did so to a surprisingly large degree.

Early in 1836, just as the New Poor Law was starting to be put into force, Dr James Somerville, Inspector of Anatomy under the Anatomy Act, informed the Home Office that owing to an oversight in the framing of the Poor Law Commission's regulations the operation of the Anatomy Act was seriously impeded. The regulations specifically stated that the workhouse master was to 'inform the friends of the Pauper of his or her decease in order that they may remove the body for interment'. Somerville asked that the Poor Law Commission be requested to change the wording of the regulations and remove the specific instruction that the pauper's friends be informed of his or her death. Needless to say this would enable the pauper's corpse to be classified as 'unclaimed' and sent to one or other of the registered anatomy schools. In March 1836 the Poor Law Commission met with Dr Somerville and agreed to make the changes he suggested.[34]

Of course the Anatomy Act was simply enabling legislation and there was no compulsion on the workhouse masters, Guardians, or anyone else to give over the unclaimed bodies of the poor for dissection. In fact there appears to have been a marked reluctance on the part of many Boards of Guardians to supply pauper bodies for dissection. In November 1837 the Home Office again took a hand. They expressed concern to the Poor Law Commission that the composition of the Union Boards under the New Poor Law had materially obstructed the supply of unclaimed bodies to the anatomy schools. The Poor Law Commission was instructed to do all in its power to prevail on the Boards of Guardians to allow pauper bodies to be used for dissection.[35]

Despite the good offices of the Home Secretary and the Poor Law Commission, the Inspector of Anatomy's problems were not at an end. A disgruntled surgeon and an inventor of an 'antiseptic' method for preserving bodies for dissection, William Roberts, began to publicise the connection between the workhouses and the anatomy schools. In a letter marked 'secret', Somerville informed the eminent anatomist and physiologist, Richard Grainger, of Roberts' activities.

[W]e have now Mr Roberts most actively putting in form his threat to blow up the Anatomical Schools, by placarding their nefarious transactions. My name is now placarded full length throughout the Metropolis, I receive constantly notices from the Vestries, that they require me to give explanations. For all this I was fully prepared, but not for the fact, that Mr Roberts has somehow obtained a pretty correct information *[sic]* of what is going on in the schools – in the meetings of the committee. The usual theme of the Roberts declaration is the very disgusting mode of treating the remains, the mockery of the interment &c.

Somerville suggested to Grainger that he speak to his students about the importance of treating the dead human body with marked respect.[36]

Although it is clear that the Poor Law Commissioners and the Home Office were prepared to accommodate the Inspector of Anatomy – to go along with his proposals and actively work to increase the supply of bodies – I do not think we can say that the Anatomy Act and the New Poor Law were designed to work in harmony or that they were part of a co-ordinated conspiracy against the poor and labouring populations. There is no doubt that the two pieces of legislation were capable of inflicting great hardship and cruelty. But we must also recognise that fundamentally the aims of the two Acts were opposed. The Anatomy Act sought to increase the number of corpses available for anatomical study, and most of these corpses were to be obtained from amongst recipients of poor relief. The New Poor Law's intention, on the other hand, was to reduce the number of paupers. If it had been successful it would necessarily have reduced the number of potential corpses available for dissection. Ruth Richardson has posed the question of whether the Anatomy Act (like the principle of 'less eligibility' which underpinned the New Poor Law regulations) had the effect of keeping people out of the workhouse.[37] I doubt it would have had much effect in that regard. Anyone who could possibly avoid it did not go into the workhouse. Dire necessity drove people into the workhouse; the Anatomy Act only succeeded in making them more fearful once they were there.

V

The 1834 Poor Law was perceived as part of a general attack on the wages and conditions of the labouring population of England and Wales. It combined with the factory system, the New Police, and the Anatomy Act to oppress and exploit working men and women. Lawrence Pitkethly was only one of many opponents of the New Poor Law who drew attention to this when he attacked the rich or those linked to them [who think they] have the power to dispose of their fellow creatures as they would dead matter [,] namely to transport them from the land of their birth, cast them into horrid bastiles and starve them and bring them to a lingering death in cells excluded from family and friends and given to the doctors for dissection after being starved or poisoned . . .

The political significance of the New Poor Law ultimately lay not only in its role as an instrument of exploitation and oppression, but also in the fact that it was perceived as such by working men and women. By being able to point to the apparent connections between the New Poor Law and the factory system, and the New Police, and the Anatomy Act, it became a symbol of class oppression to the working men and women of early Victorian Britain. Samuel Bower, an old popular radical who had been present at Peterloo, told a meeting at Bradford in March 1837, just after the New Poor Law had first appeared in the north of England,

that to injure or abolish this greatest of the poor man's rights [the Old Poor Law] is calculated to weaken or destroy the tie of allegiance which binds him to the government of the King, [and] to undermine every kindly feeling which subsists between the different classes of society . . .

By 1841 a bitter Richard Oastler, the Tory radical who had tried all his life to maintain the old bonds, observed:

The working classes are now ... at war with all the superior classes. They are alienated and hostile, heart and soul.

The 1834 New Poor Law had played a central role in producing this state of affairs.[38]

Notes

1. [Anon.], *A Petition to Parliament Against the New Poor Law Act* (n.p., Bradford, [1835]).
2. M. Hovell, *The Chartist Movement* (Manchester University Press, Manchester, 1970), p.85.

3. S. Roberts, *The Anti-Bastile, An Address to the Inhabitants of the Ecclesall Bierlow Union* (n.p., Sheffield, 1841), p.10; S. Roberts, *The Pauper's Advocate; A Cry from the Brink of the Grave against the New Poor Law* (Sherwood, London, 1841), pp.3-4.

4. R. Oastler, *Damnation! Eternal Damnation to the Fiend-Begotten 'Coarser-Food' New Poor Law* (Hetherington, London, 1837), p.2; R. Oastler, *Convocation, The Church and the People* (n.p., London, 1860), pp.29, 34. To be fair to the Church of England, quite a few of its ministers were active opponents of the New Poor Law. They included the Reverend George Stringer Bull, vicar of Bierley; the Reverend Patrick Brontë, vicar of Haworth; the Reverend J.R. Brown, vicar of Prestbury; the Reverend Mr Clark, curate of Great Morden; the Reverend Joshua Fawcett, vicar of North Bierley, the Reverend James Furnival, vicar of St Mary's, Wigan; and the Reverend Mr F.H. Maberly, curate of Bourne in Cambridgeshire.

5. [J.R. Stephens], *Sermon Preached by the Reverend Mr Stephens . . . January 6, 1839* (n.p., London, [1839]), pp.4, 7; [J.R. Stephens], *The Political Pulpit, No. 1 . . .* (Dugdale, London, 1839), p.1.

6. J. Lawson, *Progress in Pudsey* (first published 1887; Caliban, Firle, Sussex, 1978), p.68; J. Obelkevich, *Religion and Rural Society* (Oxford University Press, London, 1976), pp.276-9.

7. Lawson, *Progress in Pudsey*, p.70.

8. F.H. Maberly, *To the Poor, and their Friends ...* (n.p., London, 1836), p.5.

9. Roberts, *Pauper's Advocate ...*, p.11.

10. *Manchester and Salford Advertiser*, 25 November 1837; M. Fletcher, *The Migration of Agricultural Labourers* (Kay, Bury, 1837), p.4.

11. W. Cobbett, *Legacy to Labourers* (first published 1834; Griffin, London, 1872), p.7.

12. Ashworth to Chadwick, 9 June 1834, PRO, MH 12/5593; 'First Annual Report of the PLC ...' *PP*, 1835 vol.XXXV, p.22

13. Table of Persons located in Yorkshire from the Agricultural Districts of the South, 1836, PRO, MH 12/15224; Walker to PLC, 9 May 1836, PLC to Walker, 20 May 1836, PRO, MH 12/14830; 'First Report of Children's Employment Commission', *PP*, 1842, vol.XV, pp.41-3; Carr to PLC, 9 July 1842, PRO, MH 12/14831.

14. Gilbert to Chadwick, 3 May 1835, Chadwick Papers, UCL, CP 808.

15. Fletcher, *Migration*, p.6.

16. Baker to PLC, 13 March and 16 May 1836, PRO, MH 12/15224.

17. *Leeds Intelligencer*, 1 April 1837; *Leeds Times*, 10 June 1837.

18. Fletcher, *Migration*, pp.4-5.

19. *Leeds Mercury*, 10 December 1836; *North Cheshire Reformer*, 8 February 1838.

20. Mott to Chadwick, 27 April 1833, Chadwick Papers, UCL, CP 1449.

21. *The Times*, 3 March 1837.

22. Weyland and Dover to Russell, 17 June 1835, Walpole to Russell, 5 August 1835, PRO, HO 52/26. See also: Dorking Magistrates to Russell, 29 July 1835, PRO, 52/26; Lutton to Kay, 17 December 1835, PRO, HO 73/2, part 1; Parry to Lewis, 1 July 1835, PRO, MH 12/8249.

23. Chadwick to Russell, August 1836, and Russell to Chadwick, 1 September 1836, Chadwick Papers, UCL, CP 1733.

24. A.P. Donajgrodzki, 'Social Control and the Bureaucratic Elite' in A.P. Donajgrodzki (ed.), *Social Control in Nineteenth Century Britain* (Croom Helm, London, 1977), p.66; Chadwick to Russell, August and 6 September 1836, Chadwick Papers, UCL, CP 1733.

25. 'First Report of the Commissioners appointed to Inquire of Establishing an efficient Constabulary Force in England and Wales', *PP*, 1839, vol.XIX, pp.180-4.

26. *The Times*, 27 February 1837.

27. *Northern Star*, 9 June 1838; J. Foster, *Class Struggle and the Industrial Revolution* (Methuen, London, 1977), p.68; [Anon.], *Series of Letters, on Rural Police and the Poor Law Amendment Act* ... (J. King, Ipswich, 1838), p.13.

28. This subject is explored in much greater detail in J.W. Knott (forthcoming), 'Popular Attitudes to Death and Dissection in Early Nineteenth Century Britain: the Anatomy Act and the Poor', *Labour History*, no.49, November 1985.

29. 'Report of the Select Committee on Anatomy', *PP*, 1828, vol.VII, p.6: Z Cope, *The Royal College of Surgeons of England* (Anthony Blond, London, 1959), p.55; 'Report S.C. Anatomy', *PP*, 1828, vol.VII, p.10.

30. *Hansard*, 3rd series, vol.IX, col.302, and vol.XII, col.316.

31. Ibid., vol.XIII, cols 825-7.

32. Proceedings of the 2nd Annual Meeting of the National Political Union, 4 February 1833, Place Papers, BL, Add.MSS.27835, f.49; *Cobbett's Two-Penny Trash*, 1 July 1832, 1 February 1832, 1 October 1830.

33. *Bolton Chronicle*, 28 January 1837; *Manchester and Salford Advertiser*, 15 April 1837; [S. Roberts], *Lectures Lectured and the Dissectors Dissected* (n.p., Sheffield, 1834), p.10.

34. Somerville to Phillips, 18 February 1836, PRO, MH 74/13; Lewis to Phillips, 4 March 1836, PRO, HO 73/51.

35. Somerville to Phillips, 12 January 1836, PRO, MH 74/13; Phillips to Lewis, 30 November 1837, PRO, MH 19/63.

36. Somerville to Grainger, 3 October 1837, PRO, MH 74/13.

37. R. Richardson, 'A Dissection of the Anatomy Act', *Studies in Labour History*, no.1 (1976), p.11.

38. Pitkethly to Broyan, 4 March 1838, PRO, HO 40/47; *The Times*, 14 March 1837; *Fleet Papers*, 16 January 1841.

I

In 1834 the members of the newly reformed Parliament attempted to solve the problems of poor relief in England and Wales by bringing the Old Poor Law into line with the precepts of political economy. They failed and in the process unleashed a storm of popular protest. Throughout southern England angry farm labourers demanded to have their 'rights' restored to them. Relieving officers were mobbed, Guardians stoned and workhouses attacked. The authorities responded with brutal repression. Special constables were sworn in, the military placed on alert and detachments of Metropolitan Police quickly moved into troubled areas. Throughout south-east England all organised protests against the 1834 Poor Law were ruthlessly crushed. The use of force did not stop the protests, however, it merely drove the protesters underground. In the Swing counties, traditional forms of rural protest – arson, intimidation, the maiming of animals – slowly took over from organised public protest. But it was in the textile manufacturing districts of northern England that the most sustained and effective opposition to the New Poor Law was to be found. Not only were the authorities confronted by an organised and militant working class with a long tradition of radical protest, but they also found themselves facing a middle class concerned about centralisation and the cost of supporting an expanded poor law bureaucracy. There were protest meetings, demonstrations and mass petitions. When London failed to heed their call for repeal the northern opponents of the New Poor Law moved to defeat the legislation locally. The authorities responded in turn by drafting Metropolitan Police and troops into the area. The opposition forces in the north were not easily cowed however, and after a series of violent clashes the implementation of the 1834 Poor Law in the manufacturing districts of northern England ground to a halt.

Who were these opponents of the New Poor Law who challenged the power of the state and (in the north, at least) eventually forced the government to compromise? And, even more importantly, what was their motivation? As with any popular movement the problems of determining the social composition of the protesters (let alone why they protested) are immense. In the case of the campaign of popular

269

opposition to the 1834 Poor Law, source limitations and the scale of the protests add to our difficulties. Nevertheless it is possible to identify some significant characteristics of the anti-poor law protests. It is quite clear, for instance, that opposition to the New Poor Law tended to be centred on towns and villages rather than large cities, that workers in the handicraft trades were more active than those employed in factory production, that working women were just as vigorous in their opposition as men, and that paupers (those actually in receipt of poor relief) were conspicuously absent from the campaign of protests.

Poor law protests were in essence community protests. Poor relief under the Old Poor Law had developed over two hundred years of local administration into a personal service in which the poorer members of a community were relieved in familiar surroundings by people who were for the most part personally known to them. This personal contact meant that the parish officials were unusually well placed to judge the circumstances and needs of a particular pauper. It also meant that the paupers could, if necessary, bring moral (or even physical) pressure to bear on those administering relief. The result was a flexible system of poor relief in which familial values and a moral concern for the needs of the poor and destitute guided the type and amount of assistance given. The 1834 Poor Law with its insistence on a uniform system of relief directly challenged the notion that the level of support should be based on individual need. This was more than an attack on the poor themselves, who were now faced with the prospect of only obtaining relief in a workhouse; it was an attack on that network of customary rights and obligations which helped bind a community together. By denying a community's right to care for its less fortunate members, the New Poor Law threatened the very existence of that community. In such circumstances it is not surprising that government officials observed farm labourers and tradespeople, shopkeepers and small farmers, banding together to oppose the new system of poor relief.[1] Admittedly the squire and the large farmer tended to support the New Poor Law, but in the Swing counties at least they had long ago ceased to acknowledge any community of interest between themselves and other local inhabitants. Lacking the support of the landowning classes, the organised protests of rural communities in southern England were, of course, doomed to failure.

Community opposition also characterised the anti-poor law protests in the north of England. Communities in the industrial north, like those in the agricultural south, had developed their own flexible systems of poor relief based on individual need. And these northern communities would also have felt themselves to be threatened by the 1834 Poor Law's attempt to destroy that web of mutual rights and obligations which helped hold communities together. It is no accident, for instance, that all the leaders of the anti-poor law movement in the north of England (with the exception of Feargus O'Connor) had been drawn into the protests as a result of their involvement in the affairs of their local communities. Political representatives, paternalist employers, religious leaders, political activists and concerned working men and women could all find common cause in defending the rights of their own communities. Northern opposition to the New Poor Law differed from that in the south in two significant respects however. First the radical traditions of northern workers ensured that opponents of the legislation had the organisational skills (and ideological insights) necessary to mount and sustain an effective campaign against it. And secondly many respectable inhabitants, particularly those with radical or Tory sympathies, were prepared to speak out against the new poor relief regulations. The result was an extremely well organised opposition campaign which, in its early stages at least, enjoyed widespread community support.

The strongholds of the campaign of popular opposition to the 1834 Poor Law in the north of England were the small weaving towns and outwork villages, not the large cities. This is not to say that the inhabitants of places like Leeds and Manchester were totally unconcerned about the New Poor Law, but simply that conditions in these large urban centres were not conducive to the creation of effective local campaigns. Cities with large and highly mobile populations could not hope to nurture the tight-knit social networks that were to be found in smaller towns and villages. And without close community feeling it was difficult to mount a strong opposition campaign. It was also the case that city fears over the New Poor Law were different from those found in smaller communities. Necessity had previously forced most of the large cities to rationalise their own systems of relief. City parishes had been amalgamated and centralised bureaucracies created to control the administration of poor relief.[2] As a result a personalised relief system had long ago ceased to exist in the large cities and city paupers were quite used to dealing with officials who were personally unknown to them. Even fears about the loss of local autonomy were likely to cause less concern because the boundaries for the new city Poor Law Unions tended to be based on existing administrative arrangements. It is true that the central committees responsible for co-ordinating the anti-poor law protests were usually located in the large cities, but this was only for reasons of convenience. Towns like Oldham, Todmorden, Dewsbury and Huddersfield with their clusters of outlying villages provided the mass support necessary to stage those protests.

Within the towns and villages it was handicraft workers, rather than those employed in factories, who proved to be the most active opponents of the 1834 Poor Law. All textile workers had reason to be grateful for the protection the Old Poor Law provided during the periodic slumps to which the cotton, woollen, linen and silk industries were prone. But it was those employed in the depressed handicraft trades who had most to be grateful about, and consequently the most to fear from the New Poor Law. The allowance system had reached its most advanced form in the industrial north of England, supplementing the wages of poorly paid handloom weavers and other victims of technological change. As a result the Old Poor Law had come to assume a crucial role in maintaining the domestic economy of depressed handicraft workers and their families. Not all outworkers in the textile industry were regular recipients of relief under the allowance system of course, but it was important to all of them that such assistance be available in an emergency. The psychological support provided by the Old Poor law was as important as any concrete benefits which might flow from it. Factory workers were also less likely to fear the ideological implications of the New Poor Law than handicraft workers. While outworkers viewed the new factories and the new poor relief regulations as part of a new and oppressive economic system, factory workers were already a part of that new economy. They might seek a better deal, but they were unlikely to challenge the system itself.

One of the most striking features of the campaign of popular opposition to the 1834 Poor Law was the protesters' searching inquiry to understand the ideology which lay behind the legislation. Throughout Britain popular opponents recognised that there was something sinister and frighteningly different about the New Poor Law, but it was only in the manufacturing districts of the north that working men and women had the strong sense of shared identity and the conceptual tools necessary to undertake a sustained ideological critique of the Act. In their search to explain the 1834 Poor Law to themselves, the northern workers were also constantly refining their understanding of their own shared identity, rights and interests. The precepts of Christianity, popular radicalism and utopian socialism were all marshalled to attack the New Poor Law. The 'rights of the poor' were supported by Holy Scripture, claimed religious leaders like the Reverend J.R. Stephens. Matthew Fletcher, on the other hand, found a different precedent, insisting that the poor had 'natural rights' which needed 'not the aid of human law'. And the Barnsley linen weaver, Joseph Crabtree, conceived of the nation as an enormous Friendly Society in which the poor obtained their right to relief through having contributed to the wealth of the nation.[3] Popular radicals looked at the factory system, the Anatomy Act, the New Police and the 1834 Poor Law and viewed them all as part of a systematic attack on the wages and conditions of the labouring population. Christians saw in it the hand of Mammon and the Devil. All, men and women alike, agreed it was caused by the avarice of those in power.

Right from the beginning working women had taken an active part in the campaign of popular opposition to the 1834 Poor Law. There was nothing surprising about this of course. Working women in the north of England had a long and proud tradition of involvement in radical politics. Women had been active in the post-war radical reform movement which culminated in 'Peterloo'. And they had a long history of participation in Trade Union and Friendly Society activities. As the campaign of popular opposition to the New Poor Law got under way in northern England in late 1836 there was a revival of female radicalism.[4] Women participated in demonstrations, attended meetings and even helped get up petitions. Nor were they averse to using violence, either real or threatened. In fact women anti-poor law protesters were, if anything, more militant than the men. This is partly explained by their presuming on the privilege of their sex. While in private a man might have no inhibitions about using force against a woman, in public it was not so easy. Even the most brutal soldier or policeman would have found it difficult to cope with a determined woman protester. The militancy of working women also suggests that once aroused and set on a particular course of action they were less likely to be deflected than men.

Why were working women so angry about the New Poor Law? To start with, women were deeply insulted by the bastardy clauses and the assumptions on which they were based. They were especially offended by the implication that women were scheming creatures who would not hesitate to use their bodies for personal profit. Women were also very conscious of the fact that it was they who would have to cope with any reduction in the amount of relief under the allowance system. Women were responsible for overseeing the family budget in most labouring families and any challenge to the long-established system of assistance to those in the depressed outwork trades was thus a challenge to a woman's attempt to maintain herself and her family. Similarly women were quick to recognise that the New Poor Law's insistence on only obtaining relief in a workhouse threatened them much more than it did men. At a meeting of women at Elland, Yorkshire, in February 1838 this theme – that women had the most to fear from the new workhouses – was returned to again and again by the female speakers. Mary Grassby, for instance, explained that '[t]heir feelings were more susceptible and the pangs of being separated from those to whom they had been used to look for support, and from their children ... were more severe, ... than it was possible for men to feel'. Another speaker, Elizabeth Hanson, agreed and reminded the female audience of such things as the cropping of a woman's hair, the workhouse uniforms made of 'shoddy and paste', and the possibility of a sick child being bereft of its mother's attention.[5] Grassby and Hanson's concerns were very real for working women. Women had always been, and would continue to be, the major recipients of poor relief. Men might threaten vengeance of the 'bastiles', but it was the women who could expect to end up inside them.[6]

Paupers took almost no part in protests against the 1834 Poor Law. It is true that in the south of England some recipients of poor relief had demonstrated their anger over the new regulations by mobbing relieving officers and setting fire to workhouse extensions, but such activities were exceptional. What characterised most anti-poor law protests was the total absence of paupers. This is not to suggest, of course, that recipients of poor relief were unconcerned about the outcome of the campaign of popular opposition. But it does indicate the extent to which the majority of Paupers were already alienated from society. People only sought poor relief as a last resort. It was something to fall back on after all other avenues for obtaining assistance (such as help from family and friends) were exhausted. The destitute, the sick and the aged were in no position to take part in protests ... sheer survival was their concern, not the possibility of initiating political change.

The anti-poor law protesters were drawn from the ranks of potential, rather than actual recipients of poor relief. It was those who were one or more steps removed from pauperdom who had the luxury of being able to engage in political agitation. This is not to suggest, of course, that their protests against the 1834 Poor Law were any the less desperate than they would have been had actual paupers been able to participate. Working men and women in particular were not motivated by altruism and political principles alone (important as these were), they also acted for reasons of self preservation. Labouring people knew that one day they too might be forced to seek poor relief under the New Poor Law. Let me quote the words of someone who lived through the events I have attempted to describe. 'People are now prone', wrote George Holyoake in the 1880s,

> to look upon the stormy and infuriate opposition to the [New] Poor Law as based upon mere ignorance. Those who think so are too ignorant to understand the terrors of those times. It was not ignorance, it was justifiable indignation with which the [New] Poor Law scheme was regarded. Now, the mass of the people do not expect to go to the workhouse and do not intend to go there. But through the first forty years of this century almost every workman and every labourer expected to go there sooner or later. Thus the hatred of the [New] Poor Law was well founded. Its dreary punishment would fall, it was believed, not upon the idle merely, but upon the working people who by no thrift could save, nor by any industry provide for the future.[7]

II

I hope there has emerged from this account a picture of the campaign of popular opposition to the 1834 Poor Law that is different from the traditional one of 'sporadic' protests based on 'superstition and ignorance'. I have attempted to show that the anti-poor law protests were a self-conscious process guided in almost every instance by a coherent system of beliefs and assumptions; that these beliefs and assumptions contained notions about the legitimate 'rights' of the poor; and that they provided an ethical framework within which ordinary men and women were able to judge for themselves the morality of the new regulations governing poor relief. Experience, tradition and political belief all argued that the New Poor law was opposed to the interests of ordinary working men and women. It was not 'pathetic misconceptions' which guided popular opponents of the 1834 Poor Law, but their own perceived self-interest. Looked at in this way we can for the first time see that the campaign of protest was not the futile exercise it has previously been presented as. The northern protesters, for instance, actually succeeded in gaining concessions from the government . They might not have won a resounding victory, but then neither did London. Similarly, although the campaign of popular opposition to the New Poor Law began as a clash between two world views, moral economy versus political economy, we can now see that it was modified over time to emerge in Chartism as a class struggle for political representation. This in the end might be the real significance of the 1834 Poor Law and the campaign of popular opposition: It taught working men and women that the last vestiges of paternalism were finally dead and that henceforth they could only rely on their own actions. Together with the factory system, the New Police and the Anatomy Act, the 1834 Poor Law had become a potent symbol of class oppression.

Notes

1. Poore to Russell, 5 May 1835,and Dorking Magistrates to Russell, 29 July 1835, PRO, HO 52/26; Hanley to PLC, 8 May 1835, PRO, MH 12/13157; Gilbert to PLC, 24 May 1835, PRO, MH 12/380.
2. P.W. Anderson, 'The Leeds Workhouse under the Old Poor Law, 1730-1844', unpublished M.Phil. thesis, Leeds, 1977, and G.B. Hindle, *Provisions for the Relief of the Poor in Manchester* (Chetham Society, Manchester, 1975).
3. J.R. Stephens, *Political Pulpit, No. 10: A Sermon ... Delivered at Staley-Bridge ... June 9th, 1839* (Dugdale, London, 1839),pp.77 *The Times,* 9 January 1838 and 18 May 1837.
4. D. Thompson, 'Women and Nineteenth-Century Radical Politics: A Lost Dimension' in J. Mitchell and A. Oakley (eds), *The Rights and Wrongs of Women* (Penguin, Harmondsworth, 1976), pp.112-38.
5. *Northern Star,* 3 March 1838.
6. P. Thane, 'Women and the Poor Law in Victorian and Edwardian England', *History Workshop,* no.6 (Autumn 1978), pp.29-51.
7. G.J. Holyoake, *Life of Joseph Rayner Stephens* (William & Norgate, London, n.d.), p.59.

INDEX

Acland, James 190-1
a'Court, Colonel Charles 110, 138-9, 228
Ainsworth, Thomas, 21, 88
allowance system *see* poor relief 'Speenhamland'
Almondbury 112, 130, 132, 193
Althorp, Lord
  subject satire 234, 235, 237
Amersham 71, 72
Ampthill 67-8, 81
Anatomy Act 247, 260-5, 266
  'popular radicals' opposition to 262, 263
  popular view of 263
  Tory opposition to 262
  see also dissection
Andover Union 216-17
Anti-Poor Law Committees 103-6, 113-14, 151
  aims of 106
  Central Committee 113-114
  see also demonstrations; petitions; South Lancashire Anti-Poor Law Association; Short Time Committees
Ashton-under-Lyne 4, 96, 125, 147, 173n12
Ashworth, Henry 191, 252
  see also labour migration scheme
Assistant Commissioners 58, 65, 83, 88-9, 100
  attitude to opposition 77-8
  Treasury criticised over 217
  Royal Commission (1832) 53-4, 61n46
  see also a 'Court, Colonel Charles; Chadwick, Edwin, Gilbert, William John; Head, Sir Francis Bond; Henderson, Gilbert; Kay, Dr James; Mott, Charles; Parker, Henry Walter; Parry, Captain Sir Edward; Poor Law Commisison; Power, Alfred; Wade, Colonel; Voules, William James.

Baines, jun., Edward 123, 140 *see also* effigy burning; *Leeds Mercury*
Barnsely 20, 23, 88, 101

Basingstoke Union 75
Bastardy Clause 58
  satire on 235-6
bastiles *see* workhouses
Battyre, B.N.R. 155, 156
Beaumont, Augustus Hardin 143n12, 262
Becher, Rev. John T. 48-9
Bentham, Jeremy 45-8
  on poor relief, 45, 46, 47
  influence of 54, 55, 57, 59n2
Benthamites 51-2
  influence on the 1834 Poor Law 54, 55, 57, 59n2
Bircham 68-70
Blackburn 162
Blomfield, Rt. Rev. Charles James 52, 234-5, 237
Boards of Guardians 57, 62n59, 65-84, *passim* 89, 103, 145-72 *passim*, 177-95 *passim*, 200-18 *passim*, 253, 264
  elections 65, 145-61, 173n5, 182-6, 192
  boycott of 146-9, 182, 196n12
  see also Oldham; tactics
  irregularities at 147, 183-7, 189-90
  protests by 98, 157, 189, 215-6
  threats and violence against 69, 74-7, 82, 83, 152-6, 160, 165-6, 168-70, 171-2, 179, 192-3, 202-3, 205-6, 208-9, 213-14
  see also New Poor Law; Poor Law Commission; Poor Law Unions; Union clerk
Bolton 56, 93, 96, 191, 173n12, 263
Bower, Samuel 105, 266
boycott
  coronation day celebrations 2-3
  Guardian elections 146-9, 182, 196n12
  see also Oldham; tactics
Bradford 87, 95, 90, 102, 103-6, 112, 116, 162, 163-73 *passim*, 229, 247, 266
Bradford Observer 103, 170-2
Bradford riots 169-71
  see also riots